Legal Aspects of Child
Health

Legal Aspects of Child Health Care

Judith Hendrick

Senior Lecturer in Law
Oxford Brookes University
Oxford
UK

CHAPMAN & HALL

London · Weinheim · New York · Tokyo · Melbourne · Madras

Published by Chapman & Hall, 2–6 Boundary Row, London SE1 8HN, UK

Chapman & Hall, 2–6 Boundary Row, London SE1 8HN, UK

Chapman & Hall GmbH, Pappelallee 3, 69469 Weinheim, Germany

Chapman & Hall USA, 115 Fifth Avenue, New York NY 10003, USA

Chapman & Hall Japan, ITP-Japan, Kyowa Building, 3F, 2-2-1 Hirakawacho, Chiyoda-ku, Tokyo 102, Japan

Chapman & Hall Australia, 102 Dodds Street, South Melbourne, Victoria 3205, Australia

Chapman & Hall India, R. Seshadri, 32 Second Main Road, CIT East, Madras 600 035, India

Distributed in the USA and Canada by Singular Publishing Group Inc., 4284 41st Street, San Diego, California 92105

First edition 1997

© 1997 Judith Hendrick

Typeset in 10/12 pt Palatino by Mews Photosetting, Beckenham, Kent

Printed in Great Britain by Page Bros. (Norwich) Ltd

ISBN 0 412 58320 8   1 56593 340 0   (USA)

A catalogue record for this book is available from the British Library

Library of Congress Catalog Card Number: 96–85901

∞ Printed on permanent acid-free text paper, manufactured in accordance with ANSI/NISO Z39.48-1992 and ANSI/NISO Z39.48-1984 (Permanence of Paper).

FOR JOSIE AND EVE WITH LOVE

Contents

Preface

Article 24 of the United Nations Convention on the Rights of the Child requires states to

> recognise the right of the child to the enjoyment of the highest attainable standard of health and to facilities for the treatment of illness and rehabilitation and to strive to ensure that no child is deprived of his or her right of access to such health care services.

To implement these 'rights' states must take 'appropriate measures' which include (among other things) diminishing infant and child mortality, providing necessary medical assistance and health care to all children with the emphasis on the development of primary health care, developing preventive health care and providing education on child health nutrition.

The UN Convention was ratified by the United Kingdom in 1991 and undoubtedly represents the most important statement about the treatment of children, their protection and participation in society. In some respects, however, English law goes further than the Convention. For example, it now recognizes the rights of older children to autonomy and self-determination in certain contexts. The National Health Service Act 1977 also contains provisions to protect and promote children's health as does other legislation such as the Education Act 1993. But how effective are these and similar measures in ensuring what the British Paediatric Association state to be the purpose of the health service for children, namely that they

> reach adulthood with their potential uncompromised by illness, environmental hazard or unhealthy lifestyle?

This book attempts to provide the answer by looking at how the law regulates the relationship between health professionals and children, how it sets and maintains standards of care and how it ensures that children have access to adequate medical assistance and health care. In so doing it assesses the impact of rapid advances in medical technology, their resourcing implications and rising expectations about the success of treatment and the right to compensation when 'things go wrong'. Similarly as patients become better informed and better educated about medical matters so they also expect to be treated as more equal partners in the professional–patient relationship.

Children and young people are not immune to these developments. In health care contexts they too now increasingly expect to be involved in decision-making. It is perhaps no coincidence that the Children Act 1989 which arguably goes further than any other in enhancing children's legal status, recognizing their independent rights and autonomy, was passed in the same year as the UN Convention and implemented a few years later in 1991 just before the Convention was ratified by the UK.

But how do children's expectations affect health professionals in their day-to-day dealings with them? While it is well understood that professionals must operate within the law it has long been recognized that the 'law in action' does not always reflect 'law in the books'. Hence in practice it may be all too easy to deny children the information they need to make meaningful choices. Not surprisingly the issue of children's consent to medical treatment is thus a major recurring theme in this book which is divided into three parts.

The first part (Chapter 1) briefly outlines the legal system and includes sections on how law is classified, where it comes from and the court structure. It also examines concepts such as 'rights', 'duties' and 'powers' and how they operate in health care contexts.

The second part (Chapters 2–4) covers general aspects of professional accountability and liability, notably medical malpractice, consent and confidentiality.

The third part (Chapters 5–12) deals with specialist areas and includes chapters on family planning, assisted reproduction, prenatal injuries, genetic counselling and screening, research and transplantation, death, dying and the treatment of the incurably ill, mental health, child protection, the welfare of children in hospital, health promotion and special educational needs.

The book has two broad aims. One is to describe in outline the legal framework of medical law as it affects children. This involves describing the relevant rules and principles and the constraints which the law imposes. The second aim is to provide a practical guide to the law and how it affects the role and practice of professionals. The legal implications of their actions and decisions are therefore illustrated throughout the text by 'case studies' designed to reflect situations which may arise in practice.

The law is as at May 1996 and applies to England and Wales.

PART ONE
The Legal System

The legal system

1

CLASSIFICATION OF LAW

There are several ways of classifying the law and because classifications help those unfamiliar with the English legal system to make sense of the nature of law this chapter will begin by adopting a similar approach. But dividing the law into apparently discrete areas does have its drawbacks. First it over-simplifies the complex inter-relationship between the various different categories suggesting that there is a natural underlying unity or rationale which in practice may not exist at all. As a result it may well give a distorted picture of how the law changes and develops and how legal reasoning and processes work. Secondly, it implies, often quite wrongly, that there is no overlap between the different categories, implying, again falsely, that behaviour may have only one legal consequence whereas in practice it may have several. Thus, for example, the same act can be both a crime and a civil wrong. A third related problem is that some classifications, especially those which focus on the legal consequences of behaviour, fail to emphasize how sometimes the law is broken but the courts do not get involved nor is any legal action taken. As one commentator has aptly put it, 'The law does not police itself but relies on someone starting proceedings'. In other words a health professional may have been negligent but is not sued by the patient possibly because the harm suffered is very minimal or because the patient is unaware of his or her legal rights. In such cases while there has clearly been an unlawful act because it is not acted upon (and may not even be reported) the law appears not to be relevant.

Despite these qualifications it is still helpful to classify the law in the following ways largely because each branch of the law can have different purposes, follow different procedures and rules, be processed through different courts, impose different sanctions and remedies and, finally, be based on very different concepts.

CRIMINAL LAW

NATURE AND AIMS

Criminal law is the branch of the law which is primarily concerned to protect society from anti-social behaviour. It includes several different categories of offences, i.e. those against property, people, public order and state security. Crimes are generally regarded as affecting society as a whole. As such they can be seen as disputes between alleged offenders and the state representing the community. Put simply the criminal law aims to protect society and uphold its values by prohibiting and controlling certain behaviour as well as punishing offenders. Generally a crime can only be committed by carrying out a positive act but exceptionally a crime can also be committed by an omission, i.e. if someone fails to do something which the law requires them to do. Thus, surprisingly perhaps, if someone stands by and watches a helpless baby drown in an inch of water no crime is committed unless the person watching is the baby's parent (or other carer) in which case failing to act would undoubtedly result in criminal charges. Similarly a health professional whose gross negligence in failing to treat led to a patient's death could be criminally liable.

Offences can be further subdivided according to their seriousness. Summary offences are the most common and constitute the vast majority dealt with in the courts. They include those designed to protect consumers as well as such 'minor' offences as assault and criminal damage. Summary offences are tried in the magistrates' courts without a jury. Indictable offences are the 'major' ones such as murder and manslaughter. They are tried in the Crown court before a judge and jury. However, some less serious indictable offences can be tried either way.

CRIMINAL RESPONSIBILITY

No-one can normally be held criminally responsible (i.e. 'guilty') unless two crucial elements are established. First, the prosecution bears the burden of proof which means it must prove 'beyond reasonable doubt' that the defendant committed the wrongful act. This standard of proof is very strict since no guilty verdict can be reached unless the jury is convinced that the accused person did commit the offence. Any doubt should therefore result in an acquittal. Secondly, the prosecution must also prove that the required criminal intent is present. Although this mental element may differ from one crime to another it is generally satisfied by proving that the defendant either 'intended' to do something or was 'reckless'. There are also some offences, called 'strict liability' offences where no criminal intent or fault is required at all. These 'regulatory' offences are principally used to maintain minimum standards such as in the supply of medicines.

CHILDREN AND YOUNG PEOPLE

The criminal law divides children and young people into three distinct age groups. No child under 10 years of age can be held criminally responsible. This is simply because the law presumes that such children are too immature to have the necessary criminal intent. Nevertheless behaviour which in an older child would be criminal can have legal consequences, most notably, proceedings under the Children Act 1989 (see Chapter 11). Children between 10 and 14 are presumed to be incapable of forming criminal intent. This presumption can, however, be rebutted by proving that the child in question knew that his or her behaviour was 'seriously wrong', i.e. more than simply 'naughty'. Young people over 14 but under 18 are treated like adults and so are assumed to have normal capacity to commit crimes although they are treated differently in the courts and are likely to receive different sentences.

CIVIL LAW

NATURE AND AIMS

The other major branch of the law deals with private disputes (sometimes called civil wrongs) between individuals, and other bodies such as health authorities and NHS Trusts. The main aims of civil law are to define the rights and duties people have towards each other and to provide a system of remedies to settle disputes. In some respects, therefore, civil law shares with criminal law the aim of controlling conduct and bringing about social change. Furthermore some actions, such as an assault, can give rise to both civil and criminal liability (called 'double liability'). There are many different heads of liability under the civil law but the ones which are most likely to concern health professionals in relation to children are contract, tort and family law.

A tort arises from a breach of general duty imposed by law and irrespective of any agreement between the parties involved. The aim of tort law is to compensate those who are harmed by another's wrongful act rather than to punish the wrongdoer. Torts cover several different types of activity but in health care contexts negligence and trespass are the most important. Family law regulates the relationship between parents and children. It is especially important in relation to disputes about medical treatment and child protection.

Contracts by minors are regulated by the Minor's Contracts Act 1987 and would be enforceable should a contract for the supply of private health services be for the child's benefit.

CIVIL LIABILITY

The standard of proof in all civil cases is 'the balance of probabilities'. This is a lower standard of proof than that required in criminal cases and it means that it must be more likely than not that the alleged event or events did happen. Another aspect of civil liability is the doctrine of vicarious liability. This plays a very important role in the law of negligence since in certain situations it allows an employer to be held liable for the acts or omissions committed by his or her employee. The main aim of vicarious liability is to ensure that an injured person can obtain damages. A health authority or NHS Trust, for example, is much more likely to have the funds to pay compensation than an individual health professional (see Chapter 2).

PUBLIC LAW

Public law is concerned with the legal relationship between individuals, groups and the state. Apart from criminal law it comprises constitutional and administrative law which regulate the many different kinds of institutions through which governments operate. These so-called 'state agencies' include the police, Parliament, central and local government, the Crown, the civil service, the armed forces, local authorities, nationalized bodies such as the National Health Service and so on. Public law also covers the legal rules which are designed to protect the civil liberties and rights of citizens and enable them to question and challenge how public law agencies exercise their powers.

PRIVATE LAW

This branch of the law deals with the rights and duties of private individuals in their everyday dealings with each other. It therefore includes medical, tort and family law as well as several others, such as property, contract and trust law.

SOURCES OF LAW

English law is created through two main processes. These are: common law and legislation.

COMMON LAW

Common law is often called case-law or judge-made law as it is based on the legal principles created by the decisions of judges in individual cases. Common law is the oldest source of law. It derives its legal authority from the doctrine of binding judicial precedent – one of the most fundamental features of the English legal system. Known simply as 'precedent' this doctrine requires the courts to interpret like cases (that is cases involving the same or similar legal principles, circumstances or facts) in like manner. This means that in principle courts are legally bound to follow earlier decisions although whether a court is actually bound in practice by a particular precedent depends on its position in the court hierarchy (see below). There are, nevertheless, several ways in which a court can avoid following an 'inconvenient' precedent. It may, for example, be able to overrule a previous decision or 'distinguish' it, in other words identify material differences or distinctions which can justify a different decision.

The system of judicial precedent is said to have many advantages, in particular, flexibility, certainty and consistency. Furthermore, by responding to actual cases which are brought before the courts it can readily adjust to society's changing needs and so develop new legal rules and principles when necessary. On the other hand, because it is based on a rigid hierarchical court structure, it can result in hair-splitting as courts attempt to evade unpopular precedents by distinguishing them on what sometimes seem to be very questionable grounds. Common law can also be extremely slow in changing and can develop erratically since it evolves only when specific individual disputes are litigated and cannot, as legislation can, deal with a whole area of law in one go.

Common law has greatly contributed to the development of medical law, especially in relation to children. The landmark 1986 Gillick case for example, established the important principle that mature young people can, in certain circumstances, have an independent right to consent to medical treatment without their parents' knowledge and even against their wishes (see Chapter 3). The law of negligence has also largely developed through the common law.

LEGISLATION

Legislation is now the major source of law. It has three broad functions – to alter, revoke and create new law – but it is also the most effective way of clarifying and confirming the common law. There are two types of legislation.

ACTS OF PARLIAMENT

Acts of Parliament (Acts are also sometimes called statutes) are 'primary legislation' and all start life as Bills which have to pass through several lengthy and formal stages in both Houses of Parliament before they receive the Royal Assent and become law. Many Bills are preceded by a Green Paper which is a consultative government document and a White paper which sets out government policy. A consolidating Act brings together and re-enacts, usually with modifications, several Acts on the same subject. The purpose of this kind of Act is to simplify the law. A codifying Act involves collecting all the law on a particular subject into one Act. It is a process which almost always involves combining both the common law as well as previous Acts on the subject. Again the main purpose of codification is to simplify the law. With the exception of the law of negligence and consent child health law is largely governed by statute law.

DELEGATED LEGISLATION

Another major source of law is delegated (also called 'secondary') legislation. It includes all the rules, orders and regulations created by subordinate bodies and is usually issued in the form of statutory instruments. Delegated legislation is increasingly popular because it is the quickest and simplest way of supplementing primary legislation. Although it does not go through the same rigorous Parliamentary scrutiny as primary legislation, it is subject to various controls and can be challenged in court. One example of delegated legislation is the Midwives Rules. Another is the National Health Service (General Medical Services) Regulations 1992 which define the duties expected of GPs. Delegated legislation has the same legal force as a statute and so must be obeyed.

EUROPEAN COMMUNITY LAW

Although not a major source of child health law European Community law (in the form of Directives and Regulations) cannot be ignored as certain forms automatically take precedence and therefore override English law. Moreover much of the law concerning drugs derives from Community law, in particular liability for defective products.

'NON-LEGAL' SOURCES

Although professional practice is primarily regulated by legislation (both primary and secondary) and the common law, the legal status of which is clear and unequivocal – they are legally binding and must be followed – there are several other communications, in particular Guidance documents, health service guidelines (HSGs) and executive letters (ELs) as well as Codes of Practice which can affect professional practice. But what is their precise legal effect and status? As regards Guidance documents and circulars these can stand alone but are often linked to a particular statute or set of Regulations. If so, their main purpose is to identify areas of change, explain the statute's underlying principles and discuss its implications for policy and practice. As such they are primarily intended as statements of 'good practice' and so are expected to be followed. Although neither Guidance nor circulars have the force of law they should be complied with since to do otherwise could be used or quoted in court proceedings and so could be the basis for a legal challenge.

HSGs and ELs are normally issued by the NHS Management Executive and are much more flexible and short-lived than certain forms of delegated legislation. Health Service guidelines are the main way of communicating with the NHS and their main purpose is to convey standing guidance to NHS authorities of policy and operational matters. ELs are meant to give guidance about policy or legislative changes which need action (often urgent) and/or involve allocation of funds. Neither HSGs nor ELs have statutory force (although very exceptionally Parliament may give them the same legal effect as statutory instruments). They cannot, therefore, be described as 'law'. However, providing they are 'reasonable' and do not conflict with the law they should be complied with.

Codes of Professional Practice, such as that issued by the UKCC for the Nurse, Midwife, and Health Visitor, are rules of practical guidance which are intended to establish, maintain and improve standards of professional practice. Failure to comply with them can result in disciplinary proceedings. Codes of Practice are commonly used to supplement legislation and provide guidance on the exercise of discretion, such as, for example, the Code of Practice under the Mental Health Act 1983. They may be 'statutory' in that they are required by legislation but they are not law in the way that a statute is law. Health professionals are nevertheless expected to follow their recommendations, likewise those issued by the Royal College of Nursing in relation to paediatric nursing and the Audit Report on community child health and social services.

RIGHTS, POWERS AND DUTIES

Concepts such as 'rights', 'duties' and 'powers' are very fundamental to the operation and implementation of the law. But what do they mean when used in health care contexts? And, more importantly perhaps, can they be enforced in the courts? The concept of a 'legal right' is so fundamental to the operation of the law that it is often described as the most basic 'unit of legal currency'. Yet it has proved to be one of the most difficult to define. Nevertheless in relation to health care several 'rights' have long been recognized by the law. These include the right to consent to (and refuse) medical treatment (see Chapter 3); the right to confidentiality and of access to health records (see Chapter 4) and the right to a reasonable standard of care (see Chapter 2).

How these various 'rights' are protected will be explored in subsequent chapters but as the case of B. v. Cambridge AHA [1995] highlights (see Chapter 2) the National Health Service Act 1977 does not create any absolute rights to health service resources.

Legal duties can be imposed by statute or the common law but irrespective of their source they must be carried out. Legal duties can either be absolute (recognizable by the words 'must' and 'shall') or qualified (when words such as 'shall take reasonable steps' are used). Not surprisingly those exercising qualified duties have considerable discretion in how and when they implement them. Legal duties can also be either 'general' or 'specific'. General duties tend to be very open-ended and imprecise, whereas specific duties are much narrower and more detailed.

Several legal duties are imposed on the Secretary of State in the National Health Service Act 1977, for example, to 'continue the promotion in England and Wales of a comprehensive health service designed to secure improvement a) in the physical and mental health of the people of those countries, and b) in the prevention, diagnosis and treatment of illness, and for that purpose to provide or secure the effective provision of services in accordance with this Act' (s.1). S.3 imposes more detailed duties, in particular to provide hospital accommodation, medical, dental, nursing and ambulance services, facilities for the care of expectant and nursing mothers and young children and so on.

But attempts by aggrieved patients to enforce these statutory duties in the courts are unlikely to be successful as the following cases illustrate. In R v. Secretary of State for Social Services, ex p Hinks [1980] four patients in an orthopaedic hospital alleged that they had waited an unreasonable length of time on the waiting list, and certainly longer than was medically advisable, for hip-replacement surgery. They claimed that the Secretary of State was in breach of his duties under the National Health Service Act 1977 for failing to provide a comprehensive health service and appropriate facilities and services for orthopaedic surgery. Notwithstanding these 'duties' the Court of Appeal rejected their claim. It held that the Act did not impose an absolute duty on the minister to provide health services irrespective of Government economic policy. Instead he had a discretion in the allocation of resources and health care with which the court could only interfere if the minister had acted 'unreasonably' (which in that case he had not).

A similar decision was reached in R v. Central Birmingham HA ex p Walker [1987]. It concerned a premature baby needing heart surgery whose operation had been postponed five times because of staff shortages in a neonatal ward. The mother sought an order that the operation be performed, claiming that inadequate health resources had been allocated by the health authority resulting in her baby being denied surgery. The Court of Appeal refused to order the operation for much the same reason as in the Hinks case, namely that it would not substitute its own judgement for the judgement of those responsible for the allocation of resources (unless they had acted 'unreasonably').

In both the above cases the patients were not in immediate danger. So would a court reach a different decision if a patient's health was in jeopardy? R v. Central Birmingham Health Authority, ex p Collier [1988] was just such a case. It concerned a four-year-old suffering from a hole in the heart who was said by his consultant to be in 'desperate need' of lifesaving surgery and who would probably die without it. Although the operation had been arranged it had been cancelled three times. But yet again the Court of Appeal refused to order the health authority to carry out the operation as it decided that the legal principles involved were no different from previous cases which sought to question the allocation of resources. In other words even if there was immediate danger to health the court would only interfere if a health authority made a decision that no reasonable person or body would have made.

Finally, there was the case of Re J (a minor) (wardship: medical treatment) [1992] which also focused on the nature of a legal duty in health care but this time that of an individual health professional. J suffered an accidental fall hitting his head when he was one month old. As a result he was profoundly handicapped, both mentally and physically. He was microcephalic, had a severe form of cerebral palsy, cortical blindness and severe epilepsy. His life expectation was uncertain, but unquestionably short. A dispute arose between the consultant paediatrician and J's foster parents. The consultant considered that if J were to suffer a life-threatening event, it would be appropriate to offer ordinary resuscitation with suction, physiotherapy and antibiotics, but not prolonged life support. But J's natural mother wanted his life to be prolonged as long as possible, using all available life-saving measures. The Court of Appeal rejected her claim. One reason was that it considered it an 'abuse of its power' to compel a medical practitioner to act contrary to the fundamental duty which he owed to his patient, that was a duty to treat the patient in accordance with his own best clinical judgement.

Another was that it acknowledged the

> sad fact of life that health authorities may on occasion find that they have too few resources, either human or material or both to treat all the patients whom they would like to treat in the way in which they would like to treat them and it was their duty to make choices.

Taken together these decisions (likewise the case of B v. Cambridge AHA [1995], see further Chapter 2) make it clear that despite the legal duties contained in the National Health Service Act 1977 patients will almost certainly be unable to enforce them in the courts. This is partly because the courts are reluctant to make orders they cannot supervise but also because of their unwillingness to be drawn into policy questions about the distribution of finite resources which they have consistently regarded 'as questions for Parliament not the courts'.

Failure to provide a statutory service may, nevertheless, lead to a negligence claim or complaint proceedings (see Chapter 2).

A legal power confers a discretion on someone to do something. This means that it can, but does not have to, be exercised. If the power is exercised existing legal relationships are likely to be changed, sometimes very significantly. Legal powers are usually identified by the word 'may'. Generally a legal power has no correlative duty except in rare instances, such as the power and duty of a judge to give a decision.

Legal powers can either be 'general' or 'specific'. The former are very open-ended and imprecise whereas the latter are much narrower and more detailed. In neither case though can action be taken to enforce the power (unless it is coupled with a duty). But if the power is exercised it must be exercised properly, i.e. with reasonable care and with due regard to relevant legal processes and requirements.

Legislation governing health care frequently contains powers both general and specific. For example the National Health Service and Community Care Act 1990 lists a number of powers which NHS Trusts may or may not exercise. In particular they have specific powers to (among other things) enter into NHS contracts; undertake, commission or make facilities available for research; provide or make facilities and staff available for staff training. The Act also gives NHS Trusts a wide range of general powers such as the power to buy and sell property; accept gifts of money, land or other property; and employ staff on terms it thinks fit.

Numerous other examples of legal powers can be found in the National Health Service Act 1977. See, for example s.5 which covers school health and dental inspections. Similarly, as we shall see in Chapter 10, the Mental Health Act 1983 gives doctors, nurses and social workers very specific and extensive powers to detain people compulsorily, which do not, of course, have to be exercised. This means that although generally no-one is under a legal duty to detain mentally disordered persons, they have the legal authority to do so. Once detained, patients then have several rights (and powers) for example, to have their cases reviewed by an independent Mental Health Review Tribunal and to be told under what provisions they are being detained.

'NON-LEGAL' RIGHTS

The most notable example of these are the so-called 'rights' contained in the Patient's Charter and the Charter of the National Association for the Welfare of Children in Hospital. Like other Charters (e.g. the Citizen's Charter) these list several rights which patients are apparently entitled to. However, the 'rights' in these and other Charters such as the European Charter for Children in Hospital are deliberately expressed in non-legal and very general terms because they do not (and were never intended) to have direct legal force nor give patients rights which they could enforce in the courts. The principles they embody, however, are expected to be followed by health professionals. Nevertheless some Charter rights do, albeit in broad terms, reproduce well-established legal rights. Thus, if patients are not given a 'clear explanation of proposed treatment, including risks and any alternatives' they may be able to sue in tort and claim that medical procedures were carried out without their 'real' consent (see Chapter 3). Similarly, patients' rights of access to their health records, although adding nothing to existing legislation, may be enforceable (see Chapter 4).

THE COURT SYSTEM

Only a tiny proportion of medical disputes are dealt with in the courts since the vast majority are resolved through various complaints procedures (see Chapter 2). But despite their very minor role the courts are still regarded as the focal point of the English legal system. The court system can be classified in a number of ways.

CRIMINAL AND CIVIL COURTS

Generally civil courts deal with civil disputes and criminal courts with criminal cases although there are some courts which hear both civil and criminal cases. Whether the court is exercising its civil or criminal jurisdiction, however, it has three main functions. The first is to investigate the facts. The second is to identify and formulate the relevant legal issues and rules which involves applying the law to the facts. The relationship between law and fact can be, but is not always, straight-forward, as sometimes the line between questions of law and fact becomes blurred, particularly in medical negligence claims. This is well illustrated in the case of Whitehouse v. Jordan [1981], for example which concerned a boy born with severe brain damage. His 30-year-old mother (who was 4 ft 10½ in) was unable or refused to have an internal examination or a lateral X ray. Initially 'trial by forceps' was undertaken but after five or six attempts at this the baby was delivered by Caesarean section. After his birth the baby was found to be irretrievably brain-dam-aged. Mrs Whitehouse alleged that this was due to the senior registrar's (Mr Jordan's) negligence in pulling too hard or continuing traction too long, actions which caused the baby's head to become wedged.

Four issues had to be decided by the court: (1) did the 'trial by for-ceps' cause the damage? (a question of fact); (2) how much force was actually applied to the baby's head?; (3) what legal duty did Mr Jordan owe? (a question of law); and (4) did he breach that duty?

Questions (1) and (3) were fairly straightforward. Question (2) was more complex in that it involved the court drawing inferences from var-ious witnesses who were present at the birth. But it was question (4) which was the hardest to answer and involved the court in exercising practical judgement (neither purely factual or legal). In other words it combined both since the court had to decide what degree of 'careless-ness' a reasonably competent surgeon should be allowed before he or she is considered negligent.

The court's third function is to reach a decision, i.e. to decide 'what the law is' or 'what the law ought to be'. If there is no clear or settled law on the point the courts may have to set a precedent and possibly create a new legal principle.

FIRST INSTANCE AND APPEAL COURTS

Courts can be either first instance ones where cases are heard for the first time (also called original jurisdiction) or appeal courts. Some courts hear cases both at first instance and on appeal. An appeal system is necessary not just because judges can make mistakes (about both facts or the law) but because the law needs constantly to develop to reflect social and other changes in society. The appeal courts have considerable powers to review, adapt and create new law.

SUPERIOR AND INFERIOR COURTS

A distinctive feature of the English legal system is its hierarchical struc-ture. This means that some courts are 'superior' (or higher) courts, i.e. the House of Lords, Court of Appeal, High Court and Crown Court while others are 'inferior' (or lower) courts, i.e. county courts and magistrates' courts. The higher courts hear far fewer cases than the lower courts but deal with those which are more complex and generally more important and serious. In general the lower courts are bound to follow the decisions of the higher courts but appeals are possible so that a case which began in the lowest court can end up being heard in the most superior court.

THE COURTS

House of Lords

In cases which do not involve European Community legislation, the House of Lords is the highest court. It hears both civil and criminal appeals (on points of law of general public importance). Although very few cases actually reach the House of Lords its decisions are very important since they bind every other court in the system and can only be overruled by statute.

Court of Appeal

The Court of Appeal plays a major role in the development of the law as it hears far more appeals than the House of Lords and so is in practice the ultimate appellate court in the English legal system. As a result it has considerable influence over the pace and nature of legal reform because its decisions are binding on all courts below it in the hierarchy, i.e. all courts except the House of Lords. The Court of Appeal is generally bound by decisions of the House of Lords (unless it can distinguish them) and the European Court. The Court of Appeal has two divisions. The civil division hears appeals from all lower civil courts and has wide powers to reverse, amend and confirm their decisions. It can also order a new trial. The criminal division has similar wide powers and can confirm or quash convictions and order a retrial. Sentences too can be either confirmed, varied or reduced. In very rare cases a sentence which is considered 'unduly lenient' can be increased.

High Court

This superior court has three major divisions, each of which deals with very different kinds of cases. All divisions hear cases for the first time as well as having an appellate jurisdiction (called a Divisional Court) hearing appeals from the lower courts. As a court of first instance the Queen's Bench Division is the busiest division. It deals with major civil disputes such as tort claims (i.e. medical negligence actions). As a

Divisional Court the Queen's Bench Division has an important supervisory jurisdiction which enables it to discipline inferior courts and rectify their mistakes. This process is called 'judicial review'. The other divisions are the Family division which hears all aspects of family law including those involving children and the Chancery Division. Acting as a Court of Protection the Chancery Division also protects and manages the property of people suffering from mental disorder. Decisions in all the three High Court divisions are binding on the county courts but do not have to be followed by other High Court judges. Nevertheless in practice previous decisions are considered 'persuasive' authority and are therefore usually followed. Appeals from the High Court usually go to the Court of Appeal although some can 'leap frog' directly to the House of Lords.

Crown Court

This court tries the most serious criminal cases 'on indictment', i.e. with a jury. The Crown Court also hears criminal appeals from the magistrates' courts and appeals from youth courts. Decisions on points of law in the Crown Court are not binding but can be persuasive. The 'Old Bailey', otherwise known as the Central Criminal Court, is the Crown Court which sits in the City of London.

County courts

These courts were originally introduced to hear small civil claims quickly and cheaply. They are at the bottom of the civil court ladder but process far more claims than any other civil court. They also deal with some family matters such as divorce and certain proceedings involving children, notably care proceedings.

Magistrates' courts

Although magistrates try the vast majority of criminal cases (about 97%) their powers are fairly limited. They can only try summary offences, i.e. the less serious ones such as motoring offences or those offences which are triable either way. In both types of cases there is no jury so the magistrates, who can either be full-time, legally qualified professionals (called stipendiaries) or part-time, decide whether the accused is guilty or innocent. In passing sentence magistrates must keep within statutory limits but if they think their sentencing powers are inadequate they can commit a convicted person to the Crown Court for sentencing. Magistrates also play a part in cases which can only be tried in the Crown Court since they carry out preliminary investigations to see whether the prosecution has sufficient evidence to justify a trial.

Acting as youth courts specially trained magistrates also try children and young people charged with criminal offences. These proceedings are much less formal than those involving adults.

Magistrates' courts also have a very limited civil jurisdiction.

OTHER COURTS

The European Court

Since the United Kingdom joined the EEC the Court of Justice of the European Communities is the supreme court for matters with a European element. Its role is to ensure that Community law is enforced and interpreted uniformly throughout the Community. The Court has no jurisdiction over internal domestic cases.

Court of Human Rights

As a member of the European Convention of Human Rights it is possible for UK citizens who allege that a basic right of freedom has been violated to have their claim referred to the Court of Human Rights in Strasbourg. One recent case which was decided against Britain, i.e. it was held to be in breach of the Convention, concerned the caning of school children against the wishes of their parents.

Coroners' courts

The main function of coroners' courts is to investigate unexplained deaths (such as those allegedly caused by medical negligence) and those where death was violent, unnatural or suspicious. It also investigates deaths in prison. The Coroners Act 1988 lists the various circumstances in which coroners should be informed of a death. These include (among others) deaths of foster children, 'obscure' infant deaths including those believed to be due to sudden infant death syndrome, and stillbirths where there is some doubt about the child being born alive.

After a death has been reported a coroner may order a post-mortem examination to find out the cause of death. Depending on the outcome of this an inquest or inquiry may be held. An inquest is not a trial but is held to establish how, where and when the deceased died. Although all witnesses are under oath rules of evidence are not applied as strictly as in other courts. Sometimes a jury will be used at the inquest. If so its verdict (which need not be unanimous) can include unlawful killing as well as death from natural causes. An open verdict can also be given if it is impossible to determine the cause of death.

Tribunals

Tribunals exist alongside ordinary courts and have an increasingly important role to play in resolving disputes, particularly those of a technical nature. Considered by some to be inferior to the courts because many of them were created to provide 'instant justice' cheaply, informally, and without all the trappings of a formal court setting such as highly paid judges and inflexible procedural rules, tribunals now deal with approximately six times more disputes than the courts. There are three broad categories of tribunals, administrative tribunals (which include Mental Health Review tribunals and National Health Service tribunals) employment and domestic tribunals. Despite being outside the formal court structure, tribunals have to observe the so-called principles of 'natural justice', i.e. that no person can be a judge in his or her own cause; that each side shall have the opportunity to be heard and be given a fair hearing and that a person must be informed of what he or she is accused. To ensure that all tribunals observe these principles and do not exceed their powers or misinterpret the law they can be supervised by the courts which can also hear appeals in certain circumstances.

FURTHER READING

Gee, D.J. and Mason, J.K. (1990) *The Courts and the Doctor*, Oxford University Press, Oxford.

Farrar, J.H. and Dugdale, A.M. (1990) *Introduction to Legal Method*, Sweet & Maxwell, London.

Ingham, T. (1994) *The English Legal Process*, 5th edn, Blackstone Press, London.

Keenan, D.(1995) *Smith & Keenan's English Law*, 11th edn, Pitman, London.

PART TWO
Aspects of Professional Practice

Medical malpractice   **2**

Medical malpractice is another name for medical negligence. Until recently litigation between health professionals and patients was uncommon but over the past decade or so there has been a dramatic increase in the number of claims as well as a substantial increase in the amount of damages awarded by the courts. Whether or not this is due to a 'malpractice crisis' is hard to say, largely because all the relevant evidence is not routinely collected. Nevertheless it is undoubtedly true that health professionals are now much more likely to be sued (and be the subject of complaints procedures) than in the past. Several reasons are usually given to explain the increase. Overworked and over-tired practitioners working under increasing pressure and with less resources are more prone to make mistakes. Easier access to medical records and to lawyers who are no longer reluctant to specialize in high-profile medical litigation are equally important factors. So too is the public's increasing 'compensation awareness', resulting in a growing number of disgruntled and dissatisfied 'claims-conscious patients' expecting (often quite legitimately) to be compensated for 'life's misfortunes'. Advances in medical technology, changes, not just in patterns of consultation but also in the concept of illness itself which prompt patients to seek treatment for 'new' conditions inevitably also increase the opportunities for things to go wrong.

Because the tort system is the main method used by patients seeking compensation this chapter will focus on the law of negligence. However, it will also look, albeit briefly, at other ways by which standards are controlled, notably complaints and other disciplinary procedures and the very limited role of the criminal law.

NEGLIGENCE

The law of negligence has two broad aims. One is the so-called compensation aim which seeks to minimize the effect negligence can have on a 'victim's' life. For example, injured patients may lose all or most of their income and require long-term nursing care. Damages awarded are thus expected to compensate them for their lost earning potential and higher living expenses. The second aim is the deterrent one which seeks to reduce both the number and seriousness of medical accidents by making health professionals personally liable. In other words the threat or fear of legal action and the potential damage to professional reputations is expected to ensure that greater care is taken in treating patients. But irrespective of the merits of these aims (neither of which withstand too much scrutiny) it is clear that the tort system is by no means the best method of dealing with negligence claims. Aptly described as a 'lottery' it allows patients with justifiable claims and often very serious injuries to lose because they cannot prove fault or causation. Lengthy delays, the excessive cost of litigation and growing complexities of medical technology also explain why so many claims fail or are settled 'out of court', often for less compensation than would probably be awarded by a court. But despite the known shortcomings in the tort system and the many reform proposals (such as a no-fault scheme) it is likely to remain, at least for the foreseeable future, the main method for dealing with medical negligence.

Negligence is best defined by quoting the words of Lord Atkin in Donoghue v. Stevenson [1932]. This is undoubtedly the most famous tort case in the twentieth century because it laid down the general principles of liability for unintended harm. Basically liability arises if you fail to 'take reasonable care to avoid acts or omissions which you can reasonably foresee would be likely to injure your neighbour'.

This means that before a patient can successfully sue and obtain compensation three elements must be proved. These are:

1. that the health professional (or health authority or NHS Trust) owed a duty of care; and
2. that the defendant breached that duty; and
3. damage (which the law recognizes) was caused by the breach.

DUTY OF CARE – HEALTH PROFESSIONALS

Whether a duty of care does or does not exist is a question of law. In most health care settings this is easy to establish. Thus health professionals undoubtedly owe a duty of care to patients they are treating. This means that GPs (and their staff) owe a duty to patients on their lists (likewise those not on their lists but who they have agreed to accept or who are temporary residents). It should be noted here that 16- and 17-year-olds and children under 16 who are 'Gillick competent', i.e. sufficiently mature (see Chapter 3 for a more detailed discussion of

Gillick competence) have an independent right to apply for inclusion on a GP's list and to seek treatment from other health professionals. As for children under 16 who are not 'Gillick competent' (likewise incompetent 16- and 17-year-olds) the request for medical services on their behalf must come from someone else, usually a parent or anyone with parental responsibility or temporary care of the child. Hospital staff (as well as health authorities and NHS Trusts) also owe a duty of care to patients they are treating, whether as out-patients or in-patients. Similarly accident and emergency departments owe duties to those who seek treatment or advice – the duty arising as soon as they make their presence known to appropriate hospital staff irrespective of whether or not they have been formally admitted. The duty owed to patients arriving for treatment at a hospital without an accident and emergency department (and without any prior appointment) is arguably limited to simply ensuring their safety which, depending on the circumstances, may amount to no more than calling an ambulance. Note too that the duty of care owed to NHS patients is imposed by the law of tort. Private patients, on the other hand, have a contractual relationship with health professionals. The duty of care owed to them thus derives from a contract. Nevertheless in practice, its extent, nature and legal consequences is virtually the same.

In some situations, however, the existence of a duty of care is not so apparent. There is a common misconception, for example, that health professionals have to be good Samaritans, providing health care whenever it is needed, even if they are off duty. But this is not the case since English law does not require health professionals to 'rescue' everyone they come across who has an accident or falls ill. In short they do not have to provide treatment even if no more than first aid is needed. Exceptionally, though, GPs may have a duty of care in certain emergency situations since their terms of service require them to treat 'persons to whom they may be requested to give treatment which is immediately required owing to an accident or other emergency at any place in their practice area'. This would, for example, cover visitors temporarily in their locality.

In other cases whether or not a duty of care exists can be determined by applying Lord Atkin's 'neighbour test', derived from the famous case of Donoghue v. Stevenson (1932). This states that such a duty is owed to

> persons who are so closely and directly affected by my acts that I ought reasonably to have them in contemplation as being so affected while I am directing my mind to the acts or omissions which are called into question.

The 'neighbour test' is an objective one and involves asking a hypothetical question about what a 'reasonable' person would have done in the circumstances. Furthermore, it is not only owed to patients but extends to all those who may be affected by a health professional's actions or inactions such as other health professionals as well as patients' relatives and visitors.

> **Case study 2.1**
> Anna, a boisterous five-year-old, falls from a tree while playing in the park. She seems to be badly hurt and her mother frantically calls for help. Bertha, a GP, who is on holiday, passes the accident. Is she legally obliged to give emergency treatment? What difference would it make if Bertha was a nurse or other health professional?

Since this situation is not covered by the provisions of the NHS Terms of Service for doctors Bertha is under no legal obligation to help. But if she does decide to treat Anna then a duty of care arises. Put simply, by volunteering treatment Anna becomes Bertha's legal neighbour. Similarly if Bertha was a nurse or other health professional then unless her contract of employment imposed an obligation to treat in such situations she too would not be legally obliged to offer treatment.

DUTY OF CARE – HEALTH AUTHORITIES AND NHS TRUSTS

What happens when a patient's care is allegedly adversely affected by inadequate resources? For example, expensive treatment may be denied or an operation repeatedly postponed because of a shortage of skilled staff. Or to save money a health authority decides to close its accident and emergency service with the result that a patient's condition worsens. In such cases can it be claimed that the health authority or NHS Trust has a primary (otherwise known as direct) duty to the patient which it breached because of its failure to provide a reasonable regime of care? Although this aspect will be examined in more detail below it is worth noting here the most recent case to come before the courts on what was essentially an issue of resource allocation. B v. Cambridge HA [1995] concerned a ten-year-old girl with leukaemia with a life expectancy of about two months. She had already received chemotherapy, irradiation and a bone marrow transplant but sadly, despite a brief period of remission, suffered a relapse. In the opinion of those treating her 'no further treatment could usefully be administered'. B's father sought other medical opinions, however, one of which suggested a more hopeful prognosis – of between 10 and 20%. But this depended on further expensive treatment, including chemotherapy and a second transplant, costing altogether £75 000. The health authority refused to fund the further treatment claiming it was not in B's best interests and moreover as it was very expensive it would not be an appropriate use of the authority's limited resources. B's father sought judicial review of that decision.

Somewhat surprisingly, given previous decisions on the allocation of resources (see Hinks, Walker and Collier, Chapter 1), the High Court ordered the health authority to reconsider its decision. But within 24 hours the Court of Appeal predictably overruled the High Court's decision. Repeating once again that the courts had no right to interfere with a health authority's funding decisions providing they were rational and fair, the Court of Appeal concluded that even though in a

> perfect world any treatment which a patient or a patient's family sought, would be provided if doctors were willing to provide it, no matter how much it cost, particularly when a life was potentially at stake ... it would be shutting one's eyes to the real world if the court were to proceed on the basis that we do live in such a world.

Accordingly the Court of Appeal refused to interfere with the authority's decision as despite the action by B's father being

> wholly understandable it was nevertheless misguided to involve the court in a field of activity where it is not fitted to make a decision favourable to the patient.

Does the outcome of this case (sadly Child B died in May 1996) suggest that a patient allegedly harmed by inadequate resources can never succeed against a health authority or NHS Trust for breach of its direct duty of care? The answer depends ultimately on the particular facts of the case in question and a patient might well succeed if the lack of resources results in failure to employ competent staff, to provide reasonable facilities or to exercise proper supervision. A good example of this type of case is Bull v. Devon HA [1993]. Mrs Bull claimed that her son suffered asphyxia when he was born because his birth was delayed – for 68 minutes – due to no suitably qualified doctor being available. Maternity services in the area were divided between two sites and the system was designed to ensure that a suitably qualified doctor would be available within 20 minutes. But this system had broken down. In rejecting the health authority's claim that it had provided the best maternity service it could, given available funding, the Court of Appeal found the authority liable; in particular it emphasized that it was 'indisputable' that the authority owed a duty of care directly to Mrs Bull's son. It described the nature of the duty owed in these terms:

> the duty of the hospital is to provide a woman admitted to labour with a reasonable standard of skilled obstetric and paediatric care,

in order to ensure as far as reasonably practicable the safe delivery of the baby or babies and the health of the mother and offspring thereafter.

BREACH OF DUTY

THE MEDICAL STANDARD OF CARE

Once a duty of care has been established a patient has to prove that the duty was breached. Whether the duty derives from a contract or, as is much more likely, tort law, both categories involve breaches of the same standard of care. Both also require proof that the defendant's behaviour fell short of the required standard of care. In other words the patient did not receive the care he or she was entitled to. But proving breach of duty is much harder than showing that a duty of care was owed despite a huge volume of case law. In fact one of the earliest precedents on the medical standard of care was laid down as long ago as 1838 when the court said that:

'every person who enters into a learned profession undertakes to bring to the exercise of it a reasonable degree of care and skill'.

A more recent and well-known precedent was established in Bolam v. Friern Hospital Management Committee [1957]. The plaintiff claimed that the broken pelvis he sustained during electro-convulsive treatment could have been avoided had he been given relaxant drugs and been properly restrained. He also complained that he was not warned of the risks of treatment. Mr Bolam lost his claim as at the time there was evidence that different doctors used different techniques and methods – some used relaxant drugs, others did not. Since both approaches were equally acceptable the doctor was not negligent in choosing one method rather than the other.

In his judgement the judge laid down what is generally accepted as the guiding principle in determining the standard of care doctors owe their patients. It is:

The standard of the ordinary skilled man exercising and professing to have that special skill. A man need not possess the highest expert skill: it is well established law that it is sufficient if he exercises the ordinary skill of an ordinary man exercising that particular art.

This precedent, known simply as the Bolam test of medical negligence, is important for two main reasons. First, even though the case concerned a doctor, the principle it establishes applies equally to all other health professionals. Secondly, it sets an objective test. This means that those with a special skill must be compared with other reasonably competent practitioners who practise in the same field of medicine or sub-branch thereof, in other words those who do the same kind of work. Furthermore, the skill required of a health professional is not that of 'the man on the top of the Clapham omnibus' (this is legal jargon for what a reasonable, ordinary person would do) because that man has not got any special skill. Instead the practitioner must exercise 'the ordinary skill of his or her speciality'.

So a patient who visits a GP with a skin condition cannot expect the GP to have the skill of a consultant dermatologist. Nevertheless he or she can expect to be referred to a specialist should the condition require such action.

Whether failure to refer a patient to hospital was a breach of duty was the central issue in the case of Sa 'D v. Robinson [1989]. This concerned an 18-month-old girl who sucked hot tea from the spout of a teapot at about 5.45 one evening. Her mother immediately took her to the local GP and described what had happened. The doctor examined the inside of the child's mouth and prescribed medication to soothe the child. Mother and child then went home. During the next few hours the child became very distressed and was salivating copiously. Her mother again telephoned the surgery at about 8.00 pm and repeated details of the incident (including her concern that her daughter might choke on the mucus in her mouth) to another doctor who had come on duty. He advised propping the child up with pillows. Two hours later the mother called the duty doctor out. He examined the girl and suggested it would be best if she was admitted to hospital for observation. By this time she was finding it very difficult to breathe and when she arrived at the hospital she was seen on the paediatric ward rather than in casualty. Treatment was difficult and the toddler suffered irreversible brain damage.

The court had to decide (among other things) whether the GP who saw the child at 5.45 had breached his duty of care by failing to refer her to hospital. It decided that he was negligent because he should have realized the important difference between sucking hot tea from a spout (which might involve the inhalation of steam which could reach the throat without burning the mouth) and drinking from a cup.

Having established the relevant standard of care it is then necessary to determine how the courts actually ascertain it in individual cases.

HOW DO THE COURTS ESTABLISH THE MEDICAL STANDARD OF CARE?

The answer to this question can be found again in the Bolam case where it was stated that a doctor is not liable in negligence;

If he has acted in accordance with a practice accepted as proper by a responsible body of medical men skilled in that particular art, merely because there is a body of such opinion that takes a contrary view.

Although the case concerned a doctor the precedent it set again applies equally to other health professionals. In practice it means that practitioners can usually avoid liability if they can show that other reasonably competent professionals practising in the same branch of medicine would have acted in the same way, taking into account all the relevant circumstances, such as the patient's condition and so on. This does not of course mean that they necessarily would have acted in exactly the same way but rather that the defendant's action was within a range which was acceptable.

The 'accepted practice' precedent is important for several reasons. First, it sets a minimum standard, albeit one which is best described as 'generous', below which practitioners must not fall. Secondly, because of the courts' traditional reluctance to challenge medical practice, compliance with accepted practice is almost always conclusive proof that the health professional was not negligent. Thirdly, it has been applied to several areas of medical practice (private and NHS) including treatment, diagnosis, counselling, prognosis, and arguably consent and information giving too albeit with less certainty (see Chapter 3). Fourthly, because of the courts' tendency to rubber stamp clinical practice and defer to medical judgement, standards of care are in practice both set and regulated unilaterally by the medical profession itself – an approach which potential plaintiffs find a formidable obstacle to overcome, save in cases of gross and, therefore, indefensible negligence. There is some recent evidence, however, (see for example Bolitho v. City and Hackney HA [1993]) that despite strong reservations the courts are increasingly aware of their role in judging the propriety of clinical decision-making and thus setting medical standards of care themselves.

Case study 2.2

Mary, a nurse, is on her way to work when she passes a road accident. No ambulance is in sight and it looks as though a child may have been involved. Mary stops her car, rushes to the scene and decides to act as a good Samaritan. She discovers that the child, Ayeesha, who was not wearing a helmet when her bicycle collided with a car, has serious injuries and is unconscious. Mary carries out first aid but unfortunately Ayeesha suffers serious spinal injuries. When she finally leaves hospital she is confined to a wheelchair and unlikely ever to walk again.

Ayeesha claims that her injuries were made much worse by Mary's first aid, in particular, that Mary moved her unnecessarily when she was unconscious.

Is Mary liable? What difference would it make if Mary was a GP?

In deciding whether Mary was negligent – assuming that she caused the spinal injuries by inappropriately moving Ayeesha – the court would consider how other nurses would have acted in similar circumstances. The legal yardstick by which Mary would be judged would therefore be the standard expected of other reasonably competent nurses acting in an emergency, taking into account the lack of usual medical backup and the fact that Mary had to act on the spur of the moment.

If Mary was a GP her actions would be measured against the standards of a reasonably competent GP exercising the ordinary skill of her speciality but nevertheless taking into account the emergency circumstances. In other words the standard Mary has to reach is not the best, most experienced nor the most skilful. Nevertheless health professionals who are deemed to be specialists must exercise greater skill and expertise than is normally the case.

WHAT IF THERE IS MORE THAN ONE WAY OF DOING SOMETHING, I.E. TWO SCHOOLS OF THOUGHT?

This was in fact the central issue in the Bolam case. It is an important one because there are often several different approaches and techniques as to how a particular condition or illness could be dealt with. In such cases the law is clear – no liability will arise if the health professional has acted in accordance with a responsible body of medical opinion even though there is a body of opinion which took a contrary view. So, the fact that other professionals would have adopted a different practice is not in itself evidence of negligence. Furthermore the courts have consistently stressed that it is not for them to give a preference for one body of opinion over another (see Maynard v. West Midlands RHA [1984]. Nor is the extent to which a body of medical opinion was responsible to be determined solely by reference to the numbers of practitioners who subscribed to the views held (see Defreitas v. O'Brien and Campbell-Connolly [1995]).

Overall, therefore, this aspect of the Bolam test is a difficult one for plaintiffs to overcome. That said, however, it is clear that no doctor (or other health professional) could, as the judge in the Bolam case said,

obstinately and pig-headedly carry on with some old technique if it has been proved to be contrary to what is really substantially the whole of informed medical opinion. Otherwise you might get men today saying: 'I do not believe in anaesthetics. I do not believe in antiseptics. I am going to continue to do my surgery in the way it was done in the eighteenth century'. That clearly would be wrong.

CAN HEALTH CARE PROFESSIONALS DEVIATE FROM ACCEPTED PRACTICE?

The main issue here is whether deviation from accepted practice is conclusive evidence of negligence. This is most likely to happen when there is only one orthodox treatment but it is not used. Instead a more innovative and possibly even new and untried technique is adopted. Whether or not its use amounts to negligence depends on the extent to which it is justifiable bearing in mind all the relevant circumstances, including the factors which were (or ought to have been) known, i.e. evidence of previous trials, the seriousness of the patient's condition and his or her previous or likely response to the conventional treatment. How this principle operates can be shown by the case of Clark v. Maclennan [1983].

Following the birth of her first child Mrs Clark began to suffer stress incontinence. Her condition was particularly acute and the defendant gynaecologist performed an anterior colporrhaphy. This was carried out just over a month after birth instead of at least three months after birth which was the normal (i.e. accepted) practice. Two further operations were necessary, neither of which was successful and Mrs Clark's stress incontinence became a permanent disability. Her claim succeeded because the court decided that there was no good reason for the defendant to depart from what was the general precautionary well-established practice of not performing the operation until at least three months after birth.

DOES THE LAW TAKE INEXPERIENCE INTO ACCOUNT?

The law does not accept a defence of inexperience, lack of ability or knowledge. The leading case on this is Wilsher v. Essex AHA [1986]. The life of Martin Wilsher was probably saved by the care he received in the special-care baby unit. Born three months prematurely and suffering from various illnesses, he was looked after by a medical team consisting of two consultants, a senior registrar, several junior doctors and trained nurses. He needed extra oxygen to survive which was administered by one of the (inexperienced) junior doctors mistakenly inserting a catheter into a vein rather than an artery. This error was not spotted by the senior registrar (whose advice the junior doctor sought) and when replacing the catheter the registrar did exactly the same thing himself. As a result Martin received too much oxygen which he claimed caused retrolental fibroplasia and left him nearly blind. Although Martin lost because he failed to prove causation (see below) the case is an important one because it established several important general principles about the liability of inexperienced staff. These are as follows.

1. An objective approach to the acts of inexperienced health professionals must be applied.
2. The standard must be set according to the post occupied rather than according to the actual post-holder and his or her personal ability.
3. Inexperienced professionals occupying a post in a unit providing specialist care would therefore be required to exercise the expertise and skill which patients would normally expect from a reasonably competent person occupying such a post and holding themselves out as having the necessary skills.
4. Inexperienced professionals 'learning on the job' and thus attempting specialist skills who make a mistake (which a more experienced professional would not make), nevertheless satisfy the required standard of care if they seek the advice and help of a superior when necessary. Accordingly the junior doctor who mistakenly inserted the catheter into the vein was not liable (because he consulted the registrar) but the registrar was (because he should have known better and ought not to have repeated the mistake).
5. Employers (the health authority or NHS Trust) may be directly liable in negligence if they fail to provide a proper system of effective supervision and training for unqualified staff and a sufficient number of competent qualified staff (see below).
6. There is no such thing as team liability since this would require each team member to reach the standard of the team as a whole. Nevertheless each individual member is responsible for his or her own actions (or inactions).

Case study 2.3
A ten-year-old boy called Tom is rushed into theatre for an emergency appendectomy. The registrar John asks the theatre nurse, Jane, to carry out the operation. He says she should easily be able to do it as she has watched him do hundreds of others. Jane is unhappy about this suggestion but is reluctant to admit her fears. John goes out for a cup of coffee and Jane performs the operation. Unfortunately, things go badly wrong and although John comes back just in time to save Tom from long-term problems he does suffer much more pain and discomfort than would normally be the case and has to stay in hospital for several weeks.
Are Jane and John liable?

Assuming there was no emergency which required Jane to carry out surgery she was undoubtedly at fault for performing a task which was well beyond her competence. John too was at fault for delegating to her a task which he knew she had not been trained for. Both Jane and John would therefore be liable.

Case study 2.4
Leila is five-years-old and has leukaemia. She has been in hospital for several weeks. During that time her mother Valerie has been constantly with her and has become very familiar with the ward's routine. She has also been increasingly involved in looking after her, especially feeding and bathing her. Recently, however, she has needed intravenous treatment – a task which has hitherto always been carried out by the nurse, Miriam, as it requires skills which Valerie has not yet learnt or ever been taught. One very busy day, however, Miriam is rushed off her feet and she asks Valerie to make sure that Leila gets her dose of drugs intravenously. Although Valerie has seen Miriam carry this out many times she is not sure how to do it but she does not want to bother Miriam who seems very stressed and near to breaking point. Over the past few weeks Valerie and Miriam have become very friendly and Valerie knows she is having marital difficulties. She therefore decides to do the best she can but unfortunately she makes some mistakes and gives Leila an overdose. As a result Leila is very ill and suffers long-term consequences.
    Is Miriam liable?

This raises similar issues to the previous case study in that Miriam's liability in negligence will turn on whether or not in delegating tasks to Valerie she knew (or ought to have known) that Valerie was incapable of carrying them out. Had she properly trained or supervised Valerie in the past and was therefore reasonably sure that she was competent to carry out the treatment arguably no liability would arise. If on the other hand no such training had previously occurred – as seems to be the case here – then Miriam would be liable (although her employers would in practice be sued either in respect of their direct or vicarious liability).
    As for Valerie's liability, much again would depend on whether she knew (or ought to have known) when carrying out the treatment that she did not have the appropriate expertise. If she did but nevertheless undertook the procedure she too would be liable.

WHEN IS ACCEPTED PRACTICE JUDGED AND WHAT IS CURRENT MEDICAL KNOWLEDGE?

Often several years can have passed between the time of the alleged negligence and a trial. During that time professional practice might have significantly changed. But for legal purposes the crucial time for determining whether or not there has been a breach of duty is the date of the treatment or operation and not the trial date. This means that defendants are judged according to the standards which were accepted at the time they carried out the treatment and not later. The classic illustration of this approach is the case of Roe v. Ministry of Health [1954]. In 1947 the patient became permanently paralysed below the waist after being injected with a spinal anaesthetic. This was caused by phenol leaking through invisible cracks in the glass ampoules containing the anaesthetic but dangers of phenol leakage were unknown at the time of the operation being first written about and published in 1951. The patient sued the anaesthetist (among others) but lost his claim. This was, according to the famous words of Lord Denning because:

We must not look at the 1947 accident with 1954 spectacles

What amounts to current medical knowledge is an important related issue because it raises questions about the extent to which the law expects health professionals to keep up to date with the latest developments in their particular field. Medical journals, research articles, technical papers, practice guidelines, circulars and so on can vary enormously in both their frequency and status. There have been few cases directly on this point but as a general principle it is clear that health professionals should be aware of all 'major' relevant developments in their area. This includes health circulars, health service guidelines and executive letters whether issued by the Department of Health or NHS Executive as well as journals which are normally read by reasonably competent health professionals practising in the same branch of medicine.

A good example of the law's approach is the case of Crawford v. Board of Governors of Charing Cross Hospital [1953]. The patient suffered permanent injury (brachial palsy) as a result of how his arm was positioned during surgery. An article had appeared in the *Lancet* six months previously warning against the dangers of this method and while the anaesthetist admitted that he had read letters commenting on the article he had not actually referred back to it. The patient claimed he was negligent in failing to change his practice. The Court of Appeal rejected the patient's claim because it decided that

it would I think be putting too high a burden on a medical man to say that he has to read every article appearing in the current medical press; and it would be quite wrong to suggest that a medical man is negligent because he does not at once put into operation the suggestions which some contributor or other might make in a medical journal. The time may come in a particular case when a new recommendation may be so well proved and so well known and so well accepted that it should be adopted. But that was not so in this case.

WHEN ARE BREACHES MOST LIKELY TO OCCUR?

The borderline between a negligent and a non-negligent mistake or error can be very difficult to draw but over the years a fairly clear pattern has emerged at least as to the particular areas of medical practice which are most likely to result in negligence claims. The vast majority of claims are made by hospital patients and so most of the case law concerns accidents occurring during the course of hospital treatment or during after-care. As such they include diagnostic errors, failures to treat, drug-induced and prescribing errors, errors in the course of treatment, failures of advice and communication and inadequate record-keeping and reporting. Several categories are likely to involve children including, in particular, ward accidents, most of which arise because they are not properly supervised. Care must also be taken to ensure that the ward environment is safe – to avoid patients slipping on wet or dirty floors or hurting themselves on dangerous equipment, i.e. broken glass left lying around.

Cases concerning children also often involve burns. In one case a baby in hospital with bronchitis was put in a steam tent. He was scalded by boiling water from a steam kettle and was left with a permanent bald patch and slightly deformed ear for which he won damages. Another case concerned a thirteen-year-old with polio who could not sit up without being propped up nor move her legs although she could move her arms a little. She was left to manage a jug of hot inhalant on a tray which she had successfully done for the previous two months. This time, however, when the nurse was briefly out of the room the jug slipped and her legs were badly scalded. The girl lost her claim because it was held that the jug had been positioned carefully and properly. Furthermore she had managed on her own and it was in her own interests to do some things for herself.

Another category to involve children is more than likely to be due to a failure to protect them from risk of harm. Not surprisingly the law expects children to take less care of themselves than adults and extra precautions may be necessary such as doors which shut automatically and handles placed out of reach. Sometimes too a young patient may need constant supervision. In one case (Selfe v. Ilford & District

Management Committee [1970]) a 17-year-old took an overdose of sleeping pills and was admitted to hospital where he was put on the ground floor with an unlocked window behind him. There were 27 patients on the ward and he was grouped with three other suicide risks at one end. Three nurses were allocated to the ward (all of whom knew that the young man was a suicide risk) but all disappeared at the same time – one to the kitchen, one to the lavatory and one to attend another patient. In their absence the patient climbed through a window and eventually threw himself from a roof. He became a paraplegic and successfully sued the hospital authority for failing to provide adequate supervision.

In another case, hospital staff were found negligent for leaving a boy of six unattended in a ground-floor ward near an open window. He fell out of the window and dropped about 17ft. As a result his forehead was badly disfigured and both feet became flat, requiring special supports.

A contrasting case involved a nine-year-old girl. When an orderly left the ward for a few minutes to get the pudding course, the girl, contrary to the rules, ran down the ward and began to swing on some swing doors. Unfortunately she tripped on the stud and was seriously injured. The hospital were held not to be at fault in that as far as discipline was concerned the standard they had to meet was that of a school teacher or ordinary prudent parent. Accordingly in the circumstances, they had provided adequate supervision.

Other claims involving children may be due to the increased use of high technology, such as intensive care and inadequate pain relief.

ARE SOME CASES EASIER TO PROVE THAN OTHERS?

To succeed, the plaintiff must prove breach of the standard of care. In medical negligence cases this is no easy task but there are some cases when plaintiffs have an in-built advantage because the acts or omissions which caused them injury give rise to a presumption of negligence which the defendant then has to rebut. In other words negligence can be presumed from the mere fact that an accident happened. This is basically a rule of evidence and is generally known by its Latin name of 'res ipsa loquitor' (the thing speaks for itself). How the rule works in practice was perhaps best summed up by Lord Denning in the case of Cassidy v. Ministry of Health [1951] when he said:

> I went into hospital to be cured of two stiff fingers. I have come out with four stiff fingers, and my hand is useless. That should not have happened if due care had been used. Explain it, if you can.

Given the difficulties many patients face in identifying the cause of their injury the rule is a very useful one but it can only be used when there is no evidence to explain how the accident occurred and the injury must be of a type which normally would not have happened had proper care been taken.

The rule is typically applied in relatively extreme cases such as when swabs or instruments are left in patients or the wrong operation is performed – i.e. on the wrong limb, on the wrong side of the body. Prescribing the wrong drugs or ascribing test results to the wrong patient are other examples. It is also particularly helpful to patients when the treatment or operation is complex, where machinery is involved and the patient is unconscious. In one Canadian case, for example, a patient went into hospital with a fractured ankle and came out with an amputated leg. Given that a leg is not normally lost in such circumstances and that neither the plaintiff nor defendant were able to explain what had happened it was not difficult to apply the rule.

Similarly, it was successfully used in G v. North Tees HA [1989] when a little girl's swab became contaminated with another swab and as a result it was thought that she had been sexually abused. She was therefore subjected to a very painful internal examination, was interviewed several times by police and social workers and suffered nightmares and enuresis. In addition she developed a fear of doctors and a dread of the police. The contamination was due to the hospital practice of using one slide for two swabs.

The rule was also successful in Saunders v. Leeds Western HA [1993] when a four-year-old's heart stopped for about 30–40 minutes during a hip operation. The defendants agreed that this did not normally happen unless there was a lack of care, although they did offer an explanation – which was rejected by the court. In other words they failed to rebut the presumption of negligence.

CAUSATION

The third element in a negligence action is the causation one which must be proved irrespective of whether the claim is brought in contract or tort. It requires proof on the balance of probabilities that the defendant's breach of duty caused (or materially contributed to) the plaintiff's injury. In the simplest of cases this causal link is unproblematic for two main reasons. First, the negligent conduct does not have to be the sole cause of the injuries as long as its effect was not so minimal as to be insignificant or trivial. Secondly, the parties are competing on fairly equal terms in that the plaintiff only has to convince a court that his or her version of the truth is more than 50% likely.

The usual starting point for establishing causation is to apply the 'but for' test. That is that the defendant's breach of duty is the cause of the damage if that damage would not have occurred 'but for' the defendant's behaviour. In some cases the test works well. For example, in Edler v. Greenwich and Deptford Hospital Management Committee and another [1953] an eleven-year-old girl became ill with abdominal pains and vomiting. Her father took her to hospital where she was examined by a casualty officer. He was told of her symptoms and when asked where the pain was the girl put her hand on her stomach and moved it to and fro, wincing every time her abdomen was touched. The doctor also carried out a rectal examination but concluded there was nothing wrong. He none the less told her father to bring her back if she got worse. As her condition deteriorated she was taken to see the family's GP. He was informed of the hospital doctor's opinion and thought it was more than likely that she had gastric trouble. But by the following day her condition was such that the GP arranged for her immediate admission to hospital where she was found to have an advanced state of peritonitis and a ruptured and gangrenous appendix. She died and her father sued both the GP and the casualty officer. The casualty doctor was found negligent in failing to diagnose appendicitis – a misdiagnosis which led to the girl's death. The GP, on the other hand, was not negligent as in the circumstances he was entitled to rely on the hospital's diagnosis.

Another case where the 'but for' test was easy to apply was Mitchell v. Hounslow and Spelthorne HA [1984]. It concerned a baby girl born with spastic cerebral palsy caused by birth anoxia due to compression of the umbilical cord. Her mother was admitted to hospital in labour and was given an enema and then shown to the toilet. But no-one showed her the emergency bell and while she was there her membranes ruptured and the umbilical cord prolapsed and emerged beyond the introitus. She called out for help, but it was some minutes before her husband and a midwife found her. No pressure was applied, no warm saline gauze was wrapped round the protruding cord and no other first-aid treatment was carried out until she reached the operating theatre and had her baby delivered by Caesarian. The child sued and won because the expert evidence showed that if the midwife had applied pressure to the foetus there was a 60% (i.e. more than 50%) chance that brain damage would have been avoided.

Both the above two cases were uncomplicated in that the causal link was very apparent as it also was in the recent case of Fairhurst v. St Helens and Knowsley HA [1994] which involved a child suffering from rhesus incompatibility with her mother who was born with jaundice and, following a delayed exchange transfusion, suffered brain damage. But in many others proving a link between the injury suffered and the negligent behaviour is much more difficult, if not impossible, and certainly cannot be resolved by the simple 'but for' test. One of the main reasons is the lengthy delays – especially in cases involving events which happened at birth. Such cases typically take several years to reach trial (and if there are appeals several more years). During this time witnesses' memories may have faded and they may well have forgotten the most important facts (or even worse, they may have disappeared or died). Whitehouse v. Jordan [1981] (where baby Stuart claimed that his injuries were caused by the doctor's pulling too hard and too long, see Chapter 1, for details) took nine years to reach the House of Lords. Mrs Whitehouse's evidence consisted of what she remembered, notably being lifted up off the delivery bed by the pulling. In contrast, two expert witnesses (retired obstetricians) gave evidence based on reading the hospital notes that Mrs Whitehouse had in fact been pulled down off the bed. Mr Jordan could not remember the facts in any detail but on the basis of his notes and usual practice was certain he could not have pulled too hard. Two midwives who were present and could have been very reliable and useful neutral witnesses regrettably could not be traced so could not give evidence. Other witnesses included four consultant obstetricians who again based their evidence on the hospital notes concluded that Mr Jordan had not been negligent. Faced with this conflicting and incomplete evidence – much of which was indirect – it is perhaps not surprising that Stuart lost his case.

Nor does the 'but for' test work in the following types of cases:

THE INJURY WOULD HAVE OCCURRED ANYWAY

The classic case of this is Barnett v. Chelsea and Kensington Hospital Management Committee [1968]. Three men who had been vomiting continuously since drinking tea a few hours previously went to the casualty department. A nurse telephoned the casualty officer and said, 'There are three men complaining of vomiting after drinking tea.' The doctor replied, 'Well, I have been vomiting myself and I have not been drinking. Tell them to go home and go to bed and call in their own doctors.' Mr Barnett died a few hours later of arsenic poisoning. His widow sued. The casualty officer was undoubtedly negligent in not examining and admitting Mr Barnett but since he would have died anyway if he had been treated with due care – there was no known antidote for arsenic – the plaintiff inevitably failed to prove that the negligence caused her husband's death.

SEVERAL POSSIBLE CAUSES

Sometimes the plaintiff's case collapses because his or her injuries could have been caused by several factors unrelated to and irrespective of the defendant's negligence. In such cases even though negligence is admitted (or established) the plaintiff must still prove, on the balance of probabilities, that the defendant's behaviour caused or materially contributed to the injuries. It was precisely this that Martin Wilsher failed to do (see above). In that case it was clear that a doctor had negligently administered excess oxygen. However, even though it was well known that this could cause blindness by damaging the retina there were at least five other possible causes of blindness in premature babies. With so many potential competing causes the scientific evidence linking the negligence with the harm was at best ambivalent and at worse inconclusive. Martin, therefore, lost his case for the simple reason that his condition could have resulted from any one of a number of different causes. In other words he could not prove on the balance of probabilities that his blindness was caused by the excess oxygen he was negligently given.

TWO COMPETING CAUSES

It might be thought that if there are only two possible causes of a plaintiff's injuries he or she has a much better chance of winning. But this is not necessarily so as the case of Kay v. Ayrshire and Arran Health Board [1987] clearly demonstrates. It concerned a two-year-old boy who was rushed to hospital with pneumococcal meningitis. He was given a massive overdose of penicillin (300 000 units instead of 10 000) which quickly produced toxic effects. Although the mistake was rectified and he recovered from both the meningitis and the overdose, he became profoundly deaf which he claimed was due to the overdose. Negligence was admitted yet the boy's claim failed because his expert evidence was unable to show that a penicillin overdose had ever caused deafness, i.e. had materially contributed to it, whereas meninigitis commonly did, even when properly treated. As a result the law regarded the deafness as being solely caused by the meningitis.

'LOST OPPORTUNITY' CASES

So far the focus has been on claims that the injuries suffered were 'new' in the sense that even though patients needed treatment for some existing illness or condition (or may have been healthy to start with) it was the defendant's action which caused fresh or additional harm. But what of those cases where the claim is rather that the defendant's behaviour lost the patient a chance of a full recovery or at the very least a 'better medical result'? These so-called 'lost-opportunity' cases are especially problematic for plaintiffs because they cover cases where a cure is uncertain despite proper treatment.

The House of Lords was faced with just this problem in the controversial case of Hotson v. East Berkshire HA [1987]. Stephen, a 13-year-old boy fell 12 ft from a tree rope injuring his hip. He was taken to hospital and examined but his fracture was not spotted. He was sent home but returned five days later when, following an X-ray, his injury was correctly diagnosed and treated – but unfortunately not so as to prevent major permanent disability of his hip joint. Stephen conceded that even if his hip injury had been correctly diagnosed and treated when he first went to hospital he may still have had only a 25% chance of being cured. This meant that in effect what he had been deprived of was a 25% chance of a full recovery (rather than certain cure). His claim was rejected because he could not prove on the balance of probabilities that the delayed treatment was at least a material contributory cause of his disability. This was because there was a 75% chance he would have suffered from avascular necrosis even if he had been properly treated when he first attended hospital. In short he could not establish that it was more than 50% likely that 'but for' the delayed treatment he would have fully recovered.

INJURIES MUST BE FORSEEABLE

Before patients can receive compensation they must also show that the injuries suffered were of a type which were 'reasonably foreseeable'. What this means is that were not too remote, i.e. more extensive, of a different type or occurred in a different manner from that which would normally be forseen. In the vast majority of medical negligence cases this is easy to establish as the complaint will be either that the patient is no better because, for example, the original condition or illness has not been cured or prevented, or alternatively because some new injury has been inflicted. In rare cases, however, a consequence may be too remote and therefore not the responsibility of the defendant, notably because the so-called 'chain of causation' has been broken – by some act, either of the patient, or a third party. Although a well-established principle of tort law, which is usually known by its Latin tag of 'novus actus interveniens' (meaning a new act intervening), the courts have been very reluctant to allow defendants to take advantage of it in medical negligence cases. Note too that there is an exception to the forseeability rule, notably the 'thin skull' rule which requires the defendant to take 'his victim as he finds him'.

What lawyers call 'nervous shock' is a type of injury which has only fairly recently been accepted by the courts as forseeable in respect of those who 'witness' medical accidents. In this context claims for nervous shock are usually made by parents who suffer psychiatric illness due to the defendant's negligence which harms their child. For such claims to succeed several criteria must be satisfied. These are quite restrictive and if the Law Commission's proposals are eventually accepted will be relaxed. In the meantime, however, the plaintiff must prove that: their nervous shock can be classified as a recognized psychiatric illness; other 'reasonable' people would have reacted in the same way; the illness is caused by an event which is both horrific and sudden and finally there must be a reasonable degree of proximity between the plaintiff and the victim.

One case where damages were awarded for nervous shock is S v. Distillers Company (Biochemical) Ltd [1973] in which a mother received compensation for the shock suffered as a result of giving birth to a child who was born without arms after she took the drug thalidomide during her pregnancy. Another is Krali v. McGrath [1986] in which following what was described as 'a particularly horrendous piece of mismanagement' one of the plaintiff's twins died eight weeks after birth. The plaintiff was awarded damages for nervous shock as a result of seeing and being told what had happened to her son. In the most recent case of Tredget and Tredget v. Bexley HA [1994] substantial damages for nervous shock were won by both parents who 'witnessed' the avoidable death of their baby two days after birth.

Finally it is worth noting that if a child dies as a result of medical negligence a bereavement claim – currently fixed at £7500 – may be payable to parents under the Fatal Accidents Act 1976.

PROCEDURAL AND PRACTICAL ASPECTS OF NEGLIGENCE CLAIMS

The legal principles which govern liability are obviously very important but so are some of the practical and procedural aspects of medical litigation. Those covered here in outline are the following:

- When must patients bring their claims?
- What can they be compensated for?
- What happens if patients are partly to blame for their injuries?
- Whom should patients sue?

WHEN MUST PATIENTS BRING THEIR CLAIMS?

The normal rule is that victims of personal injury must begin their claims no later than three years from the date of the alleged negligence. But this simple rule immediately raises two major problems. First, what happens if patients do not realize they have suffered harm? Usually patients realize fairly quickly that they have suffered harm – such as after anaesthetic accidents or other surgical mistakes. But in other cases the harm may take many years to come to light, especially where a patient has had prolonged treatment, suffers repercussions from treatment completed years earlier or has a long-term disease. In one case, for example, a two-year-old girl was seen by her GP several times in one week because of abdominal pains. At the end of the week she had to be admitted to hospital for appendicitis. Her appendix had perforated. Twenty years later she discovered that she could not conceive due to adhesions from the original undiagnosed appendicitis. Despite the long gap she was allowed to bring her claim because the Limitation Act 1980 says that the three-year time limit does not start to run until patients find out (or should have found out) that their injuries were 'significant' (i.e. sufficiently serious to justify starting proceedings). In this case the plaintiff did not find out about the harm until twenty years after it actually occurred so that is when the time started to run.

The second problem is a related one. What happens if patients do not know what caused their injuries? In such cases although they may know that they have suffered harm they may be unaware of what actually caused it. Again the Limitation Act 1980 allows an exception here in that the three-year rule starts from the time the patient discovers (or ought to have discovered) the relevant facts, i.e. the negligence which caused the harm.

Finally there are two other circumstances which allow an extension of the usual time limits both of which are relevant to children. One applies to injured patients under 18 for whom the period does not start to run until they are 18. So this means they must begin their claims at any time before their twenty-first birthday. The other covers injured patients who are mentally incompetent. For them the three-year period starts when they are no longer capable of managing their affairs. If they are incompetent throughout their lives proceedings can be taken on their behalf at any time. See, for example, Headford v. Bristol and District HA [1995] in which proceedings were started 28 years after the date of the alleged negligence.

WHAT CAN PATIENTS RECEIVE COMPENSATION FOR?

Patients who win their negligence actions normally receive compensation (known in law as damages). Damages are generally awarded in the form of a 'once and for all' lump sum which cannot be varied. This can be problematic in medical litigation because it is not uncommon for there to be considerable uncertainty at the time the amount is calculated about the victim's post-accident life expectation and needs. One way out of this difficulty is to award provisional damages which can be increased if necessary. Another is a 'structured settlement' under which some or all of a lump sum is used to buy an annuity as a result of which regular periodic payments can be made.

The amounts awarded are assessed by the judge who tries the case. Amounts are based on a tariff system which provides clear guidelines as to what are considered the current standard levels of awards for particular injuries. In the past damages in excess of £1 million were exceedingly rare but now they are much more common, especially in cases where a baby is brain damaged at birth or a young person with a promising career ahead suffers irreversible and catastrophic brain damage. In 1995, for example, £1.4 million was awarded to a fourteen-year-old boy who suffered cerebral palsy as a result of complications during a Caesarian. Soon after that a young woman of 22 was awarded £1.5 million after she was left blind and unable to walk or speak due to oxygen starvation during an operation when she was five. More recently a girl of 18 who was unable to speak due to cerebral palsy caused at birth received £1.65 million.

But what types (or heads as they are usually called) of damage can patients be compensated for? There are several different ways of categorizing damages, for example, 'special' damages cover losses and expenses which have actually been incurred and an estimate of any future expenses and losses, including loss of earnings, whereas general damages are made up of compensation for pain, suffering and loss of amenities.

Another major distinction is between non-financial and financial losses. Non-financial losses consist of pain and suffering and loss of amenities. The amount awarded for pain – which can either relate to the injury itself or consequential treatment – will be reduced if it can be controlled by drugs and may be eliminated altogether if the patient is unconscious. 'Suffering' is typically interpreted very broadly and so can include, for example, embarrassment, humiliation and mental anguish. Awards for loss of amenities (sometimes referred to as loss of faculty or function) are expected to compensate for everything which reduces the plaintiff's enjoyment of life. It therefore can include damages for inability (or reduced capacity) to carry out sporting or other activities, loss of enjoyment of work and the like. Interestingly too no account is taken under this head of whether or not the victim appreciates or is aware of his or her fate. So a person in a coma or with little or no awareness of the injuries suffered can still receive significant damages under this head even though the money can be of no practical benefit.

As to financial losses these are likely to affect children, especially those who have been badly injured, in two main ways. Actual and future earnings may be lost through reduced (or possibly even destroyed) capacity to work. In addition they may be at a disadvantage when competing for jobs and this too must be taken into account. In some cases the life expectancy of the plaintiff is also considerably reduced but even so damages for loss of earnings are still recoverable for the so-called 'lost years', i.e. the years when the plaintiff will in fact be dead but would (had it not been for the negligence) have been alive and working. Recoverable expenses can cover virtually anything but they must be reasonable. They commonly include amounts for increased travelling costs, medical and nursing care, special clothing, diet, equipment and so on. Note that if nursing care is given free – it is not uncommon in accidents involving children for one or both parents to give up work to look after them – the commercial cost of that care is still recoverable even though no money has actually changed hands. Medical expenses can similarly be recovered even if a patient could have used NHS facilities. Housing costs can also increase dramatically, particularly if accommodation has to be specially adapted. Related additional expenditure such as maintenance and running costs can also increase and it may be necessary to pay someone to carry out ordinary household repairs, decorations and such like which the plaintiff, had he or she not been injured, might well have carried out himself or herself.

OTHER COMPENSATION SCHEMES – VACCINE DAMAGE PAYMENTS

In the 1970s public confidence in the government's vaccination programme suffered a serious setback because of adverse publicity linking whooping cough vaccine to brain damage. As a consequence there was a significant drop in the number of children being vaccinated. A state-funded vaccine damage scheme was therefore introduced allowing compensation to be paid in certain circumstances without proof of fault. Under the Vaccine Damage Payments Act 1979 a fixed sum of £30 000 is payable irrespective of the medical condition and personal circumstances of the victim. However, to qualify for compensation applicants have to establish that they have been severely disabled – defined as being no less than 80% – as a result of being vaccinated (after July 1948) against certain specified diseases, namely diphtheria, tetanus, whooping cough, poliomyelitis, measles, rubella, tuberculosis and smallpox. Despite its good intentions the scheme is none the less fundamentally flawed because a causal link between the vaccine and the disability must be proved on the balance of probabilities. In practice this can be an impossible hurdle to overcome – as the case of Loveday v. Renton [1990] in which a claim arising from whooping cough vaccine failed clearly shows. Furthermore claims must be made within a specified time. These time limits must be strictly adhered to, otherwise a claim can be invalidated – as has happened in many cases.

WHAT HAPPENS IF A PATIENT CONTRIBUTES TO HIS OR HER INJURIES

Contributory negligence is a well-established principle of tort law which operates as a partial defence. It covers situations where the plaintiff fails to take care and so adds to his or her own injuries. As a result it is considered fair that the damages payable by the defendant should be reduced by an amount that the law considers represents the plaintiff's share of responsibility. In other words blame is apportioned between the plaintiff and the defendant.

There is no reason why in principle this concept should not be used in health care contexts, especially as patients now increasingly expect to play a part in their own health care and treatment – and so can be expected to take more of the blame when they have 'helped' things go wrong. But there are no English cases where it has been successful, even though there are several ways in which patients may in practice contribute to their injuries. For example, patients may ignore instructions about taking medication (or keeping to a particular diet): or forget to attend follow-up appointments. Alternatively they may not answer questions truthfully – about their medical history, symptoms or known allergic reactions. In some cases too, patients may refuse consent to diagnostic investigations or recommended treatment and leave hospital against medical advice.

With so few relevant precedents it is difficult to speculate how a court would deal with these allegations. Certainly a defendant would have a difficult task in that proof (on the balance of probabilities) would be required not just that the patient failed to take reasonable care but also that he or she ought to have realized what impact this failure would have. And in those cases which involve patient 'non-compliance' – a term used to describe those situations where patients do not follow instructions – the outcome of the case would probably turn on the extent to which a court considers that the defendant should have anticipated the patient's behaviour.

But what about contributory negligence by children? In the past the courts have been very unwilling to find children contributorily negligent, largely because the law does not consider them to be as responsible and careful as adults nor expect them to take as much care of their own health and safety. This is especially so when very young children are involved. None the less there is no age below which it can be said as a matter of law that children cannot be found to have contributed to their own injuries.

Case study 2.5

Errol is eight years old. While on a school trip he develops a serious infection for which he is given a penicillin injection by a local newly qualified GP, Maureen. Maureen does not ask Errol whether he has ever had an allergic reaction to penicillin, nor does she make any other enquiries to establish whether he could be hypersensitive to it. Errol has a bad allergic reaction and nearly dies. He also has to miss several weeks of school.

He sues Maureen who claims that Errol contributed to the harm he suffered because he did not tell her that he was allergic to penicillin.

Is a court likely to reduce Errol's damages on the basis that he was partly to blame? Would it make any difference if Errol was 17?

A court would almost certainly not expect an eight-year-old to volunteer information about his hypersensitivity to penicillin, especially as Maureen had not asked him any specific questions about it. Errol is therefore unlikely to be found contributorily negligent.

If Errol was 17 then the court would have to decide whether any 'ordinary' young person of a similar age and understanding could reasonably be expected to take precautions for his own safety, in other words tell a doctor (without being asked) of penicillin hypersensitivity. While a 17-year-old would clearly be expected to be wiser and more responsible than an eight-year-old it is at least arguable that no minor could be expected to know of the potential dangers of receiving penicillin if he or she was allergic to it. Another issue here would be whether Errol should have realized that penicillin treatment was normally given to treat his condition – assuming that is that Maureen did not tell him.

WHO SHOULD PATIENTS SUE?

In deciding whom to sue patients may have several choices. One is to sue the health professional whose negligence caused their injuries. If more than one was at fault then each is individually responsible for his or her own negligence. Individual practitioners are rarely sued in practice, however, as patients usually sue their employers under the doctrine of vicarious liability (see below). The third possibility is to sue a hospital, health authority or NHS Trust directly irrespective of any vicarious liability. These three alternatives will now be looked at separately.

INDIVIDUAL LIABILITY

All health professionals are personally liable for their negligence. In some cases a practitioner may be solely responsible such as a GP in a single-doctor practice. GPs working in partnership, however, are all jointly responsible for each other's negligence. A nurse, other health professional, likewise anyone else working in the practice, can also be sued personally. If the negligence occurs in hospital (in-patient or out-patient) then if the individual responsible can be identified he or she is again personally accountable. Typically though negligence will occur in the course of treatment, say in the operating theatre, when several health professionals may have been involved, in which case they will each be personally responsible for their own negligence and liability can be apportioned between them. But in some cases it may be more difficult or maybe even impossible to pin responsibility on any particular individual. In such cases the doctrine of vicarious liability and the principle of direct liability may be the only way of ensuring that a patient gets compensation.

VICARIOUS LIABILITY

Under the doctrine of vicarious liability employers are legally responsible for their employees' negligence. This does not mean, however, that negligent employees can escape responsibility because employers normally have the right to recover from them the amount paid out on their behalf – although this rarely happens in practice. Vicarious liability has long been recognized in tort law, yet it has only fairly recently been applied in health care settings. What it means is that employers in the health service, notably NHS employers (health authorities, NHS Trusts), private hospitals and GP practices employing their own staff, are indirectly liable for the negligent acts or omissions of their employees (whether clinical or non-clinical) providing the negligence occurred in the course of their employment. This raises two questions – who is an employee and what is the meaning of the phrase 'course of employment'?

An employee is a person who is engaged by an employer under a **'contract of service'**. So, for example, in a GP practice employees typically include not just other health professionals such as nurses but also receptionists and secretaries. In hospital settings it is also usually fairly easy to identify employees and as a general rule hospital authorities are vicariously liable for all their staff (full-time and part-time) whether medical or otherwise. Less clear, however, is the position of those working in private hospitals where the negligence may be caused by an employee or an 'independent contractor' with whom patients may have their own private contractual arrangements. Similarly it may be difficult to identify who employs agency nurses as their employer could be either the hospital where they are currently working or the supplying agency. None the less in practice it is more than likely that the hospital will be vicariously liable for their negligence.

Health professionals who are not employees are known as 'independent contractors'. This means that they are self-employed and working under a '**contract for services**'. The most obvious examples of independent contractors in the health service are GPs who are not employees of health authorities. Locums and deputies are also generally not employed by GPs and so usually there can be no question of the practice being vicariously liable for their negligent conduct (although in some circumstances they may be directly liable, see below). Other health professionals working in the private sector or independently may or may not be employees, depending on the terms under which they work.

As to what amounts in law to 'course of employment' it is now clear that even if employees improperly perform their jobs, in other words carry them out negligently or fraudulently, then the employer will still be vicariously liable. Disobeying orders too – even if an employee has been expressly forbidden from doing something – will also not normally exempt an employer from vicarious liability, providing the act (or omission) was considered to be within the scope of their employment. Sometimes, employees do something which they have no express authority to do but which nevertheless is intended to benefit the employer's business or property in some way. Unless the means used are so excessive that no employer could have expected such action to be taken, the employer will be vicariously liable.

Case study 2.6
Dolores, a nurse, was out walking her dog late one Saturday afternoon when she comes across an accident. Tommy, a young boy of six, has fallen from a slide and hurt his head. His mother Julie wants to take him to the doctor as he seems badly shaken and has gone very pale. Dolores tells her not to worry as it was only a superficial scratch and anyway 'bumps on the head always look much worse than they really are'. She puts a plaster on Tommy's head and says that since he lives very near her she'll drop in later to see how he is. The next day she visits Tommy round about midday. He has been asleep since the accident but Julie says he was very sick before he went to bed. Dolores still insists that nothing is wrong and that he would be fine in the morning. Later that night Julie takes Tommy to casualty but as a result of the delay he suffers serious long-term injuries.

Is Dolores, who was employed as a nurse at the local hospital, acting in the course of her employment?

Assuming that Dolores was under no legal obligation to provide treatment (which is almost certainly the case), it is clear that she acted as a good Samaritan. As such she is not acting in the course of her employment and therefore her employers are not vicariously liable for her negligence.

Case study 2.7

Maureen, a registrar, has just come on duty and is desperate to have her first cigarette of the day. Because of the hospital's no smoking policy she goes into the toilet which is just next to the children's ward. While there she suddenly remembers something urgent and rushes out, leaving her cigarette which is still alight next to the sink. Meanwhile, Charlie, who has managed to get out of the ward wanders into the toilet where he finds the cigarette. He has several puffs but then drops it on his foot and burns himself.

Was Maureen acting in the 'course of her employment'?

Leaving aside the issue of how Charlie managed to get out of the ward and who should be responsible for not supervising him properly the answer would almost certainly be yes. Maureen may have been doing something she had been told not to do but she could nevertheless still claim that she was doing the job she was employed to do albeit in an unauthorized and exceptionally negligent way.

HEALTH AUTHORITIES AND NHS TRUSTS

The final option open to victims of medical malpractice is to sue hospitals, health authorities and NHS Trusts directly. Direct duties (often also referred to as primary duties) are non-delegable which means they cannot be discharged by delegating them to someone else. There are two types of direct liability. The first, and in practice the most common, is imposed when organizational, operational or administrative failures in a hospital result in the inadequate delivery of a reasonable standard of health care. In other words the employer has not provided enough competent and qualified staff, an effective and adequate level of instruction and supervision, reasonable facilities and equipment or a safe system of work. One example which concerned a hospital's negligent system of management was Wilsher v. Essex HA [1987] (as previously noted) in which a baby born prematurely received inappropriate treatment partly as a result of the inadequate supervision of an inexperienced doctor. Another is Bull v. Devon AHA [1993] (see above) in which a health authority's organization of its maternity services (which were split on two sites) resulted in over an hour's delay before a consultant arrived. As a consequence the plaintiff suffered brain damage during birth and the health authority was held liable.

While this type of direct liability is now well-established the second is more controversial despite being given strong judicial support by Lord Denning as long ago as 1951. In the case of Cassidy v. Ministry of Health [1951] he was very keen to impose direct liability whenever a patient's care fell below a reasonable standard of care and irrespective of who was negligent, be it an employee, independent contractor, agency nurse or anyone else. This second type of liability is contentious because it goes well beyond requiring hospitals and authorities simply to take reasonable care when appointing and retaining staff to ensure that they are competent and so on (as the first type of direct duty does). Instead it imposes a much more onerous and potentially far-reaching liability which in effect makes such hospitals and authorities guarantee that care will be taken whenever a patient is accepted for treatment, irrespective of who treated them and however difficult it may be to identify who was actually responsible for the patient's injuries.

If this second wide interpretation of direct liability is correct it could mean that GPs would be directly liable for any negligence caused by their locums even if they had exercised reasonable care in choosing them. Similarly it would make private hospitals or clinics directly liable to patients who suffer harm again irrespective of who caused it (i.e. an employee or independent contractor). Even more contentiously perhaps it is at least arguable that NHS patients who receive negligent services from the private sector could pursue a claim against the NHS Trust or health authority with whom the arrangement was made.

Case study 2.8

Rebecca, a ten-year-old girl, was hit on the head by a spanner. She was taken to the local hospital and was seen by the casualty officer Omar. He cleaned the wound and inserted several stitches and then sent her home. After the accident Rebecca suffered from bad headaches and dizziness and missed several weeks of school. She was eventually diagnosed as having a depressed fracture and a hole in her skull and had to have an operation. While Omar admits that he was negligent in failing to arrange for an X-ray and treating Rebecca's injury as though it were just a minor cut on the head, he claims that the hospital was to blame because pressure on resources had resulted in a cutback on staff and he was working under a lot of pressure. In short he was overworked, overstretched and overtired.

Could the health authority be directly liable to Rebecca?

As a general rule lack of resources can never be a defence, whatever the impact on individual health professionals – who may as a consequence work longer hours, do jobs they are not qualified for and so on. This is because patients are entitled to a reasonable standard of care which should be assessed objectively (i.e. in accordance with the Bolam standard). That said, however, if lack of resources made it impossible for Omar to meet the Bolam standard, in other words made misdiagnosis unavoidable, then he may be able to avoid personal liability. Instead the courts might impose direct liability on the health authority who through their failure to provide an adequate system of health care have breached their primary duty to Rebecca.

Omar's personal liability would turn on such factors as whether he made appropriate representations about his concerns over staff shortages and the potential risk to patients: whether the negligent treatment could have been avoided had additional precautions been taken or priorities been differently assessed.

CRIMINAL NEGLIGENCE

Very exceptionally health professionals may find themselves facing serious criminal charges. In the past prosecutions were very rare but now, when a patient dies as a result of a medical 'mistake', there is an increasing possibility that the responsible practitioner will be charged with the criminal offence of involuntary manslaughter. But what level of negligence is required before such a charge is brought? Traditionally only what has been described as 'gross' or 'extreme' negligence, i.e. something going well beyond the civil test of negligence has been regarded as sufficient. In other words conduct which is so outrageous and deplorable that society would expect the accused to be punished. But what precise state of mind – the so-called mental element (usually known by its Latin tag of *'mens rea'*) – needs to be proved?

Some guidance on this has now been given following the case of R v. Prentice and Sulman [1993] (see also R v. Adomoko [1995]) in which it was held that in future, health professionals should only be convicted of manslaughter on proof of any one of four states of mind. These are: indifference to an obvious risk of injury to health; or actual foresight of the risk coupled with determination nevertheless to run it; or appreciation of the risk coupled with an intention to avoid it but also coupled with a high degree of negligence in the attempt at avoidance; or inattention or failure to consider a serious risk which went beyond 'mere inadvertence' in respect of an obvious and important matter which the defendant's duty demanded he should have addressed.

This 'new' test as to what constitutes gross negligence is one for the jury to decide. As Lord Mackay said in the Adomoko case the jury has to consider whether the breach of duty should be characterised as gross negligence and therefore a crime. This will depend on the seriousness of the breach committed by the defendant in all the circumstances in which the defendant was placed when it occurred.

COMPLAINTS AND DISCIPLINARY PROCEEDINGS

In this section alternative ways in which victims of medical accidents can seek redress are briefly examined as are other procedures which can be taken to ensure professional accountability.

COMPLAINTS PROCEDURES

Following the publication of the 1994 Wilson Report on NHS Complaints Procedures new proposals for dealing with complaints were introduced in April 1996. The new system (which will not be concerned with disciplinary matters) is both simpler and fairer, embodying the principles recommended in the report, namely, responsiveness, cost effectiveness, accessibility, impartiality, simplicity, speed, confidentiality and accountability. It is also intended to be given wide publicity. It will consist of a two-stage procedure overseen by the Health Service Commissioner. In the first stage provider services should try to resolve the complaint as quickly as possible. In the second complainants will have the option of asking for a further review which may include the establishment of a panel to reconsider the complaint.

Note too that from April 1996 a new standard on complaints was introduced in the Patients' Charter.

Children and complaints

Claims on behalf of incompetent minors will normally be made by their parents or those with parental responsibility. Once competent there is no reason why they should not pursue their own complaints.

Complaints about GPs

Most complaints against family practitioners are brought against GPs. These were dealt with by the Family Health Services Authorities but as from April 1996 have been carried out by new health authorities. They are governed by detailed regulations. Complaints can relate to any aspect of a GP's care and treatment but must allege a breach of his or her terms of service. In practice complaints are typically about failures to make a home visit, refer patients to a consultant or make the correct diagnosis. Allegations of discourtesy or rudeness are outside the terms of service but may be dealt with by informal conciliation processes. Complaints must normally be made in writing and within certain time limits.

Health Service Commissioner

The functions of the Health Service Commissioner (HSC) are very broad and his or her powers extensive. He or she can investigate allegations of injustice or hardship suffered either as a result of a failure of a relevant body to provide a service or as a result of the way the service was provided. The HSC can also investigate allegations of maladministration. The term is not defined but appears to cover 'bias, neglect, inattention, delay, incompetence, ineptitude'. It is thus broad enough to include various types of conduct ranging from not following agreed policies to giving wrong information and failing to respond adequately to a complaint previously made. Although the HSC's powers are wide there are certain limitations, most notably that he or she cannot normally, for example, investigate cases which patients can pursue in the courts nor those concerning the exercise of clinical judgement. Complaints about GPs are also outside its jurisdiction. In practice many complaints are about delays, lack of communication, discharge arrangements, poor supervision of patients and such like.

The new complaints procedure has extended the jurisdiction of the HSC to all complaints by or on behalf of NHS patients and so will include clinical complaints against all NHS staff and all complaints against family health service practitioners.

DISCIPLINARY PROCEDURES – PROFESSIONAL MISCONDUCT

Allegations of professional misconduct concerning health professionals working either in the NHS or privately are dealt with by the relevant Council. Complaints about doctors, which can come from a variety of sources such as the police, patients and other doctors or health professionals, are referred to the General Medical Council (GMC) which is an independent statutory body. It has wide disciplinary powers. If a doctor is found guilty of 'serious professional misconduct' – a term which is not defined but can cover anything from abuse of personal relationships with patients and breach of professional confidence to clinical errors and improper delegation of duties to nurses and others – he or she may be 'struck off' the register. Less draconian disciplinary actions are also possible and in practice much more common. These include putting conditions on a doctor's registration and suspension. Note that the GMC is also responsible for maintaining and improving standards of professional practice.

Complaints, which again can come from several sources – about the professional misconduct and fitness to practise of nurses, midwives and health visitors – are dealt within accordance with the procedures set up by the United Kingdom Central Council for Nursing, Midwifery and Health Visiting (UKCC). The Council has several major functions which include protecting the public from unsafe members and establishing standards of training and professional conduct. Acting through various committees it considers (among other things) allegations of professional misconduct defined as 'conduct unworthy of a registered nurse, midwife, or health visitor'. Sanctions can range from a formal caution, interim suspension to removal from the register.

FURTHER READING

BMA (1992) *Rights and Responsibilities of Doctors*, British Medical Association, London.

Department of Health (1994) *Being Heard. The Report of a Review Committee on NHS Complaints Procedures*, HMSO, London.

Dingwall, R., Fenn, P. and Quam, L. (1991) *Medical Negligence: A Review and Bibliography*, Oxford Centre for Social and Legal Studies, Oxford.

Dugdale, A. and Stanton, K. (1996) *Professional Negligence*, 3rd edn, Butterworths, London.

General Medical Council (1993) *'Blue Book' (Professional Conduct and Discipline: Fitness to Practise)*.

Jones, M. (1991) *Medical Negligence*, Sweet & Maxwell, London.

Lewis, C. (1988) *Medical Negligence, A Plaintiff's Guide*, Frank Cass, London.

Nelson-Jones, R. and Burton, F. (1990) *Medical Negligence Case Law*, Fourmat Publishing, London.

Newdick, C. (1995) *Who Should We Treat? Law, Patients and Resources in the NHS*, Oxford University Press, Oxford.

Powers, M. and Harris, N. (1994) *Medical Negligence*, Butterworths, London.

Renyer, R.L. (1993) *Children and Personal Injury Litigation, Butterworths*, London.

Teff, H. (1995) *Reasonable Care*, Oxford University Press, Oxford.

United Kingdom Central Council for Nursing, Midwifery and Health Visiting (1993) *Complaints about Professional Conduct*, London, UKCC.

Consent to treatment 3

It is only within the last decade that the independent right of children and young people to give consent to medical treatment has been recognized both by the common law – in the case of Gillick v. West Norfolk and Wisbech AHA [1986] – and in legislation, namely the Children Act 1989. According to the Court of Appeal in Re W [1992] (see page 67) the concept of consent serves two quite distinct but related functions. Its 'clinical' function is based on the belief that the patient's co-operation, faith or at least confidence in the efficiency of the treatment is a major factor contributing to the treatment's success whereas its legal function is to protect health professionals from criminal charges and civil claims. In principle the law of consent means that every competent patient is entitled to decide whether to accept or reject treatment irrespective of the wisdom of his or her decision, the reasons for which can be rational, irrational, unknown or even non-existent. But in practice (as will be seen below) the law's commitment to the autonomy of children and young people is far from total. This chapter will begin, however, by describing the general legal principles of the law of consent.

GENERAL PRINCIPLES

The law defines the term 'treatment' very broadly to include surgical, medical, or dental treatment as well as examination, investigation and diagnostic procedures (and any other procedure which is ancillary to such treatment such as anaesthesia). For consent to be legally valid certain criteria must be fulfilled. If they are not then any physical contact with a patient may result in criminal charges or a civil action for trespass. In summary the criteria are as follows.

CONSENT MUST BE EFFECTIVELY OBTAINED

The law does not prescribe what form consent should take except under the Mental Health Act 1983, the Abortion Act 1967 and the Human

Fertilisation and Embryology Act 1990 (despite the widely held but mistaken assumption that written consent is necessary for most operations). Consequently it can take any one of several different forms even though in practice the type of treatment proposed usually determines how it is actually obtained. Basically consent can be either express or implied. Express consent means that consent has clearly and explicitly been given by the patient – either by word of mouth (verbally) or in written form (the consent form). Express verbal consent is typically used for routine minor procedures such as injections and blood tests, likewise other routine day-to-day procedures such as washing patients, turning them over and so forth.

If treatment or other invasive procedures are proposed, such as general anaesthesia, surgery, certain forms of drug therapy and the like, express written consent is normally obtained. While not legally necessary – and so not required to conform to any specific format – standard consent forms are now used throughout the health service. They have several advantages, in particular they directly draw patients' attention to the procedures in question and so provide very strong, albeit not conclusive, evidence that consent was actually sought and obtained. As such they can provide a valuable record of what was agreed should the question of consent subsequently be in dispute. However, a patient's signature on the consent form may well be legally worthless and therefore ineffective as would occur, for example, if he or she was not given appropriate information or explanation, was lied to or was incapable of understanding what was involved.

In many cases patients do not give their express consent, i.e. they do not say anything nor sign any form. Nevertheless their agreement can be implied from their actions (a nod of the head, for example), circumstances or behaviour. In practice this form of consent is very common and is typically relied on for all types of minor procedures such as when patients roll up their sleeves or hold up a bare arm for an injection. There are dangers, though, in too readily assuming that a patient has implicitly given consent or that silence does in fact mean consent as in practice it may not, especially if the surrounding circumstances obviously suggest otherwise or if it turns out that the patient had no idea of what was happening. Nor can it now be assumed (as it was commonly in the past) that patients who, by implication or even expressly, give their general consent to a blood sample being taken are at the same time consenting to all the various different tests which might be thought necessary. Hence in 1993 the General Medical Council firmly rejected HIV testing unless express consent was obtained save 'in the most exceptional circumstances, where a test is imperative in order to secure the safety of persons other than the patient, and where it is not possible for the prior consent of the patient to be obtained'. Similar guidance was also issued by the UKCC in 1994 which again stressed that testing without consent was only acceptable in 'rare and exceptional circumstances where this was necessary in the patient's interests'.

Note finally that consent, whether express or implied, can be withdrawn at any time before or even during the relevant medical procedure. If this happens, fresh consent has to be obtained before treatment can be given or reinstated.

CONSENT MUST BE VOLUNTARY

For consent to be valid it must be freely given, i.e. obtained without force, undue pressure or influence (religious or otherwise) and irrespective of who applies it, for example, relatives or health professionals. This aspect of consent was recently summed up by the Court of Appeal in the case of Re T [1992] when it said:

> The real question in each case is 'Does the patient really mean what he says or is he merely saying it for a quiet life or to satisfy someone else or because the advice and persuasion to which he has been subjected is such that he can no longer think and decide for himself?' In other words, 'Is it a decision expressed in form only, not in reality?'

The answer will, of course, turn on several factors, in particular, the personalities of individuals concerned, the institutional setting, the effect of pain, tiredness, drugs and so on. The relationship of the 'persuader' to the patient may also be of crucial importance, be it a parent, spouse or religious adviser. It was just such a relationship which was the central issue in Re T which concerned the refusal of consent by a 20-year-old pregnant woman who was injured in a car accident when she was 34 weeks pregnant. She was admitted to hospital where, following an emergency Caesarian, her baby was stillborn. Soon afterwards her condition deteriorated (she developed an abscess on her lungs) but as she had refused a blood transfusion on religious grounds a court order was sought overriding her refusal. The issue before the court was whether T's refusal had been freely given, i.e. was it truly voluntary and genuine? Was it based on her own wishes, bearing in mind that she was an ex Jehovah's Witness who retained some beliefs – although these were described as neither 'so deep-seated or so fundamental as to constitute an immutable decision by her as to her way of life – or her way of death'?

The Court of Appeal decided that her refusal did not represent her own independent decision because 'her will had been overborne' by the undue influence exerted by her mother (who was described as a 'fervent, deeply committed' Jehovah's Witness) in the time she had spent alone with her shortly after she was admitted to the hospital. Furthermore as a result of the various drugs she had taken (including sedatives) she was in any event in no fit state to make a decision. This meant that the hospital could lawfully administer blood to her if it was in her best interests.

WHAT INFORMATION MUST PATIENTS BE GIVEN

Central to the law of consent is the controversial issue of how much information should be given to patients to enable them to give free consent. While few would dispute that patients cannot make balanced judgements if their choices are based on false, misleading or distorted information, there is far less agreement as to what exactly must be explained. Should patients be told every little detail about the proposed treatment and its alternatives, every single risk or side effect however small or remote? Or can some information be kept from them? If so, what?

These and related questions raise fundamental issues which inevitably lead to a discussion of the concept of 'informed consent'. Despite not as yet being part of English law a brief explanation of what is generally understood by the concept is appropriate if only because of its extensive use in medico-legal literature and the increasing reference to it in case law. The concept was first coined in the American case of Salgo v Leland Stanford, Jr, University Board of Trustees [1957] where the court held that a patient needs adequate information, i.e. facts about the nature of proposed treatment, its risks and alternatives in order to make an intelligent choice about whether or not to have it. Importantly – and what arguably makes the consent 'informed' – is that the standard of disclosure is based on the so-called 'prudent patient' test. In other words patients should be given the information which they, i.e. those with that particular illness or condition, would expect and want to know, rather than what the doctor thinks they ought to receive (which is the 'professional' test). In its most extreme form the patient-orientated test results in patients being as fully informed as possible. In practice, however, this patient-centred test is undermined as information is commonly withheld by health professionals relying on 'therapeutic privilege' (see below).

What information English law requires to be disclosed was finally settled in Sidaway v. Board of Governors of Bethlem and Royal Hospital [1985]. It concerned a woman who suffered severe disability as a result of an operation in 1974 to cure persistent pain in her neck, arm and shoulder.

One of the recognized risks of the operation was damage to a nerve root, assessed in crude percentage terms as between 1% and 2%.

Another more serious risk – to the spinal cord – was said to be less than 1% likely. Mrs Sidaway was told of the first risk but not the second. Unfortunately her spinal cord was damaged (even though the operation was carried out with all due care). She sued in negligence on the basis that she would not have had the operation had she been told of that risk. The case took just over nine years to reach the House of Lords by which time the surgeon who had performed the operation had died. Nevertheless the House of Lords held that he had acted reasonably in not revealing the very small risk to the spinal cord because in 1974 it was common medical practice not to do so. In short the surgeon was not negligent because he had acted in accordance with a practice accepted as proper by a responsible body of skilled and experienced neuro-surgeons.

The duty of disclosure is therefore determined by the familiar Bolam test in so far as it applies to the specific needs of a particular patient. In effect then, just as with diagnosis and treatment, doctors (and other health professionals) can set their own standards. Moreover it was also decided (in Gold v. Haringey HA [1987]) that the Bolam test applied to disclosure of information even when the treatment in question was non-therapeutic. That said, however, there is some evidence that the courts may in the future be prepared to take a more critical approach to 'accepted practice'. In Smith v. Tunbridge Wells HA [1994], for example, albeit only a High Court decision, the judge held the defendant in breach of his duty because he failed to warn a patient of a risk even though that omission was a practice accepted by a body of doctors at the time.

But what in practice does the Bolam test mean? What information has to be disclosed? According to the Sidaway case it seems that patients must be given 'adequate' or 'sufficient' information, i.e. be told in broad terms about the nature and effect of the procedure and its likely risks. This includes one 'so obviously necessary to an informed choice on the part of the patient that no reasonably prudent medical man would fail to make it'. As a general rule therefore the more serious the risk of harm, the more likely it should be disclosed (even if, in percentage terms it is very remote). So patients should always be told of 'substantial' risks (sometimes these are referred to as material risks or 'grave adverse consequences') .

Some guidance on what information should be disclosed is also given in HC (90)22 which states that patients are entitled to receive 'sufficient information in a way that they can understand about the proposed treatments, the possible alternatives and any substantial or usual inherent risks so that they can make a balanced judgement'. They should also be told of 'dangers which may be special in kind or magnitude or special to that particular patient'.

Therapeutic privilege

Although it should be assumed that most patients would wish to be well informed in some instances it might be justifiable to withhold certain information. Known as 'therapeutic' or professional privilege non-disclosure may be acceptable if revealing certain facts might harm the patient, i.e. damage his or her health or cause psychological harm or distress. Likewise, as the HC (90)22 recommends, a patient's ability to appreciate the significance of information should be assessed before information is disclosed to take into account those who may be shocked, in pain or have impaired sight or hearing or speech (Chapter 2, para. 2).

Answering questions

In the past there was some authority for suggesting that when a patient specifically requested information and asked a direct question about possible risks, then there was a greater obligation to answer that enquiry fully and truthfully. But in the latest case on this issue, namely Blyth v. Bloomsbury AHA [1987], the Court of Appeal rejected any distinction between patients who ask questions and those who do not. This means that although patients should not be misled or lied to, the standard of disclosure is again a matter of clinical judgement and so is governed by the Bolam test. Nevertheless there is some evidence that in this context too this test may be challenged – assuming, that is, that English courts eventually adopt an approach taken recently by the Australian High Court in Rogers v. Whitaker [1992]. Here the judge refused to follow the Bolam test and found the defendant surgeon negligent for failing to warn the plaintiff (who had 'incessantly questioned' him) of a one in 14000 chance of damage to her good eye. The risk materialized and she became virtually blind. The court held that (subject to therapeutic privilege) a doctor has a duty to warn of material risks 'on a reasonable patient' basis. As such it in effect adopted the prudent patient test which interestingly it applied whether or not questions (specific or general) were asked.

PATIENTS MUST BE MENTALLY COMPETENT

For consent to be valid patients must be mentally competent (the words capacity and competence are used interchangeably). Although the law presumes that adults have capacity the term has not been defined by statute. Nevertheless a broad test for capacity was first provided in Re F (Sterilisation) [1990] a case which involved the non-consensual sterilization of a 36-year-old mentally incompetent woman. The House of Lords held that to be legally competent in relation to medical procedures a patient had to be able to understand the 'nature or purpose of an operation or other treatment'. More recently in Re C [1994] the High Court expanded this test by introducing a three-stage approach. The case concerned a 68-year-old Broadmoor patient with paranoid schizophrenia and a gangrenous foot. The recommended treatment was amputation without which there was an estimated 85% risk of death. But C refused consent and applied to court for an injunction preventing amputation without his express written consent. Notwithstanding his mental illness and his delusions which included the belief that he had an international medical practice, the court granted the injunction because it considered C to be legally competent. This was because he was able to comprehend and retain the information he had been given; he believed it, and he had weighed up the information, balancing risks and needs to arrive at a choice.

In practice what this means is that the patient should be able to understand what the medical treatment is, its purpose and nature and why it is being proposed; understand its principal benefits, risks and alternatives; understand in broad terms what will be the consequences of not receiving the proposed treatment; retain the information for long enough to make an effective choice; and make a free choice.

In assessing competence the following points are also relevant.

- A person suffering from mental disorder is not necessarily incapable of understanding, and his or her capacity has to be judged individually in the light of the nature of the decision required and mental state at the time.
- A person's ability to understand may vary from time to time but this in itself should not constitute incapacity since competence should be assessed at the time the treatment is proposed.
- Any assessment of competence must be made in relation to specific treatment proposed.
- A patient may be competent even if his or her decision seems irrational, unreasonable or the reasons for it are unknown.
- The degree of understanding varies with the nature of the treatment. Furthermore it seems that there is no legal requirement that the patient actually understands the nature of the proposed treatment and so forth, merely that he or she has the capacity to do so.
- Although it may be good practice to consult relatives when an adult patient is incompetent any consent given or refused by them on the patient's behalf has no legal validity. None the less relatives' views may be of some value in so far as they provide evidence of the patient's own wishes.

Finally the Law Commission's definition of mental incapacity is also worth noting even if it is unlikely to be incorporated into legislation in the near future. It is: if at the material time the patient is (a) unable by reason of mental disability to make a decision for himself or herself on the matter in question; or (b) he or she is unable to communicate his or her decision on that matter because he or she is unconscious or for any other reason.

EXCEPTIONS TO THE PRINCIPLE OF CONSENT

In certain circumstances patients can be treated without their consent. These include the following.

THE UNCONSCIOUS PATIENT

It is well settled that health professionals faced with an unconscious adult patient (who is thus unable to give or withhold consent) can give such emergency medical treatment as is necessary to save his or her life and health. But treatment must be limited to that which is necessary to meet the emergency and so cannot include any treatment which could be postponed until the patient was in a position to make a decision for himself or herself. Note also that even in an emergency treatment cannot be carried out to which it is known that the patient would object if in a position to do so.

LEGISLATION

The most important legislation here is the Mental Health Act 1983 which contains several provisions authorizing non-consensual medical treatment (for mental disorder) for those compulsorily detained (see Chapter 10). The Public Health (Control of Disease) Act 1984 also provides for the compulsory examination, removal to hospital, and detention in hospital of people with notifiable diseases.

INCOMPETENT PATIENTS

Where adult patients are incapable of giving consent because they lack capacity then medical treatment can be given which is (a) necessary and (b) in their 'best interests' providing it does not conflict with the known wishes of the patient. Necessity in this context is not limited to emergency treatment but also covers any treatment which 'preserves the life, health or well-being of the patient' (see Re F above). As such it includes minor routine procedures as well as major surgery. The patient's best interests is determined by the Bolam test and thus must accord with a practice accepted by a responsible body of relevant medical opinion.

MINORS

In certain cases involving children under 18 consent may be sought from either those with parental responsibility or the court (see below).

REFUSING CONSENT

While it is a well-recognized principle that competent adults have the legal right to refuse treatment, the courts have only recently given some general guidelines as to the factors which health professionals should consider in such situations. In Re T (see above) the Court of Appeal said that doctors should give 'very careful and detailed consideration to the patient's capacity at the time of the decision'. Other relevant factors include an assessment of the true scope and basis of the refusal, i.e. whether the patient intended it to apply to the particular circumstances which had arisen; whether the refusal was based on false assumptions or those which had not been realized; whether the patient's refusal represented his or her own 'true' decision or had it been reached because of, for example, undue influence; whether the patient's capacity had been temporarily reduced to a level below that which was needed for a refusal of that significance. Finally in cases where there was doubt as to a patient's competence and where failure to treat threatened the patient's life or irreparable damage to his or her health the court's assistance should be sought. In an emergency this can be provided very quickly as happened in the case of Re S [1992].

This concerned a 'born-again Christian', 30-year-old pregnant mother of two whose third baby was six days overdue. She was competent but refused surgery on religious grounds. But despite her 'informed refusal' a Caesarian was performed to save both the foetus – who was in transverse lie – and the mother who faced the 'gravest risk of a ruptured uterus'. With no English case directly on the point the High Court reached a decision in just 20 minutes that the operation could be performed without the mother's consent relying mainly on the discredited American case of Re AC [1990].

Re S was a very controversial decision not only because it failed to save the foetus – who died in utero – but also because it undermined one of the most cherished principles of medical law, namely the right of conscious competent adult patients to control what happens to their bodies. In practice, however, Re S is very unlikely to be followed until such time as the Court of Appeal or House of Lords endorses its approach, namely to make the interests of an unborn child determinative and thereby give it an independent legal personality.

ACTING WITHOUT CONSENT

Except in the circumstances outlined above health professionals who treat patients without consent can face criminal charges or be sued for damages if treatment involves physical contact.

CRIMINAL LIABILITY

Criminal prosecutions for non-consensual medical treatment are almost never brought even though in theory health professionals could be charged with various offences under the Offences Against The Person Act 1861 or for the common law crimes of assault and battery.

CIVIL LIABILITY

In tort law an action for 'medical battery' arises when there has been no consent at all. In other words the patient has not given either express or implied consent to treatment. Although rare in practice such actions would be appropriate if, for example, a patient was treated despite his or her express refusal or, because of a mix up in a patient's notes, the wrong operation was performed on the wrong patient. In one case a claim in battery succeeded when a patient asked to be injected in the right arm but was instead injected in her left. Another concerned an operation on a patient's back when he had only consented to toe surgery. The reasons why the plaintiffs in all these cases were successful were twofold. First, the contested procedures were wholly unconnected with (and totally different from) those agreed to. Secondly, they could not be defended on the grounds of necessity in that treatment without consent on an unconscious patient is only justified if a condition is discovered which must be treated immediately to save the patient's life or health and which cannot be postponed until he or she recovers consciousness. Actions for battery cannot be brought, however, once the patient has been informed 'in broad terms' of the nature of the treatment. Nevertheless those patients who do claim have a much easier task than those who have to base their claim on negligence (see below) because patients suing for battery do not have to suffer any loss – and so do not have to prove causation. Damages are also assessed differently in battery as a patient can recover all direct damages however remote or unforseen.

Almost all consent-related claims are in practice likely to be based on negligence. They are appropriate where the patient did give consent – which is why an action for battery cannot be taken – but he or she claims that the consent is inherently flawed. The 'flaw' can take several different forms but will typically be that certain crucial information was not disclosed, such as the risks associated with the treatment and so on. But, as was noted above, patients are not entitled to know everything about their treatment as the standard of disclosure is determined by the Bolam test. This means that a negligence action will almost always fail if the defendant acted in accordance with a practice accepted at the time as proper by a body of skilled and experienced practitioners.

But even supposing that a patient can prove breach of the duty of disclosure he or she still has to overcome what is in practice an almost insurmountable hurdle, namely, the causation element. In a consent-related action this means convincing a court on the balance of probabilities that the defendant's failure to disclose certain information caused the harm. Or to put it another way the patient would not have agreed to the treatment had the relevant information been given. What this means is that if it can be shown that the patient would have consented anyway – despite being deprived of the relevant information – then the claim will fail.

CHILDREN AND CONSENT

The independent rights of under-age children to determine their own medical treatment were, or so it was thought, finally settled by the combined effect of the landmark Gillick case in 1986 and, just a few years later, the Children Act 1989. Although the Gillick case concerned consent to contraceptive treatment, its impact went well beyond that largely because of the concept of 'Gillick competence' which it introduced. Hence after the case it was widely assumed that in certain circum-stances, children had the right to consent not just to contraceptive advice and treatment without their parents' knowledge or consent, but also to all other forms of medical treatment. Moreover it was also assumed that a 'Gillick competent' child had as much legal right to refuse treatment as to consent to it. The law's commitment to advancing children's rights also appeared to be strengthened by the Children Act 1989 which, while not generally making children's wishes determinative, nevertheless con-siderably strengthened their rights to be independently consulted about decisions which affected them. Less equivocally, several provisions relating to medical, psychiatric or other examinations appeared to give mature children an absolute statutory right of informed refusal.

But just over a decade later the law's apparent commitment to the principle of autonomy has been shown to be far less strong than was originally supposed. This is because in several cases it has become clear how in practice the courts are prepared to deny children their 'right' to control medical decisions. Thus if children's wishes are considered not to be in their best interests, the temptation to challenge their legal capacity becomes almost irresistible. Once dismissed as incompetent their wishes can be ignored and decisions can be made on their behalf. More contro-versial, however, is that the courts have overridden the refusal of mature children even when there is no doubt about their competency. But, despite these developments, the concept of 'Gillick competence' is still largely intact in that it plays a major part in relation to giving consent (as opposed to refusing consent) in respect of children under 16. Given the complexity of the law it is, however, necessary to separate children into three different age groups.

16- AND 17-YEAR-OLDS

GIVING CONSENT

Children generally achieve adult status at 18 but in relation to medical treatment young people reach maturity at a younger age by virtue of the Family Law Reform Act 1969. This Act gives 16- and 17-year olds the same rights to consent to medical treatment as adults, providing they are competent (see assessment of competence p. 60), which like adults they are assumed to be until shown otherwise. But under the Family Law Reform Act the concept of 'treatment' is more limited. Thus although it includes 'surgical, medical or dental treatment and any procedure undertaken for the purpose of diagnosis and procedures such as the administration of anaesthetics which are ancillary to treatment', it is not wide enough to cover the giving of blood, taking of a blood sample, tissue or organ donation, cosmetic surgery or use of the body for experimentation or research. Consent for these and other non-therapeutic procedures would nevertheless be covered by the concept of 'Gillick competence' (even though that concept is generally applied to under 16-year-olds) except for the taking of blood samples which again is covered by the Family Law Reform Act 1969. s. 21 of that Act allows competent 16- and 17-year olds to give consent to the taking of 'bodily samples' which are defined as 'bodily fluids or tissues taken for scientific tests'. The effect of the Family Law Reform Act 1969 is significant in that the consent of competent 16- and 17-year-olds cannot be overridden by their parents (or others with parental responsibility) who consequently have no power of veto. On the other hand it can be overridden by a court.

If a 16- or 17-year old is incompetent consent can be given on his or her behalf by a 'proxy' – almost always in practice someone with 'parental responsibility'. Two questions are therefore relevant here. The first is, who has parental responsibility and the second is, who can give consent when no one has parental responsibility? The term 'parental responsibility' was introduced by the Children Act 1989. If a child is legitimate (a legitimate child is one whose parents were either married at the time of the child's conception or birth, or who married after that time) both parents automatically have parental responsibility. When a child's parents are not married only the mother automatically has parental responsibility but the father can acquire it in several ways, for example, by marrying the mother, obtaining a court order or making a parental responsibility agreement with the mother. Other people, including local authorities, adoptive and surrogate parents can also acquire parental responsibility as can grandparents and step-parents. If more than one person has it then as a general rule each of them can act alone and give consent to medical treatment without consulting the other (or others).

Except in an emergency when health professionals can treat an incompetent 16- or 17-year-old (who is, for example, unconscious) without consent the power to give consent to treatment may be given by any person who, despite not having parental responsibility, is none the less currently caring for the young person. Statutory authority for this is contained in s. 3(5) of the Children Act 1989 which allows consent to be given by a temporary 'de facto' carer for what is 'reasonable in all the circumstances of the case for the purpose of safeguarding or promoting the child's welfare'.

REFUSING CONSENT

Competent 16- and 17-year olds were once thought to have the same rights to refuse treatment as adults. But several poignant cases in the early 1990s have established that the Family Law Reform Act 1969 only gives mature young people partial autonomy. Thus while it undoubtedly gives them a right to consent to treatment it does not give them a right of refusal. This is because their informed refusal can be overridden by someone who has the power to consent on their behalf, namely anyone with parental responsibility or the court.

One of the first cases to establish this was Re W (Medical treatment) [1992]. It concerned a 16-year-old anorexic girl who before the case came to court had been fed (with her consent) by a naso-gastric tube and had her arms encased in plaster. But by the time the case was heard by the Court of Appeal she was refusing such 'treatment' and apart from drinking 12 cups of tea a day had refused all food for the previous nine days. As a result her weight had dropped to 35 kgs which for a girl of 1.7 metres was dangerously low. Medical opinion was unanimous that if she continued to refuse food, within a week her capacity to have children would be seriously at risk and a little later her life might be in danger. Given these circumstances and the fact that the anorexia was said to be capable of destroying her ability to make an informed choice, the court concluded that her refusal could be overridden. In addition the case established the following principles:

- even when a person reached 16, if he or she refused consent then anyone with parental responsibility, likewise a court, could override his or her refusal and give consent (irrespective of the minor's competence) on their behalf until the age of 18;

- a young person's refusal is a very important consideration in making clinical judgements and its importance increases with age and maturity.

Unsurprisingly Re W was a controversial decision. First, it significantly undermined the autonomy principle by returning to the pre-Gillick era of parental paternalism, i.e. giving important decision-making powers back to parents. Secondly, it left the law in an uncertain state, in particular as regards the kinds of circumstances in which a child's wishes could be overridden. While the justification for over-ruling W's wishes were regarded by many as indisputable – her health was rapidly deteriorating and her life was in danger – the Court of Appeal failed to give clear guidance on what other kinds of cases would also justify such action. According to one Law Lord a court would be justified in overriding a child's wishes whenever 'his or her welfare is threatened by a serious and imminent risk that it will suffer grave and irreversible mental or physical harm'. Similarly another thought the courts' intervention justifiable where refusal of treatment would 'in all probability lead to the death of a child or to severe permanent injury'. But typically Lord Donaldson took a much broader view of the court's powers. He implied that they could be invoked whenever the court thinks it is in a child's 'best interests'.

The extent of a parent's (and others with parental responsibility) power to give valid consent and thus override children's informed refusal is also unclear. Undoubtedly health professionals could rely on their consent whenever a child faced a life-threatening condition but beyond that the legal position is uncertain except in relation to treatments in the so-called special category such as sterilization where the court's prior permission is required (see below). But notwithstanding the uncertain state of the law it is generally assumed that whenever treatment is in a child's 'best interests' health care professionals could act on the basis of consent by anyone with parental responsibility.

Case study 3.1
Jason is 17. Last night he was involved in a serious car accident and was rushed to casualty. It became clear fairly soon that he needed a blood transfusion but he is adamant that he will not have one because of his religious beliefs – for the past two years he has been a very committed Jehovah's Witness. Hospital staff are very anxious that without treatment he will die and they contact his parents, Freda and Gerry. Freda thinks that her son's wishes should be respected but Gerry tells the hospital that they have his authority to proceed with the blood transfusion.

Must the hospital respect Jason's wishes, given that he is competent to make his own medical decisions? Can health professionals ignore Jason's wishes and rely on Gerry's consent? What if Jason's parents cannot be found or if they both refuse consent? Who can give consent on his behalf?

Even though Jason is competent his refusal of treatment can be overridden as his rights under the Family Law Reform Act 1969 (s. 8) do not give him an absolute right to refuse treatment. Jason's wishes should nevertheless be carefully considered and should be a very important factor in deciding whether to give treatment.

Health professionals could rely on Gerry's consent despite Freda's refusal if he had parental responsibility for Jason. This is because s.8(3) of the Family Law Reform Act 1969 is generally assumed to preserve the right of a parent to give consent. Gerry would have parental responsibility for Jason if he was married to Freda, for example, or if not because he had subsequently acquired parental responsibility in one of the ways specified in the Children Act 1989. Note that as long as one person with parental responsibility gives consent that makes treatment lawful even if others with parental responsibility disagree. In other words it is not necessary to obtain the consent of all those with parental responsibility as the consent of only one will do.

If neither of Jason's parents can be contacted or if they both refuse consent then the court's permission should be sought. In an emergency proceedings can be started very quickly. Note too that in non-urgent cases disputed treatment should be postponed until the dispute has been resolved by court proceedings if necessary.

CHILDREN UNDER 16

GIVING CONSENT

Children under the age of 16 can give a valid consent to treatment providing they are 'Gillick competent'. This concept was established in the Gillick case which reached the House of Lords in 1986. Mrs Gillick sought a declaration that a DHSS circular advising doctors that they could give contraceptive advice and treatment to girls under 16 without their parents' knowledge or consent, was unlawful because it deprived parents of their parental authority. Mrs Gillick lost in the High Court, won in the Court of Appeal and lost again in the House of Lords because it rejected the claim that parental authority was absolute. The basis of the House of Lords judgement was that parental rights were recognized in law only so far as they were needed to protect children. They were not a 'reward' of parenthood but were rather a 'dwindling' right which 'yielded to the child's right to make his own decisions when he reaches a sufficient understanding and intelligence to be capable of making up his own mind'.

'Gillick competent' children were thus legally entitled, in certain circumstances, to determine their own medical treatment. But what does 'Gillick competence' mean? What is the precise legal test of capacity? Although used extensively in medico-legal literature and case law there is still uncertainty as to what the concept means. There is some authority, for example, for asserting that the Gillick test requires a higher standard of informed understanding than is required for adults – because they not only have to understand medical issues such as the purpose of treatment but also wider issues, such as moral and social implications. Another difficult area is that of fluctuating capacity which was the main issue in the controversial case of Re R [1991] (see page 71).

Notwithstanding this uncertainty it is widely assumed that the 'Gillick' test is passed when a child has the capacity to understand the nature of the proposed treatment, i.e. the intellectual and emotional maturity to have a full understanding and appreciation both of the treatment, in terms of its intended and possible side effects and, equally important, the anticipated consequences of a failure to treat. Capacity is thus a flexible concept which is not determined by applying any fixed or rigid criteria but involves instead an individual assessment of the child's ability to understand in relation to the specific treatment proposed.

Guidance to lawyers and doctors on 'Gillick competence' issued jointly in 1995 by the Law Society and British Medical Association states that from the viewpoint of good practice assessment of capacity should include consideration of the young person's ability to understand that there is a choice and that choices have consequences; willingness and ability to make a choice (including the option of choosing that someone else makes treatment decisions); understanding the nature and purpose of proposed procedure; understanding of the proposed procedure's risks and side effects; understanding of the alternatives to the proposed procedure and the risks attached to them, and the consequences of no treatment; and freedom from pressure.

Other points to bear in mind when assessing 'Gillick competence' are the following:

- Although age is not an automatic indicator of competence the ability to understand will normally increase with age and maturity.
- The degree of understanding and intelligence required will inevitably vary depending on the complexity of the proposed treatment and the risks associated with it.

- Competence, according to Re R [1991] is a developmental concept which must be assessed on a broad, long-term basis taking into account a child's whole medical history, background and mental state. This means that a child is not 'Gillick' competent if his or her capacity to understand fluctuates on a day-to-day or week-to-week basis. Re R concerned a girl of 15 who suffered from cyclical mental illness. Her behaviour was at times aggressive, violent and suicidal but in the less acute phases of her illness she was sufficiently rational to give valid consent to treatment. Nevertheless despite her moments of lucidity the Court of Appeal overruled her refusal of treatment (medication) without which she would undoubtedly return to her psychotic state. As Lord Donaldson said: 'No child who was only competent on a good day can pass the "Gillick" test.'

- Advice in HC 90(22) which states that treatment without parental knowledge is exceptional and that health professionals should make every effort to persuade the child to allow his or her parents to be informed, except in circumstances where it is clearly not in the child's best interests to do so.

Note finally that a court, but not a person with parental responsibility, can override a 'Gillick' competent child's consent.

Case study 3.2
Janis is nearly 15½. Since the age of 14 she has been going out with Joe who is just 16. Last month she found out that she was pregnant. Although she and Joe intend to get married one day and have a family they realize that they are both very young and that now would not be the right time to start a family. Janis therefore reluctantly decides to have an abortion. But when she tells her parents they are horrified, especially her mother, Frances, who considers abortion wrong and something that Janis will always regret. The next day Frances rushes to see the family's GP saying she would be willing to look after her grandchild and anyway since she's Janis's mother she has the right to stop her having an abortion.

Does Janis have the right to consent to an abortion? Even if she does can her consent be overridden by Frances or anyone else? What difference would it make if Janis was just 13?

If Janis is 'Gillick competent' she has the right to give valid consent to treatment although her pregnancy can only be terminated if the criteria in the Abortion Act 1967 apply.

If Janis is 'Gillick competent' her consent cannot be overridden by anyone with parental responsibility but the court could overrule her and prevent the abortion if it considered one to be contrary to her best interests.

If Janis was only 13 then she would still be independently able to give consent provided she was 'Gillick competent'. In the case of Re B (abortion) [1991], for example, a girl as young as 12 was held to be mature enough to give consent to an abortion despite her mother's opposition. If Janis is not 'Gillick competent' anyone with parental responsibility can give consent on her behalf.

Case study 3.3
Pauline will shortly be 16. She has been in the care of a local authority since she was 10 years old and has been a drug addict for the previous two years. Her boyfriend has just died of AIDS and she decides to have an HIV antibody test. But the local authority think Pauline is far too young to understand the implications of a test and want to stop her having one.

Can Pauline consent to an HIV test?
Can the local authority stop her?

If Pauline is considered 'Gillick competent' then she can give a valid consent to an HIV test. Given the serious consequences of a diagnosis of HIV and the crisis it might precipitate for Pauline, however, the degree of understanding she will be expected to have will be considerable and certainly higher than that which would be required for minor surgery.

If Pauline is the subject of a care order then the local authority will have parental responsibility for her which they will share with others (usually her parents). While this would give the local authority the right to consent to an HIV test on Pauline's behalf if she was not 'Gillick competent' it does not give it the right to override her consent if she was. However, the local authority could apply to court which would make whatever order it considered would safeguard and promote Pauline's welfare.

REFUSING CONSENT

Just as with competent 16- and 17-year-olds, the rights of 'Gillick competent' children under 16 to refuse consent to treatment can be overridden both by a court and any person with parental responsibility. However, in such cases as Lord Donaldson stressed in Re W [1992] 'the child's views are of the utmost importance and consequently a very significant factor in deciding whether to give the proposed treatment'.

Case study 3.4

Moira is 15. She has thalassaemia and requires monthly blood transfusions and daily injections. She has been accommodated by the local authority for the previous six months and lives with foster parents. Recently she has been finding the treatment increasingly debilitating and distressing and has not kept properly to the regime. Last week she decided to refuse all further treatment, a decision her mother supports but not the local authority. Health professionals consider her to be 'Gillick competent' but are anxious to continue treatment without which Moira will die.

Can Moira's refusal be overridden? If so by whom?

Even if Moira is 'Gillick competent' her refusal can be overridden either by anyone with parental responsibility or the court. But in this case the only person with parental responsibility is Moira's mother who is also refusing consent. The local authority does not have parental responsibility for Moira because she is only being voluntarily accommodated (if Moira was the subject of a care order the local authority would have parental responsibility for her). Accordingly it does not have the power to override Moira's refusal of treatment. Nevertheless application could be made to the court (either by the local authority or the hospital) for permission to carry out the treatment.

CHILDREN UNDER 16 – NOT 'GILLICK COMPETENT'

GIVING CONSENT

If children are not 'Gillick competent' permission for treatment has to be sought from a proxy – normally a person with parental responsibility, exceptionally a child's temporary carer (under s.3(5) Children Act 1989) or the court. But what is the scope of a proxy's powers? The first broad answer to this is to be found in the Children and Young Person's Act 1933 (s.1) which sets a minimal standard of parental care and imposes criminal sanctions on any person over 16 who has responsibility for a child under the age of 16 who (among other things) 'wilfully assaults, ill-treats, neglects, abandons or exposes him ... in a manner likely to cause him unnecessary suffering or injury to health'. In effect this imposes a duty to obtain essential medical assistance for that child. Other guidance on the limits of a proxy's powers is derived from case law and is that the right to consent to treatment must be exercised in the child's 'best interests'.

The concept of 'best interests' has yet to be definitively defined although broad guidelines were given in relation to a severely handicapped baby (see Re J [1990], Chapter 9). None the less there are certain procedures which are unquestionably within its scope, such as any treatment which is 'therapeutic', i.e. intended to benefit the child. This would cover treatment for a specific condition such as a physical illness (or psychiatric disorder) as well as diagnostic procedures and preventive measures like vaccinations. More questionable are those procedures which are arguably non-therapeutic such as organ or tissue donation, cosmetic surgery, testing for genetic disorders, and certain research involving children. To authorize cosmetic surgery for a five-year-old girl in the hope that her chances of being a successful actress would therefore improve would, for example, go well beyond the limits of a proxy's power. Similarly unlawful would be any procedure which is prohibited by statute, such as the Female Circumcision Act 1985.

Note also that there are some procedures – in the so-called 'special category' – for which the court's prior approval is required. This includes sterilization to prevent a pregnancy and *inter vivos* organ donation for transplant but not abortion nor therapeutic treatment which has the effect of making the patient sterile.

REFUSAL OR ABSENCE OF CONSENT

In rare cases no-one with parental responsibility (or temporary care) may be available to give consent. For example, an unconscious child is brought into casualty following a road accident in which both her parents have died. In such cases consent is not required because the situation is an 'emergency' one in which treatment can be carried out provided it is necessary to safeguard the life and health of the child and does not go beyond what is required to end the emergency. Non-consensual treatment is also lawful where a child has been abandoned, neglected or abused. In such cases, however, a local authority is likely to take compulsory protective action thereby acquiring parental responsibility and the legal authority to give consent.

More problematic are those cases where a parent refuses consent to treatment and there is no one else with parental responsibility who is prepared to give the necessary consent. This happened in Re S [1993] when parents of a 4½-year-old child with T-cell leukaemia refused consent to a blood transfusion for religious reasons (the court overrode their refusal). In such situations an application should be made to court under its inherent jurisdiction (rather than under the Children Act 1989) for permission to carry out the proposed treatment. But when a child's life is in immediate danger and there is no time to make a court application the procedure recommended in HC (90)22 should be followed, namely that hospital authorities should rely on the clinical judgement of the relevant health professional after full discussion with the parents. In addition, written supporting evidence from a medical colleague should be obtained that the child is in danger if the treatment is withheld. The need to treat should also be discussed with the parents in the presence of a witness who should countersign the record of the discussion in the clinical notes.

Case study 3.5
Nathan was born prematurely. He is now nine months old but suffers from respiratory distress syndrome. Doctors think a blood transfusion may be necessary but his parents, because of their religious beliefs, are refusing to consent.
    Can the hospital authorities override Nathan's parents refusal?

If Nathan's life is in immediate danger then health professionals can treat him without his parents' (or the court's) consent – on the basis that they are acting in his best interests in an emergency. The procedure outlined in HC (90)22 should none the less be followed. If treatment can be postponed without endangering Nathan's life then the court's permission should first be sought (see Re O (medical treatment) (1993) for a case with similar facts).

ROLE OF THE COURT

Consent-related disputes involving children under 18 are rarely taken to court but there have been several examples in recent years where the court's protective and supervisory functions have been invoked, notably in the following types of cases:

- when parents (or others with parental responsibility such as a local authority) and competent children disagree about proposed treatment – *for example a 15-year-old wants an abortion which her parents oppose;*
- when parents and health professionals disagree about proposed treatment for an incompetent child – *for example, parents refuse consent for a life-saving blood transfusion to be given to their three-year-old son;*
- when a Gillick mature minor (or competent 16 and 17-year-olds) refuse life-saving treatment and there is no one with parental responsibility available to provide the necessary consent – *for example a 16-year-old cancer patient refuses treatment, a decision supported by his parents;*
- when there is doubt about the validity of a child's consent or refusal – *for example a 14-year-old with fluctuating capacity refuses to take prescribed drugs;*

- when the medical treatment sought has such serious implications (i.e. 'special category' cases) that the court's prior permission must be sought.

Once the court is involved it has a wide discretion but any decision must be in the child's best interests. Accordingly it can:

- override parental opposition to treatment and so give permission for it to be carried out;
- override a competent minor's informed refusal (whether he or she is over or under 16) and authorize treatment;
- override any consent that has been given, whether by a parent (or other person with parental responsibility) or competent minor and thus prevent treatment being initiated or continued;
- authorize treatment in the 'special category';
- control media publicity so as to prevent identification of a patient or his or her carers.

While the court's powers are thus very extensive in that it retains the ultimate decision-making power and can consequently both review decisions made by others and impose its own view of a child's best interests it is subject to one very important limitation. That is that save in the most exceptional circumstances it will never order a health professional (likewise a health authority or NHS Trust) to adopt a course of treatment which is, in the clinical judgement of those concerned, contra-indicated as not being in the patient's best interests (see Re J [1992] Chapter 1).

CONSENT AND THE CHILDREN ACT 1989

Several provisions in the Children Act 1989, namely those in Part IV and V dealing with child protection (see Chapter 11) enable the court to include in court orders directions about medical and psychiatric examinations and assessments (and exceptionally also treatment). The orders in question are: interim care and supervision orders; full supervision orders; child assessment and emergency protection orders. But whatever the context the Act specifically states that children with 'sufficient understanding to make an informed decision' can refuse to submit to them. This, it was widely assumed, meant that children who satisfied the statutory competency test had an absolute right to refuse medical and other examinations. But notwithstanding the unambiguous language of the Act they too can have their wishes overridden. Thus in South Glamorgan County Council v. W. and B [1993] the court over-ruled the wishes of a 15-year-old girl with severe behavioural problems. She had refused to undergo various medical and psychiatric examinations and assessments but, despite being of sufficient understanding to make an informed refusal (i.e. she was competent), the court overruled her refusal since without the medical and other examinations she was likely to suffer serious harm. In short they were in her best interests and the court could therefore order her to submit to them.

FURTHER READING

Alderson, P. (1990) *Choosing for Children*, Oxford University Press, Oxford.

Brazier, M. (1991) 'Competence, consent and proxy consents'. In M. Brazier and M. Lobjoit (eds) *Protecting the Vulnerable*, Routledge, London.

British Medical Association and the Law Society (1995) *Assessment of Mental Capacity: Guidance for Doctors and Lawyers*, BMA, London.

Department of Health (1990) *A Guide to Consent for Examination and Treatment*, HC (90) 22, HMSO, London.

Hendrick, J. (1993) *Child Care Law for Health Professionals*, Radcliffe Medical Press, Oxford.

Kennedy, I. (1992) 'Consent to treatment'. in C. Dyer (ed.) *Doctors, Patients and the Law*, Blackwell Science Ltd, Oxford.

Law Commission (1995) *Mental Incapacity* (Report 231), HMSO, London.

Montgomery, J. (1994) 'Children's legal rights in health care and research: the retreat from Gillick'. In SSRU, *Children's Decisions in Health Care*, University of London.

Confidentiality and medical records

4

Patients have a legitimate expectation that the information they give to health professionals will be kept secret. This expectation is an essential element of the professional–patient relationship and one of the most fundamental principles of health care which was first enshrined in the famous Hippocratic Oath in the fifth century BC. More up-to-date guidance for practitioners is now contained in the General Medical Council's (GMC's) 'Blue Book' and the UKCC Code of Professional Conduct for Nurses, Midwives and Health Visitors. The duty of confidentiality is based on the assumption that unless patients can trust professionals to respect their privacy some may withhold important, but embarrassing details or, worse still, may not seek essential medical care at all. A 15-year-old, for example, who wants to go on the pill – which she knows her parents would oppose – is unlikely to go to the family doctor if she thinks her parents will be told.

The duty of confidentiality is also a well-established legal right recognized both by the common law and more recently by statute. In Hunter v. Mann [1974] for example, the judge said:

> the doctor is under a duty not to disclose, without the consent of the patient, information which he, the doctor has gained in his professional capacity.

None the less the law acknowledges that there may be some circumstances when confidential information can be revealed. In other words the duty of confidentiality is not absolute. Supposing, for example, a baby is brought to the surgery with a broken arm and other injuries which the mother claims were caused when the baby fell out of her high chair. The GP suspects that the baby is being abused. Does the GP have a discretion (or even a duty) to report his or her suspicions? Before dealing with this and other exceptions to the duty of confidentiality the right of children to have their confidences respected will be outlined.

CHILDREN AND CONFIDENTIALITY

Whether or not a duty of confidentiality is owed to children turns on the maturity of the child in question. It is therefore necessary to divide children into three categories: 16- and 17-year-olds, 'Gillick competent' under-16-year olds and incompetent children under 16.

16- AND 17-YEAR-OLDS

Adolescents in this age group have the same rights as adults in relation to consent to treatment. As such they also have a corresponding right to confidentiality. But the duty of confidentiality only arises if they are competent. If not then just as with incompetent adult patients the duty to act in the patient's best interests (see below) may mean that confidential information can be disclosed to relatives (normally their parents).

'GILLICK COMPETENT' UNDER-16-YEAR-OLDS

As great a duty of confidence is owed to Gillick mature minors as competent 16- and 17-year-olds, i.e. they are treated as adults. This is because the law assumes that if they are mature enough to consent to treatment then they also have sufficient understanding and intelligence to enter into a confidential relationship. Again therefore a duty of confidence is owed to them.

INCOMPETENT UNDER-16-YEAR-OLDS

A child who fails to pass the 'Gillick' competency test (and is therefore not competent to consent to treatment) may nevertheless have sufficient maturity to form a relationship of confidence, i.e. to understand what it means to trust someone with 'secret' information. If so, there is some legal authority for saying that a duty of confidence is owed. Moreover irrespective of the legal position, professional guidance issued by the GMC and BMA strongly supports respecting confidentiality concerning consultations even when child patients are too immature to consent to treatment.

Very young children who are neither 'Gillick competent' nor capable of forming a relationship of confidence are not owed a duty of confidence, the effect of which is that confidential information can normally be disclosed to their parents (or others with parental responsibility).

WHAT INFORMATION MUST BE KEPT CONFIDENTIAL?

Surprisingly, perhaps given the long recognized right to confidentiality, there is no authoritative legal definition of 'confidential information'.

Case law has none the less shown that the courts will generally enforce a duty of confidentiality where:

1. information is not a matter of public knowledge; or
2. information is given to an individual in a situation where there is an obligation not to disclose the information without consent;
3. where protecting confidentiality is in the public interest.

Whether or not information can be 'confidential' after a person's death depends on the particular circumstances in question but the general consensus is that death does not release health professionals from their duty to maintain confidentiality. Factors which should be considered when determining what can be disclosed include the nature of the information when the patient died and the extent to which it has already been revealed in published material.

EXCEPTIONS TO THE DUTY OF CONFIDENTIALITY

In some circumstances the law recognizes that confidential information can (and in some cases must) be disclosed. Exceptions to the principle of confidentiality were first implicitly recognized in the Hippocratic Oath as they also are now in the GMC's 'Blue Book' and the UKKC's advisory paper on Confidentiality. The exceptions which are the most problematic in practice and most likely to affect children are those which allow disclosure with the consent of the patient, in the patient's interests, in the public interest and those which are required by law.

These will be discussed below although there are other permissible disclosures including those related to medical research, audit and teaching.

CONSENT OF THE PATIENT

If patients consent (which can be express, implied, in writing or verbal) to confidential information being disclosed then health professionals can act on that permission, providing of course, that it has been freely given, not obtained by undue pressure or influence and the patient understands the consequences of information being revealed.

Case study 4.1
Karena is a mature 14-year-old who has been going out with her 16-year-old boyfriend for several months. She wants contraceptive advice but is reluctant to see her GP for fear that he will tell her mother, Victoria, who she knows strongly opposes girls under 16 taking the pill. None the less she finally decides that she has no option but to go and see him. During the consultation, however,

Norman, the GP, implies, although he does not expressly say so, that he will not prescribe the pill unless Victoria is informed. Unhappily Karena agrees.

Is Karena's consent valid?

Does she have the right to see another GP for contraceptive advice and treatment?

Assuming that Karena is 'Gillick competent' she is mature enough to give consent to treatment and to enter into a confidential relationship. Consequently Norman owes her a duty of confidence. If she consents to Victoria being told disclosure is justifiable but that consent must be voluntary – which in this case seems doubtful because the pressure exerted by Norman may be almost irresistible. This is so despite the guidelines contained in health circular LAC (86(3)) which urges health professionals to try and persuade under-age girls to inform their parents or allow them to be informed that treatment is being sought. Norman has not complied with the guidelines in that he has pressurized Karena into giving her consent, i.e. encouraged her to believe that she will not get contraception unless confidentiality is breached.

If Karena's consent is not valid, or if she refuses to let Norman tell Victoria, disclosure will have to be justified on other grounds.

As regards consulting another GP for contraceptive services there is nothing to stop Karena exercising this option if she is unwilling to see Norman. Indeed Karena may be well advised to do this. However, any other GP she consults should explain to her that it is in her interests for Norman, under whose care she remains, to be informed if contraception is prescribed. He should also be told about any other medical condition which is discovered which requires investigation and treatment.

Although consent to disclosure is typically explicit sometimes this is impractical and it has to be implied. A common example of implied consent is when information has to be shared between all health professionals (and others) who are responsible for the patient's clinical management or otherwise involved in his or her care. The assumption here is that patients realize that relevant confidential information has to be passed back and forth between all those members of the 'team' caring for them and thus implicitly give consent to its disclosure. Nevertheless care must be taken to ensure that only those who 'need to know' are given information. In other words information should not be revealed to everyone at random but only to those who need the information to carry out their particular health care or related tasks. So, for example, details of a patient's medical condition can be revealed but not intimate details of their private lives which have no bearing whatsoever on their care. Moreover when confidential information is shared between health professionals and they know or ought to know that it is confidential then they are equally bound by the duty of confidentiality. If patients refuse consent to information being disclosed, their refusal must be respected (assuming they are competent) and justification for disclosure will have to be sought under other grounds.

Case Study 4.2
Stella is 15 and in care. Recently she has been diagnosed as HIV positive but despite appropriate counselling refuses to let her GP be told about her HIV status or to tell John, her 16-year-old boyfriend. The local authority is very concerned about her refusal, especially as John is also in care. Accordingly his health and well-being is just as much a priority as Stella's as it has a legal obligation to promote and safeguard the welfare of all the children in its care.
  Must Stella's request for privacy be respected?

GMC guidance on HIV infection and AIDS advises doctors that if patients refuse to allow their GP to be informed of their diagnoses then their wishes should be respected. Exceptionally, however, disclosure without consent of the patient is justified, most notably when 'failure to disclose would put the health of any of the health care team at serious risk'. In Stella's case disclosure could therefore arguably be justified on a 'need to know' basis. But who should be included in this category? Potentially it can include a wide range of people including those members of the local authority child welfare team who are caring for Stella.
  As regards telling John, GMC guidance (which is endorsed in DOH guidance) again recognizes an exception to the duty of confidentiality 'when there is a serious and identifiable risk to a specific individual who, if not so informed, would be exposed to infection'. The guidance also stresses how the doctor must discuss with the patient the question of informing his or her partner but if consent to disclosure is still withheld the doctor 'may consider it a duty to seek to ensure that any sexual partner is informed' irrespective of the patient's wishes.
  If John was told by a doctor of Stella's diagnosis he or she would be able to justify the disclosure without her consent on the basis of 'public interest' (see page 85), providing every effort had been made to persuade her beforehand of the need to tell him.
  Note too DOH guidance LAC (88)17 on children and HIV which states that if a young person does not give consent to information being disclosed their wishes should only be overruled if: the child

is at risk of significant harm if disclosure is not made; there is a legal requirement for information to be disclosed; public information requires disclosure in order to prevent others being put at risk.

DISCLOSURES IN THE PATIENT'S INTERESTS

In some circumstances close relatives, some other person such as a patient's carer, or more rarely an unrelated third party (such as a helper taking the patient out for the day) might need to be given confidential information. Normally non-consensual disclosure is justified if patients are too young and immature or too ill and thus unable to make treatment decisions themselves. Alternatively mental illness might prevent them from understanding what treatment would involve. Although relatives have no right to consent on behalf of adult patients they may be the best people to consult on treatment options and will therefore invariably need to have confidential information disclosed to them. In respect of patients who are very young disclosure to their parents will almost always be in their best interests.

While the law therefore clearly recognizes disclosure in the patient's interests the scope of this exception is unclear, especially in relation to mature children and adolescents. This is because although few would disagree that discussing a five-year-old's need for a tonsillectomy with her parents is in her interests there is likely to be less agreement about whether a 14-year-old who wants an abortion has a right to confidentiality. Equally problematic are cases where a health professional suspects that a child has been abused. In such circumstances disclosure to a third party, say the local authority, is almost always going to be in the child's interests.

> **Case study 4.3**
> Auriel is nearly two-years old and is taken to her GP, Bridgit, with a broken arm. While examining her Bridgit discovers several old bruises which she suspects may have been intentionally inflicted. She discusses her concerns with Simmy, the practice nurse who, having treated Auriel the previous day for a small burn caused by hot water, agrees that she too noticed what she thought were probably old cigarette burns.
>
> Can either Bridgit or Simmy breach confidentiality and report their suspicions – that Auriel's mother has deliberately harmed her – to an appropriate person, i.e. social services or the NSPCC?

Auriel is too young to enter into a confidential relationship with health professionals and thus cannot consent to information about her being disclosed. None the less there can be little doubt that disclosure would be in her interests and would therefore be justifiable providing health professionals comply with the procedures and recommendations in their professional Codes, the document *Working Together: A Guide to Arrangements for Inter-agency Co-operation for the Protection of Children from Abuse* and its Addendum: *Child Protection: Medical Responsibilities* (see Chapter 11). As guidance from the GMC states:

> in such circumstances the patient's interests are paramount and will usually require the doctor to disclose relevant information to an appropriate responsible person or an officer of a statutory agency.

DISCLOSURES REQUIRED BY LAW

This exception covers disclosures which are required by statute. These include those concerned with the prevention and detection of crime; the identity of drivers involved in road accidents; prevention of terrorism, and the collection of statistical data such as the number of drug addicts, abortions and infectious diseases. It also includes disclosures which are required in the course of judicial and quasi-judicial proceedings. In relation to child patients the legal proceedings which are most likely to involve practitioners are personal injury claims arising from medical negligence. These may require disclosure of 'any documents which are relevant to an issue arising or likely to arise out of a claim'. As such computerized documents as well as manually held documents including medical, nursing, anaesthetic and surgical notes, laboratory tests, X-ray films, consent forms and other correspondence may have to be disclosed. There are, however, two important limitations (or privileged exceptions) which restrict the court's powers. It generally cannot order disclosure of information protected by legal professional privilege nor that which is protected by the so-called public interest immunity. If called upon to disclose confidential information health professionals may either have to testify in legal proceedings, giving oral testimony through examination or cross examination – or produce documents.

A good example of how the public interest immunity works is that of D v. NSPCC [1978] where the Society followed up a complaint about the alleged ill-treatment of a 14-month-old girl. The girl's parents were visited and her mother, whose health was badly affected by the investigation, later sued the Society, claiming that it had been negligent. The case went up to the House of Lords who supported the Society's refusal to reveal the identity of the informant on the basis that disclosure would prevent other informants coming forward which would be contrary to the public interest.

DISCLOSURES IN THE PUBLIC INTEREST

This is the largest exception to the duty of confidentiality and probably the most contentious, mainly because its scope is so broad and uncertain since it can be (and is in practice) used to justify any disclosure which is thought to be for the 'good of society' or in the interests of the community as a whole. The little case law that there is on confidentiality shows how breaches are considered lawful whenever the public interest in disclosure outweighs the public interest in respecting confidences. In other words this exception involves balancing one public interest with another. But what is meant by the term 'public interest'? In the absence of any precise statutory or other definition the only guidance is that provided in two leading cases which is at best only very general.

The first case, X v. Y [1988] concerned two GPs with AIDS who were still practising. Details of their condition were passed on to a tabloid newspaper by a health service employee. The paper wanted to identify them, claiming that the public (and particularly the GPs' patients) had an interest in knowing who they were. The health authority sought, and obtained, an order preventing the doctors being named. In agreeing to grant a permanent injunction the court identified two public interests. The first was the freedom of the press and the related interest in having an informed public debate about AIDS (which according to the court was happening in any event and would not be significantly enhanced by naming the doctors). But notwithstanding the importance of that public interest, another public interest, notably that of preserving confidentiality, substantially outweighed it. Otherwise actual or potential AIDS sufferers could be deterred from seeking treatment or counselling through fear of being identified. If so the public would ultimately suffer through increased spread of the disease.

The other case, W. v. Edgell [1990] concerned a psychiatric patient, W, who was being detained indefinitely in a secure hospital as a result of a conviction for seriously injuring two people and shooting and killing five others ten years previously. Following his application to a mental health tribunal a report was prepared about his mental state. This strongly opposed any transfer to a regional secure unit – which was the first step towards W's eventual release – due to his longstanding and continuing abnormal interest in firearms and home-made bombs. In short Edgell claimed that, notwithstanding the opinion of the medical officer responsible for W, that he no longer presented a danger; his view was that W was still a dangerous man who needed further treatment. After seeing the report W withdrew his application but when Edgell discovered that the report was to remain confidential he sent a copy to the hospital where W was held without his permission. Finally the report reached the Home Secretary (the person with ultimate control over W's release, who in turn sent it to the Tribunal). W sued Edgell for breach of confidence but the Court of Appeal rejected his claim on the basis that the duty of confidentiality owed to W was outweighed by the overriding public interest in public safety. This required the report to be disclosed to the relevant authorities responsible for making decisions about W's future because it contained important information about his mental state.

Taken together these two cases provide useful guidelines as to the interpretation of 'public interest' and the kinds of circumstances when it is sufficiently compelling to justify disclosure. They are as follows.

- While the 'public interest' can justify breach of confidence disclosure must nevertheless be limited – to the relevant person or authorities. In other words it will only rarely be lawful to disclose information to the world at large.
- Before disclosure can be justified there must be a 'real' or 'genuine' risk of danger to the public even though that danger does not have to be imminent.
- Arguably the risk to the public must be to their physical safety, i.e. a danger of physical harm such as injury or disease.

Note too the GMC guidelines in the Blue Book which justify disclosure if failure to do so would 'expose the patient or someone else, to a risk of death or serious harm'. Similar guidance is contained in the UKCC Advisory paper which describes the public interest as encompassing matters such as 'serious crime, child abuse and drug trafficking'. In cases of doubt however, it is probably wise to seek legal advice and if necessary apply to court for a declaration that the proposed disclosure is lawful.

In practice concerns about breach of confidentiality typically focus on reporting crime to the police and 'helping them with their enquiries'. This is because in the course of their work health professionals may well acquire information or gain evidence that a patient has committed or is about to commit a crime. A patient seeking treatment may, for example, admit that he or she has received injuries while carrying out a burglary, or this may be obvious from the nature of the injuries. Practitioners working in the community might also come across a crime, stolen hospital property for example, or drugs which could not have been obtained legally.

Case study 4.4

Una, a 12-year-old girl is attacked and assaulted on her way home from school. She is taken to the local hospital's casualty department. Although she is suffering from shock she is sure she knows who attacked her because even though he was wearing a mask she recognized a distinctive large mole just above his lip. She even thinks she knows his name – Angus – because he used to go to her school but was expelled. Una tells a nurse, Gillian, all about what happened to her and her suspicions about who attacked her. Shortly afterwards a young man with a large mole seeks treatment for minor wounds to his face and arms. As soon as Gillian starts to treat him she instantly recognizes him and is not sure whether she has a legal duty to report him to the police. Failing that if the police make enquiries about him must she co-operate?

The general rule is that apart from the statutory disclosures outlined above there is no legal duty to report crime to the police. This means that the decision whether or not to inform the police is a matter for the individual health professional. It is, therefore, up to Gillian to decide what to do, bearing in mind the severity of the attack and so forth. She should, however, follow any relevant hospital policy (if appropriate) and also consider the possible consequences of breaching confidence, notably a complaint or claim by Angus and possibly even disciplinary action. Before doing anything Gillian would be well advised to seek guidance from her supervisor and employing authority.

If the police ask Gillian questions about Angus then she must not give false or misleading information since to do so would constitute an obstruction. If she were called as a witness in court proceedings she would, however, have to give evidence. Otherwise apart from the provisions of the Police and Criminal Evidence Act 1984 – which apply to medical records and human tissue or fluid taken for the purposes of diagnosis or treatment which a court has ordered must be produced – Gillian does not have to help the police by answering their questions or showing them any confidential information.

Case study 4.5
John is 17. Last week he told his psychiatrist, Mona, that he wanted to kill his mother, Tanya. Does Mona have a legal duty to warn Tanya, the potential victim and/or the police of the danger posed by John?

Although in a 1976 American case (Tarasoff v. Regents of the University of California) a psychologist who failed to warn a potential victim of a death threat made by a student was successfully sued by her parents when she was murdered – the claim being that their daughter should have been warned or that the student should have been committed – most commentators doubt if the English courts would adopt a similar approach especially if the threats were directed at the public at large. If they were aimed at a particular individual, however, a claim is more likely to succeed (but is by no means certain). Liability would turn on the law of negligence in particular foreseeability of harm to the victim, whether the threats were genuine, and whether there was a real risk they would be carried out. But the greatest hurdle would be in establishing that a health professional was under a legal duty to inform the potential victim, or the relevant authorities of the danger posed. However, given the absence of any general legal obligation to act as a 'good Samaritan', i.e. except where a special relationship exists (such as between a parent and child) no-one is legally bound to rescue another person, even if he or she could do so with little effort or danger, it is unlikely that any court would impose a legal duty on Mona to inform Tanya (or the appropriate authorities) of the danger from her son.

REMEDIES FOR BREACH OF CONFIDENTIALITY

Given the uncertainty surrounding much of the law of confidentiality, and in particular when disclosure is justified, it is not surprising that few patients have taken legal action to enforce their rights and even fewer have been successful. In principle, however, remedies are available both to prevent a threatened breach of confidence and where a breach has already occurred.

Threatened breaches can be stopped by the court granting an injunction. An injunction is a court order which orders someone either to do or stop doing a particular act. There are two types of injunctions, interlocutory and perpetual (or permanent as they are sometimes called). Both are available only at the court's discretion which means that patients have no automatic right to them. An interlocutory injunction is a temporary measure which lasts until the dispute is heard at a full trial. A permanent injunction, like the other which was granted in the case of X v. Y (above) does not necessarily mean that it lasts for ever but rather that a particular dispute over disclosure has been settled and a court has ruled in the patient's favour by granting the injunction.

An alternative remedy which is in theory available once a breach of confidence has actually occurred is an award of damages. Otherwise the most appropriate remedy for a patient would be to lodge a complaint alleging professional misconduct which could result ultimately in disciplinary proceedings.

MEDICAL RECORDS

Leaving aside the question of ownership of records, the vast majority of which belong either to the Secretary of State, relevant health authority or NHS Trust (ownership of private patients' records depends on the contractual relationship between the doctor, patient and relevant clinic or hospital), many patients now regard the right to see their medical records as a fundamental health care right. There are several reasons for this. First, irrespective of actual ownership, much more information is now routinely collected and stored, especially electronically, than in the past. As a consequence more confidential information is now potentially accessible, not just to health professionals but also to a wide range of other health service staff such as managers, administrators and so forth, many of whom are not bound by any professional code of practice preventing disclosure – although their contracts of employment are likely to prohibit breaches of confidentiality. Secondly, sometimes information stored on record can be inaccurate or misleading and patients now increasingly expect to be able to 'set the record straight' or at least check what has been said about them, particularly if they suspect that an offensive or defamatory comment has been recorded.

The main statutes dealing with access to medical records are the Data Protection Act 1984 and the Access to Health Records Act 1990. Guidance has also been issued by the Department of Health on personal child health records. The only other related statute is the Access to Medical Reports Act 1988 which applies to medical reports compiled for employment or insurance purposes. Its relevance to children is thus very limited.

Note that under common law patients do not have an absolute right of access to health records. (See R v. Mid-Glamorgan Health Services Authority and South Glamorgan Health Authority ex parte Martin [1994].

ACCESS TO HEALTH RECORDS ACT 1990

This Act applies to both private and NHS patients but only to health records compiled after 1 November 1991 which are kept in manual form, i.e. non-computerized. Its main purpose is to give patients (or their authorized representatives) the right to see their records. They also have the right to ask for inaccurate records to be corrected. Before looking in outline at the Act's main provisions several important terms need to be defined. These are:

- 'health record' means 'any information relating to a patient's physical or mental health made by or on behalf of a health professional in respect of the patient's care';

- **'care'** means 'examination, investigation, diagnosis and treatment'; and
- **'health professional'** means most registered health professionals such as doctors, dentists, opticians, nurses, midwives, health visitors, chiropodists, clinical psychologists, psychotherapists, chemists and art and music therapists among others.

The Act is not limited to health records of NHS patients and applies equally to the private health sector and to health professionals' private practice records. However, it only applies to records made in connection with a patient's care and not, for example made in the course of, say, the investigation of a crime.

RIGHTS GRANTED

Under the Act a right to access includes being allowed to inspect health records, being given a copy of them and an explanation of any terms which are unintelligible – possibly because of bad handwriting or use of medical jargon or abbreviations – without such explanation. Additionally patients can request that 'inaccurate' records, i.e. those which are misleading, incorrect or incomplete, be corrected. While the 'holder' of the record who will usually be the patient's GP, health authority or NHS Trust does not have to comply (if he or she thinks the recorded information is accurate) a note must be made recording the patient's comments. Duties of consultation with appropriate health professionals are also imposed in certain circumstances.

WHO CAN APPLY?

The main categories are patients themselves and those authorized on their behalf.

Child applicants

No specific reference is made in the Act to 16- and 17-year-olds but since they are treated like adults in relation to consent to treatment it is assumed that providing they are competent they should be considered to have the same rights of access as adult patients. If they are not competent then someone appointed on their behalf can apply which will normally be their parents. Young people under 16 can apply independently but will only be given access if, in the opinion of the record-holder, they are 'capable of understanding the nature of the application'. Unhelpfully there is no statutory explanation of what this means but it is at least arguable that a relatively low level of understanding is all that is required. But irrespective of the maturity which a child must have before he or she can apply for access another provision in the Act, notably s 5(3), is generally assumed to give child patients the power to prevent their parents seeing their records. It prevents disclosure of information previously given by a child which she or he expected would be kept confidential. The same provision also prevents disclosure of the results of investigations or examinations which the child consented to in the expectation they would not be disclosed.

Applications by those with parental responsibility

Anyone with parental responsibility for a child can apply for access to his or her record (see s. 3(1)(c)) but access should not be given unless the record-holder is satisfied that the child consents or is incapable of understanding the nature of the application but access would be in the child's best interests (see s. 4(2)). It is therefore this later provision which authorizes access to parents in respect of very young children or older ones who lack the capacity to understand what an application for access means (and to whom s.5(3) does not apply).

> **Case study 4.6**
> Vikram is 15. Does he have a right to apply for access to his health records?
> What difference would it make if he was 13?
> Can his mother, Nicole, apply for access to his record?
> What formalities must be complied with?

Providing Vikram is capable of understanding the nature of the application he can apply for access himself.

If Vikram was 13 then again he could apply providing he had the requisite understanding. Whether or not he was sufficiently mature would be an issue for the record-holder to decide.

Nicole can also apply for access as she has parental responsibility for Vikram irrespective of her marital status. However, Vikram must consent unless he is incapable of understanding the nature of the application, in which case Nicole should only be given access if it was in Vikram's best interests. In cases of applications by those with parental responsibility Health Service Guidance (HSG) (91)6 states that there is a need for the rights of the child to confidentiality to be balanced against the parental responsibility to ensure that only accurate and non-prejudicial information is recorded about the child.

Although applications for access will almost always initially be made orally, such a request does not amount to an application under the Act which should be made in writing using the model form included in Appendix 1 of HCG (91) 6. If Vikram was making his own application he would have to sign it. Otherwise Nicole's signature is required, in which case she would have to confirm either that Vikram had consented to her application or was incapable of understanding the request. Subject to any exceptions which might apply, access must be granted within 21 days if the record was made within 40 days of the application. In any other cases the record must be made available within 40 days of the application.

Finally it should be noted that even though the Access to Health Records Act 1900 gives patients new statutory rights of access to their records it does not prohibit informal voluntary arrangements whereby at the end of treatment a patient may ask what has been recorded about them and are allowed access at the discretion of the health professional who is principally responsible for their clinical care.

IS ACCESS GUARANTEED?

Although welcomed as a significant step towards giving patients rights of access to (and control over) their records, the Act recognizes that there may be some circumstances in which information should not be revealed. In other words it does not guarantee access which can be denied (either wholly or partially). In particular access should not be given to any part of the patient's record which, in the opinion of the record-holder, would disclose information 'likely to cause serious harm to the physical or mental health of the patient or of any other individual, or if it identifies a third party (who has not consented to disclosure)'. Those denied access have a right to go to court but other than that the Act does not provide any criminal sanction for its breach and any civil claim would probably only result in nominal damages (assuming that is that the harm suffered was negligible).

While the exclusions outlined above are perhaps predictable, based as they are on the well-established principle of 'therapeutic privilege', they none the less do undermine the Act's commitment to patients' rights of access, especially as there is no statutory definition of 'serious harm'. With no guidance from case law either the term can in practice be interpreted very subjectively and so give health professionals considerable discretion.

DATA PROTECTION ACT 1984

This long and complex Act was the first to give patients the right to see their own medical records. It applies to health records (among other types of 'personal data') kept on computer and aims to protect individuals from the misuse of personal information. In particular it gives them the right to find out information about themselves, challenge it if appropriate and claim compensation in certain circumstances. The Act is based on eight fundamental principles which apart from giving individuals several rights (see below) also broadly aim to ensure that computerized personal data is: obtained and processed fairly and lawfully; adequate; accurate and kept up to date; held only for specified purposes; stored securely but only for as long as is necessary; and finally is not disclosed to unauthorized people.

Although not defined in the Act itself the term 'personal health data' appears in subsequent health circulars modifying the Act, notably Circulars (87)14; (87)26 and (89)29. It includes any personal information relating to the physical and mental health of an individual and so covers medical and nursing records, pathology laboratory records and any other health-related computerized records. Individuals whose data is stored are called 'data subjects' and those who hold it are called 'data user'.

RIGHTS GRANTED

These are enshrined in the seventh so-called 'data protection' principle and give individuals the following rights:

- to be informed whether data held includes personal data;
- to be supplied with a copy of the information;
- to have unintelligible information explained;
- to be compensated for any damage suffered as a result of inaccurate data (likewise its loss, unauthorized destruction or disclosure);
- to have inaccurate data rectified or erased.

In this context 'inaccurate' means incorrect or misleading as to any matter of fact. In certain circumstances before responding to an access application appropriate health professionals must be consulted.

WHO CAN APPLY?

In respect of health-related personal data, applicants are either patients or those acting on their behalf.

Child applicants

Surprisingly perhaps no special reference is made in the Act to child data subjects, an omission rectified by HC (89) 26 as amended by HC (89) 29. This starts with the broad principle

that all individuals, including children have the right of subject access. However, a child will not always be able to make his or her own request. The way in which the subject access will work in this situation depends on the general law relating to the legal capacity of children.

The guidance then states that whenever a child requests access it should be allowed providing he or she understands the nature of the request (subject to any possible exception, see below). Given that the Family Law Reform Act 1969 treats 16- and 17-year-olds as adults for the purpose of consenting to treatment it must normally be presumed that young people in this age group must be assumed to have the requisite capacity if they comply with the necessary formalities, i.e. request access in writing and pay the appropriate fee (currently £10).

Children under 16 can also make an independent application for access providing they understand the nature of the request. The age at which they are able to do this will depend on their maturity and intellect but it is generally assumed that if they are old enough to consent to minor treatment then they will be capable of making their own application for access.

If their capacity is uncertain then either they will have to be interviewed personally or alternatively a written declaration will have to be obtained from a 'responsible adult', usually a parent or other person with parental responsibility, confirming that the child does understand the nature of the application.

Applications by those with parental responsibility

The health circulars make it clear (which the Act does not) that those with parental responsibility can apply for access to children's records but that right normally stops once they are old enough to understand the nature of an application – which they can consequently make themselves. Even then, however, applications can be made on a mature child's behalf provided he or she has authorized the request.

But where children are not sufficiently mature to make their own applications, i.e. they lack the requisite capacity, then the combined effect of the health circulars is that it should be assumed that applications on their behalf are being made in their best interests so that the applicants can carry out their parental duties. Accordingly access should be allowed. Nevertheless in such circumstances a declaration should be obtained from the parent confirming that the child does not understand the nature of the application.

IS ACCESS GUARANTEED?

As with the Access to Health Records Act 1990 access can be denied if disclosure would be likely 'to cause serious harm to the physical or

mental health' of the data subject or another person or lead to the identification of another person (other than a health professional who has
been involved in the care of the data subject or who has consented to the
disclosure). Regrettably though, there is no explanation of what the term
'serious harm' means.

FURTHER READING

BMA (1993) *Medical Ethics Today – Its Practice and Philosophy.*

Cowley, R. (1994) *Access to Medical Records and Reports*, Radcliffe Medical Press,
Oxford.

Darley, B., Griew, A., McLoughlin, K. and Williams, J. (1994) *How to Keep a
Clinical Confidence*, HMSO, London.

Department of Health Circular (1992) *Children and HIV: Guidance for Local
Authorities*, LAC (88)17, DoH, London.

General Medical Council (1993) *Professional Conduct and Discipline: Fitness to
Practise (Blue Book).*

General Medical Council (1993) *HIV Infection and AIDS: The Ethical
Considerations*, revised edn.

Guidance issued jointly by the BMA, FPA and others (1993) *Confidentiality and
People under 16.*

Department of Health (1984) Health Service Management Circulars, Data
Protection Act 1984: Modified Access to Personal Health Information
HC(87)14, as amended by HC(87)26 and HC(89)29).

Department of Health (1991) Access to Health Records Act 1990: Health Service
Guidance (HSG) (91)6, DoH, London.

Department of Health (1993) *Guidance on Parent Held Child Health Records*,
Executive Letter (93)86.

United Kingdom Central Council for Nursing, Midwifery and Health Visiting
(1992) Code of Professional Conduct for the Nurse, Midwife and Health
Visitor, UKCC, London.

United Kingdom Central Council for Nursing, Midwifery and Health Visiting
(1987) *Confidentiality: An Elaboration of Clause 9 of the Second Edition of the
UKCC's Code of Professional Conduct for the Nurse, Midwife and Health Visitor*,
UKCC, London (now clause 10 of the June 1992 edition of the code).

PART THREE
Specialist Areas

Family planning

5

Ever since the historic 1986 Gillick case, famous, among other things, for the immortal words of one of the judges that

> there are many things which a girl under 16 needs to practise, but sex is not one of them

the law's role in regulating adolescent fertility and sexuality has been controversial. And yet the case did not, as is commonly assumed, herald a fundamental change in the provision of contraceptive advice and treatment to under-age girls. For well before then – over a decade earlier in fact – Department of Health guidance on contraception (issued in 1974) made it clear that doctors who provided such treatment to girls under 16 irrespective of their parents' wishes would not be acting unlawfully providing they acted in good faith. Similarly professional workers who referred, advised or persuaded girls under 16 to seek treatment would not be acting unlawfully either.

While the legal issues surrounding minors and contraception are now well settled, some aspects of family planning practice continue to cause controversy, in particular whether young girls, possibly as young as 12 or 13, should have the right to consent to abortions and when, if ever, it is lawful to sterilize minors without their consent.

This chapter will look at the law of family planning, i.e. contraception and sterilization. It will also cover abortion.

THE PROVISION OF FAMILY PLANNING

Since 1967 and the passing of the National Health Service (Family Planning) Act 1967 contraceptive services have been available under the NHS. Department of Health Guidance has also been issued which covers advice on services for young people. Initially these were not comprehensive but subsequent legislation has ensured the availability of all the main methods of contraception including male and female sterilization within the NHS. Doctors are not, however, legally obliged to provide contraceptive services since they are one of the four so-called 'further services' which they may (but do not have to) undertake to provide. Furthermore they have the option of offering them not just to patients already on their lists but also other patients as well. Registering with another GP for contraception may well appeal to girls under 16 who are too embarrassed to consult the family doctor or are concerned about confidentiality.

The 1967 legislation did not define the term 'family planning services' nor has it been defined since. None the less for legal purposes it is generally assumed to cover any medical intervention, whether surgical or non-surgical, which aims at intentionally preventing or interrupting the process of human reproduction. But in deciding whether or not the provisions of the Abortion Act 1967 apply, family planning practice needs to be divided into three broad categories, notably contraception, contragestion and abortifacients (see page 102).

YOUNG PEOPLE AND FAMILY PLANNING

In so far as the various family planning methods described below constitute medical treatment, two issues commonly concern health professionals. The first focuses on the law of consent and when they can rely on the sole consent of the young person without involving or consulting parents; the second concerns their potential criminal liability. Given that sexual intercourse with girls under 16 is a criminal offence, is a practitioner who gives contraceptive advice and treatment to a girl under 16 going to be prosecuted?

To answer these questions children need to be divided into three age groups.

16- AND 17-YEAR-OLDS

According to s.8 of the Family Law Reform Act 1969 16- and 17-year olds are treated like adults for the purposes of consent. So, providing they are competent, they can give a valid consent to any surgical, medical or dental treatment (which includes contraceptive advice and treatment, likewise abortion). But as was noted in Chapter 3 their consent can be overridden by a court (but no-one else). Consent for treatment for incompetent 16- and 17-year-olds must be obtained from anyone with parental responsibility (usually a parent) or a court.

It is not a criminal offence for a girl over 16 to have sexual intercourse so no question of criminal liability arises.

UNDER 16-YEAR-OLDS

Providing a young person under 16 is 'Gillick competent', i.e. sufficiently mature, both emotionally and intellectually, to understand the nature and implications of contraceptive treatment, she can validly consent to it. Family planning practitioners providing contraception to such young people should follow the guidelines laid down in the Gillick case (but now incorporated in health circular HSC 86 (1) (Family Planning services for Young People). These state that contraceptive advice and treatment can be given to under-16-year-olds without parental know-ledge or consent, provided a doctor or other health professional is satisfied that:

- they understand the advice and have sufficient maturity to under-stand what is involved in terms of the moral, social and emotional implications;
- they cannot be persuaded to inform their parents or allow them to be informed that advice is being sought;
- they would be very likely to begin or to continue having sexual inter-course with or without contraceptive treatment;
- without contraceptive advice or treatment their physical or mental health or both are likely to suffer;
- their best interests require contraceptive advice, treatment or both without parental consent.

Legally in terms of the law of consent only the first requirement has to be complied with. The remaining ones – while undoubtedly state-ments of good practice breach of which could give rise to disciplinary proceedings – are not legally significant for the purposes of obtaining consent.

As to the potential criminal liability of practitioners this is governed by the Sexual Offences Act 1956, in particular the offence of 'aiding and abetting the commission of an unlawful sexual offence'. Under the Act it is a criminal offence to have sexual intercourse with a girl under 16 irrespective of her consent (note that it is not the girl who commits the offence). If the girl is under 13 it is an absolute offence but if she is between 13 and 16 there are two qualified defences, one of which, the so-called 'young man's defence', is the most common. This applies to men under 24 who have not previously been charged with an offence of this kind and who believe the girl to be over 16. So could practitioners who give contraceptive advice and treatment to under-16-year-olds be guilty of aiding and abetting? While such a charge was always unlikely given that intercourse would either have already taken place or would be very likely to happen irrespective of the action of any family planning practitioner, the issue was finally resolved in the Gillick case where it was made clear that practitioners who provided contraception to under-age girls in good faith to protect them from the harmful effects of pregnancy would not be prosecuted.

Case study 5.1

Cody is 14 but looks much younger. For several months she has been going out with Rick, who is 19. She wants to go on the pill but has been told that because she is under 16 her GP will not prescribe it. She is also reluctant to go to her GP because her mother has told her that she has a right to be consulted and contraception could only be prescribed if she agreed.

Providing Cody is 'Gillick competent' she can make her own family planning decisions and so give consent to contraceptive treatment. The fact that she looks young for her age is irrelevant since her ability to understand the nature and implication of treatment depends on her maturity not on her looks. As to her mother's rights to be consulted the legal position is that as Cody is 'Gillick competent' she is not obliged to consult her mother nor can her mother insist that her advice be followed. Thus, even though health DOH guidelines urge family planners to try and persuade their mature under-16-year-old patients to consult with their parents, the child does not have to follow that advice and no breach of any legal duty arises if she fails to do so. Furthermore, Cody's doctors would incur no legal liability if he or she failed to try and persuade Cody to tell her mother.

LEGALITY OF FAMILY PLANNING METHODS

CONTRACEPTION

There is no legal definition of contraception but it is nevertheless assumed for legal purposes that it includes any birth control method which prevents fertilization. It therefore includes barrier methods, i.e. the condom and diaphragm (or cap) as well as oral and injectable contraceptives. Other than ensuring that under-age girls can give valid consent to treatment none of these methods presents any legal difficulties although defective contraceptive drugs might give rise to negligence claims either under the common law (see Chapter 2) or the Consumer Protection Act 1987 (see Chapter 7). However, if a doctor were to prescribe oral or injectable contraceptives without taking a full history (medical, family and menstrual) or conducting appropriate tests or examinations she or he may face a negligence claim (and possibly even criminal charges under the Sexual Offences Act 1956). In addition, for consent to be valid, side effects, risks and so forth have to be explained and, if the patient is under 16, an assessment has to be made as to her maturity according to the criteria in health circular LAC 86 (3).

POST-COITAL METHODS

Post-coital birth control, namely the so-called (but misnamed) 'morning-after' pill and the intrauterine device (IUD which is sometimes also called the IUCD) are designed to act after fertilization but before implantation. As such they prevent gestation which explains why they are commonly now referred to as 'contragestives' rather than contraceptives. The reason for the different terminology is that as they take effect after the embryo has formed but before it has been implanted they cannot be described as contraception – which prevents fertilization. Nor can they be described as abortions because the law does not regard a procedure which prevents implantation as 'an act done to procure a miscarriage'. Any act done with that intent is regarded as an abortion. In other words the law accepts – although this is not stated expressly in any statute (or case law) – that a pregnancy begins when implantation is complete, i.e. when the fertilized egg attaches itself to the wall of the uterus. Accordingly a birth control method which prevents that process beginning can lawfully be regarded as a contragestive.

In some cases, however, it can be important in legal terms to distinguish between post-coital pills and the IUD.

Post-coital pills are normally prescribed within 72 hours of unprotected intercourse. If administered within this time they prevent implantation (rather than fertilization) and so prevent a pregnancy beginning rather than interrupt an existing one. If, on the other hand, these pills were to be prescribed after a pregnancy had been established then any practitioner who prescribed them could face criminal charges of unlawfully carrying out an abortion, unless of course the Abortion Act 1967 was complied with.

The IUD also aims to prevent implantation and if fitted before intercourse it presents no special legal problems in that it does not interrupt an existing pregnancy but prevents one beginning. If one is fitted post-coitally, however, it can have the effect of dislodging an implanted embryo in which case again there may well be a criminal abortion unless the Abortion Act 1967 is complied with. But in practice any prosecution would almost certainly fail because of the difficulties of proving that when inserting the IUD the doctor believed that the woman was pregnant (it does not matter that she was not in fact pregnant, merely that the doctor thought she was). Timing in this kind of case is therefore all-important. So inserting an IUD three and a half months after unprotected intercourse at a time when a pregnancy could easily be established is much more likely to result in a successful prosecution.

Menstrual extraction is a much less common post-coital procedure. If it is carried out several weeks after unprotected intercourse when a pregnancy test could be done then any termination would have to comply with the Abortion Act 1967 because the embryo would have implanted – and so, for legal purposes a pregnancy would have started.

ABORTIFACIENTS

If anti-progesterones and anti-HCG vaccines are used to prevent implantation their legality is the same as other pre-implantation contragestive methods. If, on the other hand, they are administered so as to dislodge an implanted embryo they amount to abortions and so are only lawful if the criteria in the Abortion Act 1967 are satisfied (see below).

ABORTION

As is well known the Abortion Act 1967 radically reformed the law of abortion and made it much more widely available. It also clarified the law, thereby removing almost all the uncertainty which had previously existed as to when an abortion was or was not lawful. Legal abortions were not, of course, unknown before the Act. In 1966, for example, just before the Act came into force there were 6100 recorded abortions in NHS hospitals. To be lawful, however, these had to be done to 'preserve the life of the mother'. But with no clear legal guidance on the precise meaning of these words and conflicting professional advice doctors had little choice but to apply the law as they saw fit. Fearing prosecutions some only carried out abortions when the mother faced certain death. Others interpreted the law more liberally and performed abortions whenever the mother's physical or mental health was at risk. Given the uncertain state of the law it was perhaps inevitable that illegal abortions were fairly common although reliable figures were hard to come by.

The Abortion Act 1967 is usually described as a compromise statute. As such it failed to satisfy the demands of those who wanted 'abortion on demand' but at the same time was attacked by 'pro-life' campaigners as conceding far too much. None the less the Act did substantially liberalize the law which perhaps explains why it has been continually subject to attacks – no less than 20 – to make it more restrictive. While none of these succeeded the Act was finally changed in 1990.

In explaining abortion several questions need to be answered. These are:

- what does the word 'abortion' mean in law?
- when is an abortion legal?
- what time limits apply?
- who can perform abortions?
- does the Act contain any special provisions concerning minors?

- can health professionals refuse to participate?
- what 'rights' do fathers have?
- what 'rights' does the foetus have?
- what is the effect of failing to comply with the Abortion Act?

WHAT IS AN ABORTION?

Despite the fact that virtually every legal system in the world has laws regulating abortion very few of them actually define what it means. English law is no exception and provides no definition either in the Act itself or elsewhere. Nevertheless most legal commentaries agree that unless an abortion occurs spontaneously (in which case it is usually referred to as a miscarriage) it arises whenever a pregnancy is terminated intentionally. In other words there must be some deliberate act to end a pregnancy that has successfully started so as to prevent the birth of a living child.

WHEN IS AN ABORTION LEGAL?

Abortions are illegal unless they comply with the criteria set out in the Abortion Act 1967, i.e. if two registered practitioners have decided 'in good faith' that one or more of the grounds specified in the Act apply.

The first ground

That the pregnancy has not exceeded its 24th week and the continuation of the pregnancy would involve risk, greater than if the pregnancy were terminated, of injury to the physical or mental health of the pregnant woman or of any existing children in her family.

This ground is commonly known as the therapeutic one and accounts for the vast majority of abortions. Like the other grounds in the Act it can be interpreted either narrowly or broadly. So, although there must be some risk in continuing with the pregnancy it does not have to be a very serious one and could be as little as 1% or less. But the risks of childbirth and pregnancy are not constant. Hence the risks associated with pregnancy increase with age whereas an abortion (rather than a pregnancy) poses greater risk to younger women unless the abortion is performed during the first eight weeks of pregnancy. The meaning of 'mental health' is similarly open to different interpretation. At its most restrictive it can limit abortions to those women who otherwise would suffer some form of mental illness. It can, however (and typically is in practice), interpreted more broadly to include much less severe 'mental' conditions.

The term 'children of the family' can also be generously interpreted to include not just those born in but also outside marriage as well as any child the woman is currently looking after on a long-term basis, likewise those who are grown up but still dependent through disability. The birth of another child could adversely affect them either emotionally, financially or practically – scarce family resources could be overstretched, for example, or the mother could be unable to cope with having to care for another baby. Note too that the Act allows the woman's 'actual or reasonable forseeable environment' to be taken into account when assessing risks. Often referred to as the 'social' factors, these are almost certainly potentially wide enough to enable virtually any aspect of the woman's situation, both during the pregnancy and after the child's birth, to be considered. Her attitude towards the pregnancy (likewise that of her partner and other 'family' members) could therefore be relevant.

Finally it is important to note that under this ground there is now a time limit which means that abortions must be performed by the end of the 24th week of the pregnancy.

The second ground

> That the termination is necessary to prevent grave permanent injury to the woman's physical or mental health.

The Act being rather short on definitions gives no guidance on the meaning of 'grave permanent injury' but it is assumed that temporary, easily curable conditions are not included. A woman with hypertension who could suffer permanent kidney or possible heart damage would, on the other hand, qualify on this ground as would one suffering from, for example, cervical cancer or other conditions which could deteriorate during pregnancy. As with the first ground 'social' factors can also be considered here but there is no need to carry out any balancing exercise (between risk of terminating the pregnancy and the risk associated with continuing it).

The third ground

> That the continuation of the pregnancy would involve risk to the life of the pregnant woman, greater than if the pregnancy were terminated.

Because of the sophistication of abortion technology it is claimed that any abortion performed in the first twelve weeks is going to be less risky than continuing with the pregnancy. Consequently this ground is not difficult to satisfy but in practice it is typically reserved for such medical conditions as ectopic pregnancies or eclampsia. Note too that as with the first ground there is still a need to balance the risk of ending the pregnancy against continuing with it.

The fourth ground

That there is a substantial risk that if the child were born it would suffer from such physical or mental abnormalities as to be seriously handicapped.

This ground – usually referred to as the 'foetal ground' – is arguably one of the most difficult to interpret, largely because again the Act gives no guidance on the meaning of the terms it uses. Nor does it shed any light on when the 'abnormalities' must occur. Must they be present at birth, during childhood or can they develop much later in adult life (as in Huntington's Chorea)? While it is generally assumed that serious handicaps arising at any of these times are included, this has yet to be legally confirmed. Equally crucial but just as unclear is the meaning of 'serious handicap'? Examples commonly include Down's Syndrome or spina bifida even though their effect cannot be reliably predicted from pre-natal screening. According to one commentator a serious handicap is anything which is not negligible (a cleft palate or harelip would be negligible). The word 'substantial' means that the risk must be more likely to occur than in the first ground but with no statutory guidance much is left to the discretion of doctors and relevant professional guidance.

Requirement of good faith

Abortion on any of the above grounds is only lawful if medical practitioners have acted in 'good faith'. This requirement has been questioned in only one case since 1967. In R v. Smith [1974] a doctor was found guilty of performing an unlawful abortion on a woman whom he neither examined nor asked why she wanted an abortion. The Court said that it was the jury's task to decide whether the doctor did in fact act genuinely and honestly.

TIME LIMITS

There is now only a time limit in relation to the first ground (up to 24 weeks). Abortions on the remaining three grounds can be carried out at any time, the reason being that they are all considered 'weightier' grounds and therefore justify late terminations.

WHO CAN PERFORM AN ABORTION?

Except in emergencies abortions can only be carried out in NHS (or Trust) hospitals and other licensed places by a registered medical practitioner – a term which includes nursing staff acting under the directions of such a doctor. Unless an abortion is immediately necessary to save a woman's life or prevent grave permanent injury to her physical or mental health (in which case the decision to carry out an abortion can be made just by one doctor) two doctors have to agree that the woman qualifies under the Act. The Act therefore does not give women any legal right to have an abortion. Instead it gives doctors what is usually described as a 'gatekeeping' role allowing them the discretion to decide who should or should not have an abortion.

Note that the Abortion Regulations 1991 require practitioners who terminate pregnancies to notify the appropriate Chief Medical Officer.

CHILDREN AND THE ABORTION ACT

The Act does not distinguish between different age groups. This means that the ordinary rules as to consent apply (see Chapter 3). So, providing the criteria in the Act are satisfied, competent 16- and 17-year-old girls of can give a valid consent to an abortion (by virtue of s.8 of the Family Law Reform Act 1969) irrespective of their parents' wishes. If they are not competent but an abortion is in their best interests then anyone with parental responsibility (or a court) can consent on their behalf although in such cases it is preferable to get the court's prior consent.

As to girls under 16 they can also give consent providing they are 'Gillick competent'. If they do not have sufficient maturity anyone with parental responsibility (or the court) can give consent providing the abortion is in the minor's best interests. Again, however, because an abortion is such an important step it would be wise to seek the court's prior permission.

But what happens when there is a disagreement between a young girl and her parents about abortion? Such cases rarely reach the courts but in the two cases on this issue which have done so, the outcomes were perhaps predictable. The most recent case was Re B (abortion) [1991]. The girl at the centre of the dispute was 12. She wanted an abortion, as did her 16-year-old boyfriend and her grandparents with whom she had lived most of her life. Her mother, however, strongly opposed abortion. Medical evidence was conflicting but despite the girl's age the court overruled her mother's wishes and gave permission for the abortion to go ahead, not just, of course, because the girl wanted it but because the court thought it was in her best interests.

In a similar case a decade earlier the court also supported the minor's wishes against those of her parents. Re P (1982) concerned a 15-year-old girl in local authority care who lived in a mother and child unit with her 11-month-old son. Pregnant again she wanted an abortion (a decision supported by the local authority) which her parents, particularly her father who was a Seventh Day Adventist, vehemently opposed on religious grounds. Again the girl's wishes prevailed.

Both the above cases involved girls who wanted terminations. But what is the legal position if an under-age mature girl wants to go ahead with the pregnancy but an abortion is medically indicated? No case on this has yet come to court but in principle the legal position is clear. The abortion could be carried out against her wishes, relying on the consent either of a court or anyone with parental responsibility. Whether any health professional would perform an abortion in such circumstances is, of course, another matter, even if a court did authorize one (which is doubtful). Ultimately, however, any decision would turn on the particular facts of the case and the extent to which continuing with the pregnancy would affect the girl's health.

CAN HEALTH PROFESSIONALS REFUSE TO PARTICIPATE IN AN ABORTION?

Except in an emergency when an abortion is necessary to save a woman's life or prevent her grave permanent injury, a health professional can refuse to participate in an abortion. This is because the Act has a 'conscience clause' which allows professionals to do what would otherwise amount to a breach of their employment contract.

WHAT 'RIGHTS' DO FATHERS HAVE?

Despite several attempts by fathers to prevent their partners having abortions – on the basis that as the unborn child's father they have 'rights' too – their claims have been repeatedly rejected in the English courts, not just as a matter of public policy but also for practical reasons. It simply would not be possible to 'police' a woman throughout her pregnancy unless, of course, she was physically restrained. Nor does the father have any legal right to be consulted about a proposed abortion so that even if he cannot prevent it he can at least have some say in the decision-making process. Again there are both policy and practical reasons for this in that giving such rights without the means of enforcing it would be pointless and possibly could lead to undue pressure on the woman.

WHAT 'RIGHTS' DOES THE FOETUS HAVE?

It is now well established that, although the foetus does not have rights until it is born alive, it can sue (providing it is born alive) for certain pre-natal injuries (see Chapter 7). A child is 'born alive' if, after its birth, it exists as a live child, that is to say was breathing and living through the use of its own lungs alone. But what is the legal position when an aborted foetus is born alive? In other words there is a live abortus. While this is only likely to happen in very late abortions and so is very rare it does raise interesting questions about the potential criminal liability of health professionals. What, for example should a nurse do if she finds a living abortus in the sluice-room?

There are very few cases directly on this point. In one case a foetus aborted at 23 weeks lived for 36 hours. The coroner's verdict was that it died because it was premature and therefore medical staff were not to blame. In another case a 21-week-old foetus, which was breathing and had a heart beat, was left for three hours without assistance but no-one was prosecuted. Despite the absence of any clear precedent the legal position is, at least, in principle, clear. Although doctors have no legal duty to ensure that a foetus is born alive – even in a very late abortion when that is certainly a possibility – if an aborted foetus is born alive health professionals must take all reasonable steps to keep it alive. Otherwise they could face a charge of manslaughter (or even murder).

WHAT IS THE EFFECT OF FAILING TO COMPLY WITH THE ABORTION ACT?

Unlawful abortions are serious criminal offences and any health professional (likewise anyone else) who performs (or assists in) an abortion which is outside the Act, i.e. none of the grounds apply, will almost certainly be prosecuted.

Other criminal offences relating to abortion include administering drugs or using instruments to procure an abortion and procuring drugs to cause an abortion (contrary to ss. 58 & 59 of the Offences Against the Person Act 1861).

Case study 5.2

Joelle is just 15 and 'Gillick competent'. She is pregnant but wants an abortion. She goes to see her GP, Alan, who is very opposed to abortion and tries to persuade her not to have one. He sends her away to 'think about it long and hard' and tells her to come back and see him in a few weeks' time so that they can discuss it again. Joelle returns several weeks later but again is put under pressure by Alan to reconsider. At no time does Alan tell Joelle that he has a conscientious objection to abortion, hoping that eventually he will be able to persuade her to continue with the pregnancy.

What is the extent of Alan's legal duty to Joelle? In particular does he have a duty to refer her to another GP?

Although there is no case on this the answer would depend on Alan's terms of service. These require him, among other things, to 'arrange for the referral of patients, as appropriate, for the provision of any other service under the National Health Service Act 1977'. Since abortion services are included within 'other service' Alan is in breach of his terms of service if he does not refer Joelle to another GP (who would be prepared to consider her abortion request and who would thus sign the appropriate certificate which is required before an abortion can be carried out).

STERILIZATION

Few forms of treatment are as controversial as non-consensual sterilization. That it raises fundamental issues of law, ethics and medical practice is irrefutable and was eloquently yet succinctly acknowledged in the case of Re D [1976] when Mrs Justice Heilbron said:

> sterilization is an operation which involves the deprivation of a basic human right, namely the right to reproduce, and therefore it would if performed on a woman for non-therapeutic reasons and without her consent be a violation of that right.

When the procedure is carried out on children it is perhaps even more contentious which is why it almost always requires the court's permission. The court's involvement is thought necessary for several reasons. Briefly these are, first, unlike other forms of contraception and even though it is now possible to reverse the procedure it is generally regarded, at least by patients, as irreversible. Secondly, except in very rare cases when it is carried out to prevent or treat an illness or disease, it is non-therapeutic. Thirdly, it violates what many consider to be a basic human right, that is the right to reproduce. Fourthly, it raises uncomfortable questions about eugenics and whether the 'real' (but unexpressed) reason for the procedure is to prevent the patient's condition being inherited thereby 'improving the human stock' Fifthly, it involves major invasive surgery. Finally, whereas with competent patients it is usually performed when they are older and already have a family, incompetent (and childless) minors have the surgery at a much younger age –making it more difficult to justify as in their 'best interests'.

But what safeguards can the court provide? And why should the procedure be considered outside the scope of a parent's power of consent? Again there are several reasons. These are as follows.

- Children with intellectual disabilities are particularly vulnerable, both because of their minority and their disability.
- Even though the operation should only be performed if it is in the minor's best interests there may be greater risk of the 'wrong' decision being made. One that is based on an inaccurate or flawed assessment of a child's present or future capacity, for example, or is taken for improper reasons or motives.
- The court can ensure that the complex question of consent is fully explored and that popular misconceptions about intellectual disabilities are not too readily accepted. In other words the fact that a young woman is disabled does not automatically mean that she cannot give consent or make a meaningful refusal.
- The court provides the best forum for bringing together and considering all the expert and other relevant evidence such as the minor's medical history, circumstances and foreseeable future, the risks and consequences of pregnancy, the risks and consequences (both long- and short-term) of the operation which may be biological, social and psychological, the practicability of alternative contraceptive methods and any other relevant information.
- The court can determine the extent to which interests other than the child's should be taken into account. Primary care-givers and other family members such as brothers and sisters may, for example, have legitimate (though possibly conflicting) interests which despite being relevant to the court's decision must not prevail over those of the child.
- The court can protect health professionals who carry out the surgery from any subsequent legal liability.

Overall the court's role is essentially a protective one, to protect the minors from abuse and safeguard their best interests. But how do the courts reach their decisions? What factors do they consider?

The following two contrasting cases are good illustrations of how the courts reach their decisions.

The first, Re D [1976] was heard in 1976. It involved a handicapped 11-year-old with Sotos syndrome. She was described as mildly mentally handicapped and had an IQ of about 80. She also suffered from epilepsy, several other minor physical disabilities and was said to be emotionally unstable. Her mother was anxious that given her 'precocious' physical development she might get pregnant. Following the advice of a consultant paediatrician and gynaecologist she therefore gave her consent to sterilization. However, an educational psychologist who knew the girl well thought the operation unwarranted and made D a ward of court. The court refused to authorize the sterilization for several reasons. In particular that D's mental and physical condition was improving which meant that her future prospects were unpredictable. One day, therefore, she might well be able to make her own decisions about pregnancy and childbirth. Other persuasive factors included the irreversibility of the operation, her young age and last but by no means the least, the denial of the right to reproduce which would in all probability cause her considerable frustration and resentment in later life. In short the judge decided that the sterilization was neither medically indicated or necessary.

Just over a decade later another well-known case on the sterilization of a minor reached the House of Lords. Re B [1988] concerned a 17-year-old girl who also suffered from epilepsy and had a mental age of five or six and the communication abilities of a two-year-old. Sterilization was proposed for several reasons: she was sexually mature but could not be placed on any effective contraceptive regime; she was said to be incapable of understanding (or ever learning) the causal connection between intercourse, pregnancy and childbirth; irregular menstruation meant that it would be difficult to detect or diagnose a pregnancy in time to terminate it easily; she would be likely to panic if pregnant and could not cope with labour; a Caesarian section would not be appropriate since she had a high pain threshold and would probably pick at a wound and tear it open. In any event she would be terrified, distressed and extremely violent during normal labour. Finally she had no maternal instinct and was unlikely to develop any. Given all these factors a sterilization was in her 'best interests' and therefore lawful.

So why did the courts come to such different conclusions? Unquestionably B was much more profoundly handicapped than D and was prone to more violent and aggressive behaviour. There was also apparently no chance of any improvement in her condition so that if she ever did become pregnant an abortion would be inevitable. Interestingly though other criteria, notably the right to reproduce which was considered of fundamental importance in D's case, was much more readily dismissed. In the controversial words of one of the Law Lords:

the right of a woman to reproduce is only such when reproduction is the result of informed choice. ... to talk of the 'basic right' to reproduce of an individual who is not capable of knowing the causal connection between intercourse and childbirth, the nature of pregnancy, what is involved in delivery, unable to form any maternal instincts or to care for a child, appears to me wholly to part company with reality.

Since these two cases there have, of course, been others, none of which has caught the public's attention. And yet the issue remains controversial mainly because in these later cases the courts have been arguably more willing to authorize sterilizations without carefully assessing whether the young woman is (or would be in the future) capable of consenting to or refusing a sterilization. In other words incompetence to make decisions about sterilization is assumed rather than established. Moreover because the courts now appear to accept that sterilization is more easily reversible than it once was they no longer regard it as a 'last resort' procedure but more as a convenient contraceptive method. So-called 'social' factors are also more likely to be taken into account than previously, especially if without the operation a young woman would be subject to much more control and consequently would have less autonomy and sexual freedom.

Describing the court's approach since Re B one commentator has suggested that 'eugenics banned from the front door is being let in at the back'. Extreme though this comment might seem it is given credence in that the court has recently made it clear that its prior consent is not mandatory in all cases involving minors. This was established in the case of Re E [1991] which concerned the sterilization of a severely mentally retarded 17-year-old who suffered from a serious menstrual condition. It was held in that case that because the operation was medically indicated or therapeutic, i.e. to treat menorrhagia, her parents could consent on her behalf and the court's sanction was neither necessary nor desirable. In other words the sterilization was the 'inevitable and incidental' result of treatment rather than its primary objective.

Even in such cases, however, before proceeding, it would be advisable to get two doctors to agree, first that the operation was necessary for therapeutic purposes, secondly that it was in the patient's best interests and thirdly that no practicable less intrusive treatment was possible.

'Therapeutic' sterilizations are uncommon, however, and in the vast majority of cases the court's approval will be needed. But what factors will the court consider? Other than looking at case law – which is of limited value given that each case will turn on its own particular facts – the most authoritative guidance is that contained in a 'Practice Note' issued by the official solicitor in 1993. While this guidance has no legal force and is therefore not binding, it nevertheless provides very strong evidence of expected practice – rather like the effect of guidance issued by the DHSS or a circular. The note includes procedural guidance but more importantly outlines the kinds of factors the court should consider when a declaration is sought that a sterilization is in a patient's best interests.

Overall it would expect to be given a comprehensive profile of the patient, i.e. a full medical, psychological, and social history which should provide evidence that:

- the patient is incapable of making her own decision and is unlikely to develop sufficiently to ever make an informed decision about sterilization in the foreseeable future;
- the operation is needed because there is a 'real danger' that the patient will become pregnant;
- the patient will experience greater substantial trauma or psychological damage from a pregnancy than a sterilization;
- the patient is permanently incapable of caring for a child even with reasonable assistance;
- there is no practicable less intrusive way of preventing pregnancy. In other words sterilization is immediately necessary; the method proposed is the least invasive and will not itself cause physical or psychological damage greater than its intended beneficial effects; the sterilization is in line with current medical and scientific knowledge; and finally all less drastic contraceptives methods, including supervision, education and training must have proved 'unworkable' or 'inapplicable'.

FURTHER READING

Cusine, D.J. (1989) *New Reproductive Techniques, A Legal Perspective*, Dartmouth, Aldershot.

Department of Health HC(86)1 (Services for Young People); EL(90) MB115 (Balance of Provision in Family Planning Services).

Douglas, G. (1991) *Law, Fertility and Reproduction*, Sweet & Maxwell, London.

Keown, I.J. (1988) *Abortion, Doctors and the Law*, Cambridge University Press, Cambridge.

Mason, J.K. (1990) *Medico-Legal Aspects of Reproduction and Parenthood*, Dartmouth, Aldershot.

McLean, S.A.M. (ed.) (1989) *Legal Issues in Human Reproduction*, Dartmouth, Aldershot.

Norrie, K. McK. (1991) *Family Planning Practice and the Law*, Dartmouth, Aldershot.

Assisted reproduction   6

The birth of Louise Brown, the world's first 'test tube baby' in 1978 through in vitro fertilization (IVF) is a landmark date in the development of assisted reproduction. It attracted enormous publicity, captured the public's imagination and also marked the beginning of a lengthy process of consultation and debate which culminated in the publication of the influential Report of Enquiry into Human Fertilisation and Embryology (the Warnock Report). Most of the Report's recommendations were incorporated in the Human Fertilisation and Embryology Act 1990 which regulates almost all infertility treatment. But while Louise Brown's entry into the world was undoubtedly a major technical advance in the treatment of infertility other simpler reproductive techniques were already well established. Artificial insemination using a husband's sperm was, for example, first recorded in 1790 and the earliest account of successful insemination using donor sperm was 1884. And in the UK sperm donation had been practised, albeit on a small scale, since the late 1930s, although the first proper account did not appear in the *British Medical Journal* until 1945. Surrogacy too has a long history reputedly dating from biblical times.

The word 'infertility' is not legally defined nor is its true extent known but for legal purposes accurate figures are unnecessary nor is a definition important. It is convenient, however, to divide the various reproductive techniques into three main categories, namely, artificial insemination, in vitro fertilization and surrogacy. This chapter will focus primarily on those aspects of assisted reproduction which affect children although a brief outline of the legal framework regulating infertility treatment will also be given. As such the following questions will be addressed:

- How does the law regulate reproductive technology?
- Should the potential child's welfare determine who should have access to treatment?
- What legal rights to information do children have?

- Who are a child's legal parents?
- What legal rights do surplus foetuses have?
- Are surrogacy agreements enforceable?
- What rights do disabled children have?

The main reproductive techniques are as follows:

ARTIFICIAL INSEMINATION

As was noted above this technique is well established and so simple that it can be carried out without medical assistance. In legal terms it is the least controversial when the woman's husband's sperm is used (in which case it is known as AIH). Children are thus legitimate and so are treated for legal purposes in the same way as children conceived naturally. Artificial insemination of an unmarried woman using her partner's sperm is called AIP. Like AIH, AIP raises few legal problems other than when the partner's sperm is used after his death. None the less because of the parent's non-marital status the child is illegitimate. While the status of legitimacy has lost most of its significance in recent years some discrimination remains against illegitimate children, notably in relation to citizenship. The third form of artificial insemination involves donor sperm. Known traditionally as AID (or alternatively as AI and increasingly also as TDI – therapeutic donor insemination) this technique is more legally problematic because of the questions it raises about the legal status of children, in particular who should the law regard as the child's legal father – the donor who is the genetic father or the child's 'social' father, i.e. the one who is intended to take on the caring role?

Also included in this category (although they are sometimes treated as variants of IVF, below) are two related procedures known as gamete intra-fallopian transfer (GIFT) and zygote intra-fallopian transfer (ZIFT). GIFT involves transferring eggs and sperm which have previously been mixed together directly into the woman's fallopian tubes so that fertilization and implantation can occur in vivo. This procedure does not therefore involve the creation of an embryo outside a woman's body but can use either donated sperm or eggs (or both) in which case the child may be genetically related to only one of its parents or possibly neither. ZIFT is a very similar 'intermediate' technique in which eggs and sperm (which again may or may not be donated) are mixed outside the woman's body but transferred to the fallopian tubes at the zygote, i.e. pronuclear stage.

IN VITRO FERTILIZATION

This technique (popularly known as the 'test-tube baby' procedure) is the most common infertility treatment. It entails fertilizing an egg outside the body, i.e. in vitro (in a glass), and then transferring the embryo into the carrying mother (a process previously called 'embryo transfer' but now known as 'embryo replacement'). Traditionally the technique involved collecting eggs from a woman who produced an egg but whose fallopian tubes were damaged or blocked and fertilizing it with her husband's or partner's sperm. As the genetic and natural parentage were thus identical the child's legal status and its parentage were certain. But, if donor sperm are used questions arise as the child's legal parentage, in particular who qualifies as its legal father given that the genetic father is not the 'social' father. Identifying the child's legal mother can also be problematic. A woman who does not ovulate, for example (but is able to carry a child), could use donor eggs, fertilized with the husband's or partner's sperm. This latter technique is called 'egg donation' and is the counterpart or corollary of AID. But who should be the legal mother – the woman who provided the genetic material or the one who carried the child and gave birth to it?

Another related technique is 'embryo donation'. This procedure involves fertilizing a donated egg in vitro with donor sperm and then transferring the embryo to the woman's womb. As with egg donation the child has two potential 'mothers', the genetic mother who donated the egg and the woman who gave birth to the child (the 'carrying' mother). It also has two potential 'fathers', the genetic one who donated the sperm and the husband or partner of the carrying mother, i.e. the 'social' father.

IVF is more legally problematic than artificial insemination for several reasons. The first is that notwithstanding that legislation has now settled once and for all who in law are to be treated as a child's legal parents, anomalies still exist (see below). Secondly, the technique commonly involves the production of both surplus, i.e. 'spare' ova and embryos, the legal status of which is, in some respects, uncertain. What for example should they be used for? What legal rights do they have and how long can they be stored? And what if the gamete providers die? Should the law allow them still to be used?

SURROGACY

Although surrogacy arrangements – which cover any situation in which one woman agrees to carry a child for another – have been practised for centuries it is only recently that they have involved the various reproductive techniques outlined above. Also fairly recent is the commercialization of the practice whereby a third party (and possibly the surrogate) receives some financial benefit from the arrangement. The intention behind all surrogacy arrangements is that the child should be handed over at birth to the 'commissioning parents'. There are several different types of surrogacy. A woman can become pregnant following sexual intercourse with the commissioning father but more commonly, although still relatively straightforward, pregnancy can follow artificial insemination of the surrogate with the commissioning father's sperm. This is typically referred to as 'partial surrogacy' and is most likely to be used when the commissioning mother cannot ovulate or carry a child to term for some reason or other. In such cases the woman who gives birth to the child is also its genetic mother.

Another type of surrogacy arrangement is 'full' or total surrogacy (also called womb-leasing). Here the commissioning couple provide the gametes which are then fertilized in vitro and implanted in the surrogate (or fertilization could be in vivo as in GIFT, see page 117). This method produces a child genetically related to both commissioning parents (but not the carrying mother). Other variants of total surrogacy include those where the commissioning father is infertile and donor sperm may be used and if both commissioning parents are infertile both egg and sperm could be donated. Given the various permutations it is possible that a child could be born who is not genetically related either to the commissioning parents or the carrying mother.

THE LEGAL REGULATION OF ASSISTED REPRODUCTION

In 1991, nearly six years after the publication of the influential Warnock Committee recommendations and several government reports, the Human Fertilisation and Embryology Act 1990 came into force. Essentially a compromise measure the Act adopts a threefold approach to regulating assisted conception. This consists of the establishment of the Human Fertilisation and Embryology Authority which is largely responsible for implementing the Act, a licensing system and rigorous and detailed consent requirements. Nevertheless, despite its broad scope the Act is by no means comprehensive – it does not cover either all types of infertility treatment nor deal with all the legal issues raised by assisted reproduction. As regards infertility treatment (the Act also covers other topics most notably embryo research, see Chapter 8) it has several aims. These include balancing the potentially conflicting interests of society as a whole, children born as a result of the 'reproductive revolution' and the childless and setting and maintaining acceptable standards of treatment (especially important given the low success rates of some of the techniques). The Act also attempts to provide a clear legal framework within which scientists and health professionals can practise.

THE REGULATORY FRAMEWORK

THE HUMAN FERTILISATION AND EMBRYOLOGY AUTHORITY

The Human Fertilisation and Embryology Authority (HFEA) is an independent body which has effective control over infertility treatment as a result of its wide powers to license and supervise treatment services. It also has several other functions which include the following: monitoring and inspecting premises providing treatment; maintaining a Code of Practice (setting out the principles of good professional practice) and a register of specified information (containing details of donors or recipients of gametes or embryos and any child born as a result of treatment); publicizing treatment services; providing advice and information to those receiving treatment and those to whom licences apply; keeping under review information about embryos and finally reporting annually to the Secretary of State.

LICENSING SYSTEM

One of the principal ways in which the Act regulates infertility treatment is to prohibit certain activities altogether, i.e. they cannot be licensed at all and if carried out constitute serious criminal offences. Prohibited activities involving embryos include placing live embryos or gametes other than human ones in a woman and placing an embryo in an animal. Prohibited activities involving gametes include creating human/animal hybrids (except for the 'hamster' test which is used to establish the fertility or normality of sperm). Other 'infertility' activities which are lawful but must be licensed are those which are defined as 'treatment services', i.e. 'medical, surgical or obstetric services provided to the public or a section of the public for the purpose of assisting women to carry children'. Those requiring licences are specified in schedule 2 and include bringing about the creation of embryos in vitro, keeping embryos, using gametes, and placing any embryo in a woman. The combined effect of ss 2–4 and schedule 2 mean that the following six main types of treatments must be licensed:

- egg donation;
- embryo donation;
- in vitro fertilization (where an embryo is created outside the human body even if the couples own gametes are used);
- artificial insemination by donor
- gamete intra-fallopian transfer (where either the egg or sperm has been donated);

- surrogacy arrangements using any of the above techniques, i.e. using in vitro fertilization or the genetic material of the commissioning parents.

The Act only covers treatments using donated gametes or the creation of embryos outside the body (i.e. in vitro). Furthermore, because it only applies to treatment services which are provided 'to the public' (or a section thereof), certain reproductive techniques are not included and as such remain unregulated (except in so far as they are subject to the common law and the Surrogacy Arrangements Act 1985). They are nevertheless still lawful. These 'excluded' techniques, i.e. ones not covered by the Act, are:

- artificial insemination using a husband's or partner's sperm (i.e. AIH and AIP).
- 'do-it-yourself' artificial insemination, i.e. where the woman inseminates herself using self-help methods and does not rely on medical assistance; in such circumstances it makes no difference whether the sperm is donated or not unless it has been previously stored (in which case the Act applies);
- gamete intra-fallopian transfer (where the gametes come from the woman being treated and her husband or partner). Note that this technique and related ones may be brought within the Act in the future if the relevant regulations are ever brought into effect.

CONSENT REQUIREMENTS

The third limb of the regulatory framework focuses on consent. As regards the law of consent assisted reproduction is no different from other forms of medical treatment which involve touching patients – whether they are receiving infertility treatment or providing genetic material (i.e. embryos or gametes). As such all the essential elements which are required to make consent lawful (see Chapter 3) must be present. So, for example, a patient who is contemplating AID should, in accordance with the 'Bolam' test, be informed about the risks associated with the procedure, likewise the chances of becoming pregnant and so forth. The Human Fertilisation and Embryology Act 1990 and the HFEA's Code of Practice, however, go further than the common law by specifying, first, that consent must be in writing and secondly by providing detailed guidance on the procedure for giving consent (which includes counselling opportunities) and the kind of information which must be provided to donors of genetic material (which may or may not be the same persons as those receiving treatment) and patients having treatment. Schedule 3 is the relevant section. It covers gametes used for the purposes of treatment and received for such use as well as gametes used to create embryos in vitro. It also deals with consent relating to the storage of gametes and embryos. The Act's consent requirements are complex but basically aim to ensure that those providing genetic material have the right to decide what happens to it.

SURROGACY ARRANGEMENTS ACT 1985

Almost all surrogacy arrangements are regulated by the Surrogacy Arrangements Act 1985 (and some are also governed by the Human Fertilization and Embryology Act 1990). Put simply surrogacy involves the use of another person to produce a child but the Act defines it in rather more detail. According to s 1(2) a 'surrogate mother' is one who carries a child in pursuance of an arrangement (a) made before she began to carry the child, and (b) made with a view to any child carried in pursuance of it being handed over to, and parental responsibility being met (so far as practicable) by, another person or other persons. And by s 1(3) an arrangement is a 'surrogacy arrangement if, were a woman to whom the arrangement relates to carry a child in pursuance of it, she would be a surrogate mother'.

Given that almost all surrogacy agreements are made before conception the definitions in the Act are broad enough to catch all the most common types of arrangements irrespective of who provides the genetic material. In other words they may or may not involve a genetic link between the child and commissioning parents. Thus, for example, if the father is infertile, the surrogate's partner or an anonymous donor could provide the sperm whereas if both commissioning parents are infertile, the surrogate and her husband or partner could agree to hand over their own child, or the surrogate could carry an embryo donated by anonymous egg and sperm donors.

Usually described as a panic measure the Surrogacy Arrangements Act 1985 was passed within a few months of the 'baby Cotton' case – even though a dispute between a surrogate mother and commissioning parents had come before the English courts nearly ten years previously but was not fully reported. The case, Re C (1985), concerned an American couple – the husband was fertile but the wife had a congenital defect which prevented her ever having children – who arranged a surrogacy in England through an American commercial agency who were paid well over £10 000, half of which went to the surrogate. Through their contacts with a similar agency in England a Mrs Cotton was artificially inseminated with the commissioning father's sperm. Although there was no dispute about the baby going back to America as soon as she was born the local authority's intervention forced the father to take the case to court. The judge was concerned only with the baby's best interests but decided after all that the American couple could have custody of her. He was persuaded not just by their marital status – they were both 'professional people, highly qualified, with a very nice home in the country and another in town' but by the fact that 'far more importantly they were both excellently equipped to meet the baby's emotional needs, being warm, caring sensible people as well as highly intelligent'.

The Cotton case caused a public outcry hyped up by the media into a sordid tale of baby selling and profit-making by unscrupulous agencies. The Surrogacy Arrangements Act 1985 followed very shortly. It was passed largely to appease surrogacy's most vociferous critics – although it did incorporate many of the recommendations made in the Warnock report. The stance taken by the Act is best described as a 'sitting on the fence approach' in that it does not prohibit or make surrogacy arrangements illegal but instead tries to discourage them. First, by making surrogacy arrangements legally unenforceable, the effect of which is that the surrogate cannot be forced to give up the child if she changes her mind and a court thinks it is in the baby's best interests to stay with her (see below for how the court resolves such disputes). Secondly, by criminalizing the commercial exploitation of surrogacy which basically means outlawing commercial surrogacy agencies but not those made by non-profit-making agencies, such as a charitable infertility counselling service. Payments made to the surrogate for e.g. loss of earnings or expenses are also lawful. Put simply, paid surrogacy is not criminalized providing no broker or agent gets a fee for arranging it. Accordingly negotiating surrogacy arrangements on a commercial basis and several other related activities are criminal offences as are certain forms of advertising by or for a surrogate mother. However, the scope of the prohibitions against advertising are not clear in that although editors, proprietors or publishers clearly commit offences if they publish adverts offering or seeking surrogates it is unclear whether any offence is committed by the potential surrogate or commissioning couple.

Finally what of medically assisted surrogacy and the role of health professionals who help set up a surrogacy arrangement? While such activities are lawful they were until recently strongly discouraged. However, the British Medical Association in its new guidance on surrogacy, has taken a much less condemnatory line and there is even the possibility that surrogacy will soon be available through the National Health Service. Nevertheless, the HFEA's Code of Practice recommends that using assisted conception to initiate a surrogacy pregnancy should only be considered where it is 'physically impossible or highly undesirable for medical reasons' for the commissioning mother to carry the child.

ACCESS TO TREATMENT – THE CHILD'S WELFARE

While the law plays a fairly active role in regulating assisted reproduction it does not deal, at least directly, with who should have access to treatment. In relation to infertility treatment this is especially problematic for several reasons. First, even though such treatment is theoretically available under the National Health Service and is therefore governed by the National Health Service Act 1977 several factors, in particular its high cost, mean that in practice it almost always receives very low priority. As such it is virtually unavailable under the NHS. Secondly, those denied treatment will find legal remedies of little, if any, use as the following case illustrates. R v. Ethical Committee of St Mary's Hospital (Manchester) ex parte H [1988] concerned a woman, Mrs Harriot who had been rejected both as a potential foster and adoptive parent for two main reasons. She had several convictions for prostitution offences and her husband's children by a former liaison were in care. She sought IVF treatment but this too was refused once details of her past became known. Mrs Harriot appealed to the courts, claiming that refusing her treatment was unreasonable and unlawful. Although the court accepted that it did have the power to review the hospital's decision it saw no reason to vary it, claiming that its criteria (which were the same as those used by adoption agencies) were reasonable and had been fairly applied. These were:

> in assessing suitability ... there must be no medical, psychiatric or psychological problems which could indicate an increased probability of a couple not being able to provide satisfactory parenting to the offspring or endanger the mother's life or health if she became pregnant.

The court's decision was controversial but was perhaps not surprising given that the Act only indirectly deals with access to treatment and as such effectively gives those who provide it complete discretion in choosing prospective patients. The relevant section is s.13 (5) which requires those providing treatment: to take into account 'the welfare of any child who may be born (including the need of that child for a father), and of any other child who may be affected by the birth'.

On the face of it this seems a sensible provision in that it merely requires any prospective child's welfare to be considered and so falls well short of making its welfare paramount which is what almost all other legislation concerned with children requires. However, given that the concept of welfare is notoriously difficult to apply to children who are already in existence (and so must be even harder to apply to those who are as yet just a 'twinkle in the doctor's eye') what happens in practice is that the section operates as a 'fit parent' test. In other words it can be used to deny treatment to anyone whose lifestyle is considered 'unsuitable'.

Some guidance on assessment of prospective parents is nevertheless provided in the HFEA's Code of Practice which aims to ensure equality of access to treatment by setting out detailed selection criteria. These include a requirement that the following factors (among others) be considered: the applicants' (and that of their husband or partner, if any) commitment to having and bringing up a child, their ages and medical histories (likewise those of their families), risk of harm to projected children and the effect of a new baby upon any existing child. If these criteria are applied 'fairly and in an unprejudiced' way as the Code recommends then, at least in theory, no-one should be excluded.

ACCESS TO INFORMATION

Questions about their heritage and the identity of their genetic parents may well trouble children born as a result of assisted reproduction just as much as they concern adopted children. Yet the so-called 'discovery' rights of the former group of children to trace their origins and find out the 'truth' about their genetic ancestry are far more limited despite the fact that many of the arguments in favour of a more open process apply equally to adoptees as to children of the 'reproductive revolution'. Consequently a child's family history may be important for medical purposes, for example, in assessing the likelihood of a genetic disease being passed or a predisposition to, say, heart disease. Both groups of children may also have similar psychological or developmental needs to know their origins. Proving a blood tie may also be necessary for inheritance purposes. The question of what children should be told or have the right to find out has been one of the most problematic aspects of assisted reproduction given the need to balance several different potentially conflicting interests, namely, those of the donor, the child and his or her 'social parents'. Thus it is claimed that secrecy is important to protect parents who resort to assisted reproduction because of the possible social stigma attached to such processes. Donors should also remain anonymous otherwise they will not come forward for fear of being sought out by their 'offspring' who may make financial claims on them or disrupt their lives. Whatever the arguments for and against disclosure of information the solution adopted by the Human Fertilisation and Embryology Act is somewhere between the two 'extremes'. It does not endorse full disclosure but nor does it allow the process to be kept secret.

s. 31 is the relevant section. It is a complex provision but briefly it provides that the HFEA must keep a register of those (a) whose gametes or embryos have been used or kept, and (b) who have received 'treatment services' and (c) children who were or may have been born as a result of such treatment services.

Applicants over 18 are entitled to know (providing they have had the opportunity to be counselled) whether they have a genetic parent other than those defined by the Act as their parents and, if so, certain non-identifying information about that parent. In addition applicants between 16 and 18 (after they have been given the opportunity to be counselled) and anyone over 18 can request information about their intended spouse to establish whether they are related. The rights given to children born as a result of assisted reproduction are therefore minimal compared to adopted children who (at 18) can discover their natural parents because of their rights to a copy of their original birth certificate.

LEGAL PARENTAGE

Determining legal parentage was once a relatively straightforward process in that it could be assumed that a child's genetic (or biological) parents, i.e. those whose sperm and eggs led to its birth, were also those whom the law recognized as his or her legal parents. But advances in reproductive technology, in particular egg and embryo donation, have made it increasingly difficult to establish legal parentage. In addition the law now distinguishes between legal parentage (or parenthood as it is commonly called) which is the status of being a parent and parental responsibility which acknowledges the 'rights, duties, powers, responsibilities and authority' certain people have in relation to children.

The term 'parents' can be ascribed to any one of the following:

- **genetic parents**: (also called biological parents) who provide the gametes or embryo resulting in the child's conception.
- **social parents**: those with no genetic link to the child but who perform the caring role either now – as foster or adoptive parents, for example – or in the future as and when an infertile couple make a surrogacy arrangement;
- **'carrying' mothers** (also called birth or gestational mothers): are not intended to perform any caring function once the child is born since their role is to carry and give birth to it. Carrying mothers may not have provided any of the child's genetic make-up (some or all of which could have been provided by another couple).

Legal parentage does not necessarily determine with whom a child shall live. In other words the law provides no guarantee that a child's legal parents can exercise all the legal rights and duties of parenthood (which can be exercised only by those with 'parental responsibility').

Nevertheless, establishing legal parentage is important for several reasons. First, legislation (which may either create rights or impose duties) may refer to a child's 'parents'. For example, in the Child Support Act 1991 the term 'parent' is defined as any person who is in law the mother or father of a child. Secondly, establishing legal parentage may be the essential first step to acquiring parental responsibility. Thus if an unmarried man claims that he is a child's father and applies to court for a 'parental responsibility' order his application can only proceed if he can establish that he is the child's legal father. Only then can he be granted the order and so acquire the legal authority to make decisions about his child (unless, of course he has acquired parental responsibility through another route, i.e. agreement with the mother). This is because only those with parental responsibility have the right to care for children on a day-to-day basis. In other words to decide how to meet their physical and emotional needs, whom they should see, where they go to school, what religion they should follow and what medical treatment they should (or should not) have and so forth. The third reason for establishing legal parentage is that it may arise in disputes about inheritance rights, succession to property and immigration status.

The Human Fertilisation and Embryology Act 1990 introduced new rules about legal parentage as well as clarifying the legal status of children born as a result of egg donation and embryo transfer. In summary these are as follows.

THE LEGAL MOTHER

s. 27 provides that the woman who is carrying or has carried a child as a result of the placing in her of an embryo or of sperm and eggs, and no other woman, is to be treated as the mother of the child. However, for the purposes of the Act a woman is not to be treated as carrying a child until the embryo has become implanted. This provision therefore makes it clear that the woman who carries and gives birth to the child is its legal mother notwithstanding egg donation. Implicitly it also means that a woman is regarded as a legal mother if she gives birth to a child to whom she is the genetic mother. The legal status of the carrying mother is further confirmed by s.29 which provides that a woman treated as a child's mother under s.27 is to be treated in law as the mother of the child for all purposes. Note too that a child's legal mother also has automatic parental responsibility irrespective of her marital status.

This section appears deceptively simple and is almost comprehensive yet it can produce the 'wrong result' in surrogacy arrangements. This is because it makes the surrogate the legal mother and so defeats the whole purpose of the arrangement. To overcome this problem s.30 of the Human Fertilisation and Embryology Act 1990 was enacted which gives the commissioning parents the right to seek a 'parental order' (see below).

THE LEGAL FATHER

More complex provisions apply to determining legal fatherhood. s.28 aims overall to ensure a constant supply of donors by providing that there should be no legal relationship between the sperm donor and the child (notwithstanding the common law rule under which he is deemed to be the legal father). In other words donors do not have to fear that they will be held responsible for their 'offspring'. Accordingly s.28 allows two exceptions to the common law rule. The first covers married couples and provides that if the wife has a child following treatment such as artificial insemination (or any other procedure involving donated sperm such as IVF) her husband is the child's legal father. The husband can only avoid legal fatherhood if he rebuts the so-called marital presumption (i.e. that the husband of the woman who gives birth to the child is that child's father) and in addition can show that he did not consent to the treatment. In practice this latter element is most unlikely to be relied upon because even though there is no legal requirement that a husband's consent to treatment should be obtained the HFEA's Code of Practice recommends that it is. As a result clinics are rarely, if ever, going to provide treatment without the husband's consent.

As regards unmarried couples s.28 (3) provides that where donated sperm is used for a woman in the course of treatment provided for her and a man together under the licensing procedure of the Act, the woman's partner is the child's legal father. This means that he is subject to the same rights and responsibilities as any other natural father who is not married to the mother of his child. He does not, however, have automatic parental responsibility which he must then acquire in any of the ways specified in the Children Act 1989, such as by agreement with the mother or a parental responsibility order.

Another related subsection, 28(6), makes it clear that a sperm donor who has given all the relevant consents to his sperm being used (under schedule 3 of the Act) is not to be treated as the child's legal father. This means that when a child is conceived following treatment at a licensed clinic the sperm donor has no legal link with the child and no responsibilities towards it. Nor, of course, can he assert any rights over the child.

s.28 is again fairly comprehensive but there are some anomalies. For example, in some cases a sperm donor, rather than the woman's partner, will be the child's legal father, notably when an unmarried woman has a 'DIY' insemination, i.e. where she inseminates herself through 'self-help' methods outside of treatment services. Self-help can either involve sexual intercourse or the man producing sperm which the woman then inserts into her body. In such cases the woman has no partner to qualify as the legal father under s. 28(3) and even if she has one he has not received treatment together with her at a licensed clinic as is required under that section. Nor can the sperm donor avoid legal fatherhood under s.28(6) because his sperm is not being used in accordance with the Act (given that treatment is unlicensed). The intention here is to deter sperm donors from co-operating in unlicensed treatment because if they do they then become the legal father of any child born (and so liable to support it). However not all 'DIY' insemination results in the donors being the legal father since when the woman is married her husband will still be regarded as the legal father (see s.28(2)).

Rarely too some children will have no father in law at all, i.e. they will be legally fatherless. This occurs when a single woman receives infertility treatment alone at a licensed clinic. In such cases the sperm donor avoids legal fatherhood by virtue of s.28(6) but because the woman is not being treated together with her partner there is no-one to qualify as a legal father under s.28(3). Another example of a legally fatherless child is one born posthumously, i.e. when a man's sperm or an embryo created with his sperm is used after his death. The intention here is to discourage 'posthumous' births but not to prohibit them. See also Re Q (Parental Order [1996] in which a child, born of an un-married woman, acting as a surrogate mother for a married couple, who had been created from the egg of the wife fertilized by sperm donated at a clinic under a licensed arrangement, was held not to have a 'legal' father.

LEGAL PARENTAGE AND SURROGACY

A child's legal parentage in a surrogacy arrangement can be problem-atic. Not only is the surrogate the legal mother (regardless of the child's genetic make-up) but often the father's status is also unsatisfactory. Where the surrogate is married then her husband will be the legal father (assuming he consented to the procedure) even if the commissioning father's sperm was used. In contrast when the surrogate is unmarried then the commissioning father will be the legal father – but only if he had sexual intercourse with the surrogate or provided the sperm for unlicensed 'DIY' insemination since the 1990 Act does not then displace the common law rule (that the sperm donor is the legal father, see above). If on the other hand the commissioning father's sperm was used following licensed treatment then the combined effect of s.28(3) and (6) could arguably mean that neither the commissioning father nor the surrogate's partner (if any) is the child's legal father.

How, therefore, can a commissioning couple acquire legal parentage or at least the ability to exercise the rights and responsibilities of parenthood? One option is for them to adopt the child. But this is a lengthy and cumbersome process which in any event is not available to unmarried couples who want to adopt jointly. Another is to seek a residence order under the Children Act 1989. The most appropriate option is to invoke s. 30 of the Human Fertilisation and Embryology Act 1990 and apply for a 'parental order', i.e. an order that the child will be treated in law as a child of the parties. But this order will not suit all commissioning couples as a number of conditions have to be satisfied, which in practice limit its scope. First, only married couples can seek the order. Second there has to be a partial genetic link in that either the commissioning mother or father must have provided genetic material. This means that no order can be granted unless at least one of the commissioning couple has provided gametes.

RIGHTS OF THE SURPLUS FOETUS

Multiple pregnancies although rare do occur in infertility treatment. The success rate in IVF treatment is, for example, significantly higher if several embryos are implanted. Hormone treatment too can result in multiple pregnancies and there is increasing evidence that more eggs are now being used in the GIFT procedure. But, in the context of infertility treatment, what legal rights do these surplus foetuses have and is it lawful to destroy them? Known as selective reduction (also sometimes as reduction of multiple pregnancy) the practice basically involves destroying one or more foetuses so that another can develop. Even though the practice is controversial and raises similar issues as abortion it is regarded by some as both medically and socially necessary. The difficulties families face bringing up several children simultaneously and the increased possibility of handicap (or of none of the foetuses surviving) were poignantly highlighted in the widely reported experiences of Helen Pusey in 1990. She suffered temporary blindness, kidney failure and pleurisy at the end of her quadruple GIFT pregnancy. Two of the quads died, one 20 minutes after birth, the other at five months while her two surviving children have multiple handicaps. Her marriage also failed.

Although it is a well-established principle of English law that a foetus has no legal personality – and as such is not treated as a person or classified as 'property' – selective reduction was legally problematic in the past because of the uncertainty as to whether the procedure amounted to a miscarriage or a termination of pregnancy. Some argued that the practice could not be a miscarriage (and so was not a criminal offence within s.58 of the Offences Against the Person Act 1861) because the foetus was not expelled which is what the word 'miscarriage' presupposes. Nor, so it was claimed, was selective reduction caught by the Abortion Act 1967 because the pregnancy continued, i.e. the remaining foetuses were still being carried. Given the uncertainty as to the legality of the practice the Abortion Act 1967 was amended so as to make it clear that selective reduction was legal but only if it complied with the Act.

In effect this means that selective reduction is lawful either on the foetal abnormality ground, i.e. there is a substantial risk that the child would be seriously handicapped or that continuing with the pregnancy would involve risk of injury to the mother's health. Notwithstanding the legality of selective reduction, however, the practice remains controversial which perhaps explains the HFEA Code of Practice guidance that no more than three eggs or embryos should be transferred in any one cycle. It seems, therefore, that the 'rights' of the surplus foetus amount to no more than the right not to be destroyed unless the requirements of the Abortion Act 1967 are complied with.

Another aspect of assisted reproduction worth noting here is the storage of gametes and embryos. Such activities are regulated by the licensing requirements of the Human Fertilisation and Embryology Act 1990, in particular section 14 and schedule 2. Briefly, the position is that a storage licence may be granted in its own right or it can be coupled with a treatment or research licence. Either way it can permit the freezing and storage of gametes and embryos for ten years (these periods can be extended in certain circumstances). After that time, i.e. after they have passed their 'freezer date', they must be allowed to perish irrespective of the wishes of the gamete providers.

ENFORCEABILITY OF SURROGACY AGREEMENTS

There have been several well-reported cases both in England and America where the surrogate mother has refused to hand over the child to the commissioning couple. Supposing too that the surrogate refuses to keep to her side of the bargain in other ways – seeking an abortion perhaps or failing to adopt a 'safe' lifestyle or undergo pre-natal testing, the commissioning couple may also renege on the agreement – rejecting the child if it is born with disabilities or paying the surrogate less than was agreed. These kinds of problems raise two related questions. Is a surrogacy agreement legally enforceable and how do the courts decide between competing parents?

The first question is easy to answer because the Surrogacy Arrangements Act 1985 states unequivocally that 'no surrogacy agreement is enforceable by or against any of the persons making it'. This means that the parties cannot sue if individual terms are broken nor can the commissioning parents sue if the surrogate decides to keep the child. They can, however, take such a dispute to court. But the Act only applies to arrangements made before the surrogate agreed to carry the child, i.e. before it is conceived. Although these constitute the vast majority of surrogacy arrangements the common law, rather than the Act, still applies to all agreements reached after the child has been conceived. To date no English court has dealt with this issue but it is most unlikely that they would be enforced. In short the common law would follow the Act and treat any surrogacy agreement as unenforceable.

What happens when the surrogate refuses to hand the baby over? Inevitably the courts will become involved but given the small number of reported cases no guidelines have been laid down about how the court reach their decisions other than the broad 'best interests' test. Nevertheless in the case Re P (minors) [1987] the court did give some indication of the factors it considered relevant. The case concerned a married 'professional' man for whom a surrogate agreed to conceive following artificial insemination. As the pregnancy progressed she became determined to keep the twins and following a short period of indecision finally decided not to hand them over. Five months after their birth the case finally reached the court, during which time they had been cared for by the surrogate. The court considered the following to be relevant, namely the fact that she had carried the twins, looked after them successfully since birth and had bonded with them. Factors relevant to the commissioning parents included the 'shape' of their family which was 'better' because it was a two-parent family, their more affluent circumstances and better intellectual quality of their environment. But, notwithstanding these 'advantages', the judge allowed the children to stay with the surrogate being persuaded ultimately by the maternal bonding that had occurred.

RIGHTS OF 'DISABLED' CHILDREN

There are several reasons why children born as a result of assisted conception may be suffering from disabilities. With 'DIY' insemination screening is unlikely and the donated sperm may be contaminated or the donor may be the carrier of an hereditary disease. If the donor knew of his infection or genetic disease he would almost certainly be liable to the child, in which case his identity can be revealed by a court order. But, even if infertility treatment is carried out by a clinic, there is still a chance that gametes or embryos might be defective. For example, the screening procedures could be at fault, resulting in defective gametes being selected or sperm may not be properly examined. Embryos too could be damaged or a defective one may be implanted. Finally, the freezing and storage process could lead to disabilities (possibly only showing up many years later).

Given all these possibilities, what rights do children have to sue? Claims would have to be pursued under the Congenital Disabilities (Civil Liability) Act 1976 (see Chapter 7) which was amended to include disabilities caused by assisted conception. To succeed a child would have to prove that he or she has been born disabled and that the disability resulted from an act or omission in the course of the selection, keeping or use outside the body, of the embryo or of the gametes used to bring about the embryo. The amendment was intended to ensure that any disability, whether caused as a result of GIFT, IVF or artificial insemination, would be covered by the Act. However, there is some uncertainty – due to ambiguous wording – as to whether treatment other than IVF is in fact covered. Note too that all the conditions and defences which apply under the 1976 Act apply here as well. In particular, the defendant must be liable to one or both of the parents (irrespective of whether they suffered injury) but no liability arises if one or both of the parents knew of the risk of their child being born disabled. It is therefore very important that parents are given full information as to the possible risks associated with treatment. Furthermore, as with all such claims, breach of duty and causation have to be proved which can in practice be very difficult to establish.

FURTHER READING

Cusine, D. (1990) *New Reproductive Technologies: A Legal Perspective*, Aldershot, Dartmouth.

Cusine, D. (1989) Legal Issues in Human Reproduction. In S.A.M. McLean (ed.), *Legal Issues in Human Reproduction*, Aldershot, Dartmouth.

Douglas, G. (1991) *Law, Fertility and Reproduction*, Sweet & Maxwell, London.

Freeman, M. (1989) 'Is Surrogacy Exploitative?' In S.A.M. McLean (ed.), *Legal Issues in Human Reproduction*, Aldershot, Dartmouth.

Mason, J.K. (1990) *Medico-Legal Aspects of Reproduction and Parenthood*, Aldershot, Dartmouth.

Morgan, D. and Lee, R. (1991) *The Human Fertilisation and Embryology Act 1990: Abortion and Embryo Research. The New Law*, Blackstone Press, London.

Prenatal injuries

7

Few drug tragedies have attracted more national concern than Thalidomide. Prescribed as a tranquillizer or sleeping pill in pregnancy, it caused deformities, some of them very severe, in 8000 children world-wide (400 or so in Britain) born between 1959 and 1962. Many of the children had no arms or legs, some were limbless trunks without either arms or legs. A few died. The tragedy drew attention to the vulnerability of the foetus and its need for legal protection and highlighted major deficiencies in the common law. The claim against the drug company dragged on for ten years and an out-of-court settlement was only finally reached because of a media campaign as a result of which most, but by no means all, the children received compensation. One response to the tragedy was the Law Commission's 1974 Report on Injuries to Unborn Children. It recommended that liability in respect of prenatal injuries should be regulated by legislation rather than be left to the vagaries of the common law. Another was the Congenital Disabilities (Civil Liability) Act 1976 which followed a few years later. But although the deformities suffered by the Thalidomide babies shocked the world, dis-abilities and childhood death can be caused by several other factors unrelated to drugs. Furthermore as genetic screening and prenatal diagnosis become increasingly available under the NHS, inevitably the more likely it is that 'something will go wrong'.

What then are the legal consequences of negligent genetic screening and prenatal testing? Supposing parents are wrongly advised about the risks of passing on a genetic disorder? Do they (or their disabled chil-dren) have any legal remedy? And what is the legal position if the rights of pregnant women conflict with those of their unborn children? Although rare such conflicts are not unknown. These are just some of the issues and questions which can arise in this context (others were identified in the Report on Genetic Screening published in 1993 by the Nuffield Council in Bioethics.) Basically, however, they all turn on estab-lishing what legal rights unborn children have and what legal duties are owed to them. This chapter will therefore focus on the legal position of the unborn child, although it will begin with an outline of the different categories of prenatal injuries.

TYPES OF INJURIES

PRE-CONCEPTION INJURIES

Damage to either parent's reproductive capacity before conception can affect their ability to have a child. For example, a woman may be given an infected blood transfusion (e.g. causing HIV or venereal disease) or not be treated for rhesus incompatibility which causes brain damage in a subsequent child. Or her pelvis may have been damaged through negligent surgery or a previous abortion which so weakens the uterus that it ruptures and injures the child during labour. Pre-conception exposure to chemicals, excessive radiation, and X-rays could also damage sperm and cause gene mutation as could defective contraceptives. Exposure to excessive doses of radiation was the basis of two unsuccessful actions against British Nuclear Fuels Ltd in 1993. Both plaintiffs claimed that their partners' sperm had been damaged by radiation which in turn had led to cancer in their children. They lost largely because there was insufficient evidence to link the radiation to the injuries. In other words it was not possible to prove on the balance of probabilities that the radiation caused the cancer.

INJURIES DURING PREGNANCY

This category covers cases where the foetus is damaged in utero. Drugs taken by pregnant women, especially early in the pregnancy, are perhaps the most typical example. Less common are those injuries which arise from an operation which goes wrong when the mother was pregnant (as happened in the Burton case, see page 142). Also rare but nevertheless possible are those instances when a foetus is damaged in utero because of an assault on its mother. Other injuries which might affect a foetus are those which were caused by negligent infertility treatment. Usually referred to as occurrences ex utero they cover cases where a child's disability is due to the negligent selection, storage or use outside the body, of an embryo carried by the mother or of the gametes used to bring about the creation of the embryo.

INJURIES DURING BIRTH

Negligent delivery procedures are the main cause of injuries in this category such as occurred in the well-known case of Whitehouse v.

Jordan [1991] where it was alleged that brain damage was caused because the doctor pulled too hard and too long with forceps as a result of which the baby was severely disabled.

NEGLIGENT GENETIC COUNSELLING AND PRENATAL TESTING

Claims for prenatal injuries, whether occurring before or after conception, are almost always likely to give rise, if at all, to liability under the Congenital Disabilities (Civil Liability) Act 1976 (see page 138). Furthermore in all such cases it is the defendant who is responsible for the child's disabilities, i.e. his or her negligent act or omission brought about or caused the damage. But what about injuries which are not caused by the defendant but nevertheless his or her behaviour resulted in a disabled child being born? The essence of any such claim is not therefore that the defendant's actions (or inactions) actually caused the child's disabilities but rather that he or she facilitated its birth. In other words, but for the negligent conduct, a child would never have been born. These kinds of claims are called 'wrongful life' actions when brought by children and 'wrongful birth' when brought by their parents (see below).

'Wrongful life' and 'birth' actions are likely to arise out of negligent genetic counselling or prenatal foetal testing, and less frequently negligent infertility treatment. Genetic counselling involves answering questions about a medical condition or disease that is, or may be, genetic in origin, i.e. it is hereditary. The counsellor may (but does not have to) be medically qualified but regardless of his or her qualifications the advice given will depend upon a medical diagnosis or medical assessment. Information may be sought about a condition which has affected several relatives and thus seems to 'run in the family'. In such cases the counsellor is likely to be asked whether the 'clients' are carriers. If so what is the risk of the disorder being inherited by their children? But more commonly advice will be sought retrospectively after a child has already been born with the disorder. Questions then typically focus on the chances of any subsequent children inheriting the disease. In some cases too prenatal advice is sought because a woman wants to know how pregnancy might affect her health.

Prenatal testing or diagnosis involves testing whether or not a particular foetus is affected by a genetic or other disorder, i.e. congenital malformations or chromosomal abnormalities (e.g. Down's Syndrome). Screening procedures can be invasive, such as serum testing the mother's blood for alphafetoprotein (AFP), amniocentesis and chorionic villus sampling (CVS) or non-invasive, the main technique being ultrasound. Claims arising from negligent prenatal testing are likely to be pursued if, for example, foetal abnormalities are not detected because a test was carried out negligently or was wrongly interpreted. Or perhaps no test was offered at all despite being medically indicated. Thus in Salih v. Enfield HA [1991] liability was based on a failure to detect that a pregnant woman was infected with rubella. In another the mother's claim arose out of a failure to carry out an ultra-scan resulting in the birth of a baby with spina bifida. Other potential negligence claims which maternity services, in particular high-technology ones, can lead to include the safety of CVS which has been linked with limb defects and ultrasound which (given the danger of false positive scans) can result in unnecessary terminations. Consent-related claims are also a potential negligence area if women are not given full information, in particular about the exact nature of any test proposed, its effects, purpose and whether its advantages outweigh its risks.

The various claims disabled children (and their parents) can make will now be looked at but first the role of the criminal law in protecting the unborn child will be outlined.

REMEDIES

CRIMINAL LAW

Although the foetus does not have an independent legal personality – and so is not treated as a 'person' for legal purposes – several statutes aim specifically to protect it. The most important of these is the Infant Life Preservation Act 1929 which makes it a criminal offence for any person, who, with intent to destroy the life of a child capable of being born alive, by any wilful act causes a child to die before it has an existence independent of its mother. No offence is committed if the act which caused the child's death was done in good faith to save the mother's life.

Subject to the provisions of the Abortion Act 1967, The Offences Against the Person Act 1861 also makes it illegal for a pregnant woman to unlawfully administer to herself any poison or use any instrument unlawfully with intent to procure a miscarriage. It is also unlawful for another person to attempt to cause a miscarriage by similar means whether or not the woman is pregnant. In addition s.59 of the Act makes it illegal for anyone to supply or procure any poison or other noxious thing or any instrument knowing that it is to be used unlawfully to procure a miscarriage whether or not the woman is actually pregnant.

As to the mother's criminal liability for harming the foetus, should she act in any way detrimental to its well-being it is very doubtful that any criminal charge would be successful unless she contravened the Offences Against the Person Act 1861 or the Infant Life Preservation Act 1929. However, in the recent case of Attorney General's Reference (no. 3 of 1994), the Court of Appeal confirmed that the crimes of murder and manslaughter can be committed both to a child in utero and to a mother carrying a child in utero, where the child is subsequently born alive, enjoys an existence independent of the mother, thereafter dies and the injuries inflicted while in utero either caused or made a substantial contribution to the death.

THE CONGENITAL DISABILITIES (CIVIL LIABILITY) ACT 1976

Before the Act was implemented no English case had confirmed that a common law of duty of care was owed to an unborn child. It was therefore unclear whether disabled children had a cause of action for injuries sustained before birth. Their uncertain legal status was in fact one of the main reasons why the victims of the Thalidomide tragedy finally settled their negligence claim out of court. It was also an issue which the Law Commission recommended should be resolved once and for all by legislation. Accordingly s.1 of the Act establishes the right of disabled children to obtain compensation for injuries sustained before birth. In other words the Act recognizes that a duty of care is owed to unborn children. None the less despite the Act's good intentions it is a notoriously complex piece of legislation. Its major flaw is undoubtedly, however, that it retains the fault principle. Compensation therefore depends on proving both breach of duty (to a parent) and in addition causation. In any negligence claim these are very difficult, if not impossible, hurdles to overcome (see Chapter 2) but they can be even greater when the claim relates to events occurring before birth. It is thus not surprising therefore that the Act can be invoked by no more than 0.5% of all severely disabled children and is no use at all to the vast majority of children the cause of whose congenital defects are unknown.

The principle provisions of the Act can be summarized as follows. First it applies to all children born after 21 July 1976 and replaces the common law, at least for those situations covered by the Act (see below as to the continuing relevance of the common law). Secondly, only disabled children who are born 'alive' (the child must survive for at least 48 hours) can sue. So no claim can be brought on behalf of children born dead even if their death was caused by negligence (unlike their parents who may be able to sue at common law for the trauma of, e.g. still birth or miscarriage). Disability is widely defined as 'any deformity, disease or abnormality, including predisposition (whether or not susceptible of immediate prognosis) to physical or mental defect in the future'. Thirdly, whatever the disability it must have been caused by what the Act calls an 'occurrence'.

The 'occurrence' can be either a pre- or post-conception one, i.e. one which affected either parent's ability to have a normal healthy child, affected the mother during her pregnancy or affected her or the child during the course of its birth (i.e. the various types of injuries outlined at the beginning of this chapter). Because of the advances in infertility treatment the Act was amended in 1990 to include disabilities caused by acts or omissions arising from the selection, storage or use outside the body of genetic material, i.e. embryos or gametes even though it is arguable that the amendment (and therefore the Act) is limited to IVF treatment (see Chapter 6).

Fourthly, children's rights under the Act are derivative only. What this means is that the 'occurrence' must have made the defendant liable in tort to a parent. As a consequence disabled children can only sue if a duty of care owed to either of their parents is breached. Liability to children is therefore essentially a by-product of the breach of duty owed to parents. Or to put it another way if no duty is owed to parents children cannot sue irrespective of any injuries they may have suffered. But even though a child's claim relies upon negligence towards a parent it is not necessary for that parent to have actually suffered 'any actionable injury' himself or herself. In one of the commonest types of situation giving rise to liability under the Act, such as when a pregnant woman takes a drug negligently developed, prescribed or manufactured, this means that the defendant cannot avoid liability simply because the mother was unharmed – in fact her health is likely to have improved. She will, however, almost certainly suffer some damage such as nervous shock when she gives birth to a disabled baby. Moreover it is difficult to imagine any situation when the duty of care health professionals owe towards pregnant women will not also include a duty towards any foetus they are carrying. This means that any breach of duty to the mother will inevitably give rise to a cause of action by her child who is disabled as a result. The only possible exception to this general rule (i.e. that the duty to a mother encompasses one to her foetus) is where there is a conflict of interest between the two. During labour, for example, the doctor's duty towards the mother may mean that he or she has to risk harming her unborn child.

Fifthly, children cannot sue for pre-conception injuries if either or both of the parents knew of the risk of their child being born disabled. Responsibility thus rests firmly, albeit somewhat unfairly at least from the child's point of view, with the parents. If they knowingly run the risk (which can be as low as 1% or even lower) of conceiving a disabled child their child's claim is defeated irrespective of anyone else's negligence. None the less, as with every general rule there is an exception. In this case it turns on the father's knowledge. If he is aware of the risk but not the mother he will be liable to his child.

Finally, mothers (but not fathers) are given extensive immunity under the Act. The legal effect of which is that they cannot be sued by their children even though they may have caused their disabilities. There are several sound reasons for this immunity. One is that claims against mothers are unlikely ever to be pursued within 'normal' family relationships and so the Act simply reinforced what is likely to happen in practice (or not happen). Another is the risk of liability being used as a 'potent weapon' in disputes between parents. Finally, given that women are given so much advice during pregnancy, much of which is likely to be contradictory or at least not very persuasive, such as what they should or should not eat and drink and so on – it would in any event be very difficult, if not impossible, to prove they were negligent. But there is one exception to the mother's immunity namely when a child is born disabled as a result of its mother's negligent driving. This exception which arises when the mother knows she is pregnant (or ought reasonably to know) is considered 'acceptable' because of the role played by insurance (the 'real' defendant being the insurer company) and because in such cases it will be much easier both to prove cause and effect and also set the relevant standard of care.

Other points worth noting about the Act are, first, where a parent is partly to blame for a child's disabilities compensation can be reduced to take into account his or her share of the responsibility. Secondly, no action for 'wrongful life' can be taken under the Act. Thirdly, the Act incorporates the professional standard of care. This means that defendant health professionals will almost certainly be able to avoid liability if they have satisfied the 'Bolam' test. Finally, the Act retains the fault principle. Thus to succeed a child has not only to prove a breach of duty (to a parent) but also causation. As with all negligence claims, both these elements can in practice be almost insurmountable obstacles.

Case study 7.1

Janet is a 30-year-old pregnant woman who has been a voluntary patient in a psychiatric hospital several times but is now living on her own. For most of her pregnancy she has refused all offers of help from her family and has had very little antenatal care. She also often sleeps 'rough'. The local authority are very worried about the effect her lifestyle may have on her baby. Not only has she continued to take drugs and smoke very heavily but she has also repeatedly insisted that she has no intention of giving up drugs irrespective of the effect on her baby's development. There is therefore a very real chance that her baby will be harmed.

What action can the local authority take?

If Janet's baby, Gemma, is born with disabilities as a result of her drug addiction can she sue Janet under the 1976 Act?

There is no action that the local authority can take in respect of Gemma before she is born because it is not possible in English law to ward a foetus. This was established in the case of Re F (in utero) [1988] where the local authority failed in its attempt to do just that. The case concerned a 36-year-old woman with mental health problems who had led a nomadic existence wandering around Europe. She finally returned to England and settled down but the local authority became very anxious about the safety of her baby and attempted to take wardship proceedings in respect of the foetus. The Court of Appeal rejected the application saying it had no power to ward a foetus because until it was born and had an existence independent of its mother it had no legal personality. One of the main factors influencing the court's decision was the practical difficulties warding a foetus would entail – enforcing the order against her mother would mean that she would have to be effectively 'policed' throughout her pregnancy.

If Gemma was born with disabilities she cannot sue her mother under the 1976 Act even if her disabilities were caused by Janet's lifestyle during pregnancy, i.e. they were due to her negligence. This is because, except when driving a motor vehicle negligently, mothers are expressly excluded from liability under the Act.

Case study 7.2

Mariella is six weeks pregnant. She visits her GP, Jhicta, with a minor complaint and is prescribed a drug which the British National Formulary (BNF) warns should not be used at all during pregnancy or only used with caution. Jhicta fails to ask Mariella if she could be pregnant. Several months later Tom is born with serious disabilities which were undoubtedly caused by the drugs Mariella took early in her pregnancy.

Is Jhicta liable to Tom under the 1976 Act?

Jhicta owed a duty of care to Mariella to ensure that any foetus she was carrying was not harmed by drugs prescribed in pregnancy. In other words the duty owed to Mariella includes taking care not to harm her foetus. But has Jhicta breached her duty of care? This would depend on the standard of care which would be expected of a reasonably competent GP. In assessing this the Bolam test would be applied which is, in fact, incorporated in s.1(5) of the 1976 Act. This section, commonly referred to as the 'doctor's defence', allows doctors (likewise other health professionals) to avoid liability if they 'took reasonable care having due regard to the received professional opinion applicable to the particular class of case'. The section then goes on to confirm that departing from received opinion is not in itself evidence of negligence. Jhicta's liability would therefore turn on whether or not other reasonably competent GPs would have prescribed the drug, i.e. would they have been aware of the risks it posed? And even if they were aware of the risk did the potential benefit to the mother outweigh that risk? This seems unlikely given (a) that Jhicta did not even ask Mariella if she could be pregnant and (b) Mariella was only suffering from a very minor complaint.

As to the possible liability of the drug company under the Consumer Protection Act 1987, see below.

NEGLIGENCE

A question which remains as yet unsettled, at least in respect of children born **after** 21 July 1976, is what liability exists, if any, towards them under the common law. In other words once the Act applies, is recourse to the common law precluded? Leaving this question aside for the moment however, there is now no doubt that children born **before** the 1976 Act came into force can sue at common law for prenatal injuries (in fact the 1976 Act does not apply to them at all so a common law remedy is their only option). It was only recently, however, that it was confirmed that a common law duty of care was owed to a foetus. This was in Burton v. Islington HA [1991] where a dilation and curettage was carried out on a woman who was five weeks pregnant. No pregnancy test was done (the woman did not know she was pregnant) and her baby was born in 1967 with brain damage asphyxia after a failed forceps delivery. Similarly another child also born in 1967 was able to claim in respect of injuries sustained during delivery and birth (see De Martell v. Merton & Sutton HA [1991]). As a result of these two cases children born before the 1976 Act can now sue for compensation for negligent prenatal injuries at common law although few claims based on events so long ago are now likely to be pursued.

Case study 7.3

Stuart was born in 1975. His birth, per vaginam, was a difficult one and his mother claims that the severe brain damage he suffered at birth was due to negligent delivery procedures. In short a Caesarian section operation should have been carried out due to his size, the fact that he was in breech presentation position and showing signs of stress and that his mother was very small (for similar facts see the case of Hinfey v. Salford HA [1993]).

Will his claim succeed?

While, following the Burton case, a duty of care was clearly owed to Stuart as an unborn child he still has to prove on the balance of probabilities that a breach of duty occurred and that his injuries were caused by the manner in which he was delivered. As was noted in Chapter 2 proving breach (likewise causation) can be very difficult bearing in mind that the obstetric team can avoid liability by showing that it acted in accordance with the standard of care accepted as proper by a responsible body of medical opinion (i.e. the Bolam standard). Ultimately, of course, the outcome of any case will turn on its particular facts.

As to children born after 21 July 1976 (to whom the 1976 Act applies) it is unclear whether or not the common law exists as an alternative course of action. The most likely reason for using the common law would be when a child born is disabled as a result of its mother's behaviour during pregnancy (as in the case study involving Janet and Gemma). Given that liability under the Act is excluded a claim at common law would be the only way such a child could obtain compensation. Until the point is decided, however, the role of the common law remains uncertain. Several commentators claim that once the Act applies no common law remedy is possible. Others disagree and suggest that despite the 1976 Act actions can still be pursued at common law most notably in respect of those situations not covered by the Act.

Case study 7.4
Leticia is in labour and several days overdue. Due to the position of her baby a Caesarian section is recommended. In fact this operation is thought to be the only way the baby can survive unharmed. But Leticia, who is a competent adult patient, refuses the operation. Her son, Michael, is born with severe brain damage as a result of Leticia's decision.
    Who can Michael sue? What difference would it make if Michael was born in 1974, i.e. before the 1976 Act came into force?

Michael cannot sue any health professional (or the NHS Trust or hospital authority) under the 1976 Act because they have not breached their duty of care to Leticia. This is because she is entitled to refuse to accept recommended treatment and as such practitioners commit no tort if they respect her wishes. In fact they would almost certainly be liable in tort for battery if they ignored her wishes and operated without her consent (subject to Re S, see page 144). What this kind of situation therefore involves is a conflict of interest between mother and child. The duty to the mother – to exercise reasonable skill and care for her health – includes respecting her right to refuse treatment even though as a consequence Michael is harmed. As was noted above a child's rights under the Act are derivative only, i.e. they rely on negligence towards a parent (which in this case has not occurred).

Nor can Michael, despite being harmed in utero, sue Leticia under the Act because it grants immunity to mothers. As to whether Michael can sue her at common law, this as yet is unclear given the uncertainty as to the role of the common law once the Act is in force.

If Michael was born in 1975 then even though his claim would be based on the common law it is doubtful whether an action against Leticia, his mother would be successful. The courts would almost certainly be very reluctant to allow one to succeed fearing the potential, far-reaching implications of such claims – mothers who smoked or took drugs could otherwise arguably face claims by their children (assuming of course that their injuries could be proved to have been caused by their mothers' behaviour during pregnancy).

But could the precedent of Re S [1992] be used to justify operating on a competent adult without consent? In that case (see Chapter 3) the High Court overruled a mother's refusal of consent even though she was competent on the basis that an operation was thought to be the only way of saving the mother's and her unborn child's life. But Re S is a very doubtful precedent and was also specifically rejected in guidelines (1994) issued by the Ethics Committee of the Royal College of Obstetricians and Gynaecologists soon after the case. Among other things it emphasizes that a

doctor must respect the competent pregnant woman's right to choose or refuse any particular recommended course of action whilst optimising care for both mother and foetus to the best of his or her ability. A doctor would not then be culpable if these endeavours were unsuccessful even though her refusal might place her life and that of the foetus at risk.

So while it is in theory possible to plead necessity – i.e. to commit battery against the mother in order to save the child – such a course of action is certainly not recommended especially as Re S may well eventually be overruled by a higher court.

DRUG-INDUCED INJURIES

COMMON LAW REMEDIES

The deficiencies in both the 1976 Act and the law of negligence can mean that children disabled as a result of prenatal injuries receive no compensation. And if their injuries are drug induced, i.e. they were harmed in utero by a drug taken during their mothers' pregnancy, then it is even more likely that any claim based on negligence will fail (whether they are taken against the manufacturer or importer of the drug, the health professional who prescribed it or the dispensing chemist). Again proving fault is the major obstacle as drug companies will almost always be able to avoid liability by showing that at the time the drug was manufactured they followed current safety standards and so cannot be held responsible for unforseeable or unknown risks. When Thalidomide was prescribed, for example, its potential for causing foetal deformities was by no means clear since even though it had long been established that drugs could harm a foetus the evidence was far from conclusive and certainly was not universally accepted. Proving a causal link is another formidable hurdle for claimants with drug-related disabilities as it is not uncommon for several years to pass before the damage becomes evident. It was nearly twenty years, for example, before the harmful effects of diethylstilboestrol (DES) became known. It was prescribed to pregnant women to reduce the risk of a miscarriage but caused vaginal and cervical cancer in many of their daughters in utero when they took the drug. The causal link can similarly be hard to establish, in particular if a child's disabilities could have had a natural cause or if they are hypersensitive. Medical records too may be inaccurate, making it even more difficult to prove when the drug was taken and in what doses.

In some cases contract law can provide a remedy – based on the manufacturer's duty under the Sale of Goods Act 1979 and 1994 to ensure that drugs are 'fit for their purpose' and of a 'satisfactory quality'. But a contract-based claim will again almost certainly fail, especially in relation to drugs prescribed under the NHS. This is because contract-based remedies depend on the plaintiff 'purchasing' the defective goods and there is no contract between the pharmacist and the patient in relation to prescription-only drugs (where the contracts are first between the manufacturer and the wholesaler and secondly between the wholesaler and the retail chemist). On the other hand patients who buy drugs over the counter (likewise private patients who pay the chemist the full cost of the drugs they buy) can base a claim on contract law providing they can prove that the drug was unfit or of an unsatisfactory quality.

CONSUMER PROTECTION ACT 1987

The Act was passed following the growing consumer protection movement which originated in America in the 1960s and was the main impetus behind the European Community's harmonization programme and its 1985 directive on liability for defective products. The Act does not replace either contract or negligence law but is an alternative remedy. Overall it aims to make the producer of a product liable for personal injury (as well as certain property damage) caused by a defect in a product, irrespective either of the contractual position or negligence. Victims do not therefore have to prove fault as the Act introduces a scheme of strict liability. Removing the fault element was expected to make the Act a much more effective remedy or at least introduce a more sensitive and compassionate compensation system. However, liability, as we shall see, is far from absolute mainly because there are several 'defences' in the Act which significantly limit its impact and arguably allow the fault principle to return, albeit through the 'back door'.

But what are the Act's main provisions? These are best described by outlining who is liable under the Act, what they are liable for and what 'defences' they can plead.

WHO IS LIABLE?

Liability is imposed principally on the 'producers' of goods. The word 'producer' is widely defined and is intended to catch all who are involved in the production and marketing process. As such it includes not just original manufacturers (either of the finished product or components) – albeit the principal defendants in any claim – but also those who market, import, or brand-name a product. A hospital, health authority or Trust could therefore be a 'producer' of a drug sold in a hospital shop or bought wholesale and marked with the name or other distinguishing hospital feature such as its logo. Those who supply drugs are also deemed to be producers. This means that in some circumstances health authorities (likewise individual health professionals) could be liable. In the case of 'suppliers', however, liability only arises if they cannot identify the drugs' manufacturers (see further DHSS circulars (HN(88)3 and HN (FP(88)5) which provide guidance on the implications of the Act for the National Health Service).

WHAT IS A 'DEFECTIVE' PRODUCT?

The Act applies to 'products' defined as 'any goods or electricity'. The term also includes component parts and the raw materials from which products are made. Drugs are clearly within the definition but blood and human tissues are almost certainly not. It is therefore unclear whether a patient harmed by infected blood could use the Act to obtain compensation. None the less most commentators agree that blood transfusions (other than Factor V111 which is a 'product') would be treated as the provision of a service and so would not be classed as a 'product'. Consequently claims relating to infected blood should be based on negligence law and breach of statutory duty under the National Health Service Act 1977.

Having established which 'products' the Act covers the next key concept to unravel is that of a 'defect'. The Act says (s.3(1)) that a product is defective if its 'safety is not such as persons generally are entitled to expect'. Known as the 'consumer expectation test' this tells us very little except perhaps that 'safety' is a relative concept. Nor does s.3(2) provide much further guidance. It states that in deciding whether a product is defective all the circumstances shall be taken into account including 'the manner in which, and purposes for which, the product has been marketed, its get-up, the use of any mark in relation to the product and any instructions for or warnings with respect to, doing or refraining from doing anything with or in relation to the product'. Note too that the Act judges a product's safety when its producers supplied it and not at any later date, i.e. when with the benefit of hindsight previous standards would be rejected. In relation to drugs, defects can arise from their manufacture, design or presentation. Typically though, drug defects are caused by design faults in which case their 'defectiveness' will turn on several factors such as whether the risk was known at the time of production, how long development would have taken to eliminate the risk, the usefulness of the product and so on. Relevant too is the extent to which warnings and instructions given were adequate and perhaps even more important whether the risks associated with a drug were justified by its overall benefits. So the effects of cytotoxic chemotherapy may nevertheless be outweighed by its greater potential benefits (bearing in mind what is likely to happen if the drugs are not taken and the risks and benefits of alternative treatment). In contrast the side effects of a mild analgesic should be no more than minimal.

Other factors which would have to be taken into account include idiosyncratic reactions, whether these were known in advance, whether the reactions of a small number of patients are outweighed by the drug's potential benefit to the public, the size and predictability of those actually affected and whether appropriate warnings were given.

CAUSATION

Although the Act imposes strict liability the causal link must still be proved. This requires proof that the damage was caused 'wholly or partly' by the defective drug. But just as many negligence claims fail to overcome this hurdle so do those under the Act. Thus children who alleged they were brain damaged by the whooping cough vaccine failed to receive compensation because the courts did not accept that the vaccine caused their disabilities. Similarly a child harmed in utero will have to prove that it was the defendant's drug, rather than any other drug, which caused the damage. And if a child's disabilities could have been caused naturally it may be almost impossible to prove cause and effect. Note too that liability under the Act only lasts for ten years after the drug was first supplied.

DEFENCES

Even if the causal link is proved the drug's producers can plead any one of the several defences introduced by the Act. But the one most likely to be relied on in drug-related cases is the so-called 'development risk' or 'state of the art' defence. Always a controversial provision, and undoubtedly a compromise measure, it was introduced in large part because of pressure from industry, especially the pharmaceutical industry, who maintained that without it innovation would be stifled. The 'defence' allows drug companies to avoid liability if they can show that the defect could not have been known, i.e. it was undiscoverable at the time, given the state of 'scientific and technical knowledge' when the product was circulated. Not surprisingly given that many drug-induced injuries typically take several years to manifest themselves – by which time standards may well have changed – claims will often fail. If the Act had been in force when the Thalidomide tragedy occurred, for example, there is a very strong possibility that by relying on this defence the drug company could have avoided paying any compensation. Their liability under the Act turned on whether, given the then state of scientific knowledge, they should have conducted reproductive toxicity tests.

Case study 7.5
Julie is 16 and suffers very badly from serious and persistent acne. She buys a non-prescription ointment from the local chemist. On the label as well as in a leaflet enclosed with the ointment, warnings are given that effective contraception is essential to those at risk of becoming pregnant because of the potential harmful effects of the ointment on a foetus. Julie fails to read any of this information and uses lots of the ointment. She also had no idea that she is pregnant – she had unprotected sex for the first time just a month before buying the medicine. Several months later her baby Guy is born with disabilities caused by the ointment.
      Is the drug company liable under the Act?

The drug company's liability would largely depend on the adequacy of the information provided to patients and the overall benefits of the ointment, i.e. whether these outweighed its side effects. In respect of non-prescription medicines (i.e. those sold over the counter) the information must be given direct to patients, either via labels or leaflets and should include, among other things, instructions for use, precautions, contra-indications and so on. Given that this information was provided it is doubtful whether the ointment would be considered defective despite its harmful effect on Guy. In other words a drug which is inherently dangerous to a foetus can be made safe if adequate warnings and instructions for use are provided. It is just possible nevertheless that the ointment may not be considered very useful – and could even be described as cosmetic. As a consequence it is arguably defective irrespective of any warnings given.

WRONGFUL LIFE

'Wrongful life' is a claim by, or on behalf of, a child born with predictable physical or mental disabilities that, but for the defendant's negligence (in relation to genetic counselling, selection of embryos for implantation or foetal testing), the person would not have been born conceived or, having been conceived, would not have been born alive. In short these are actions by children that should not have been conceived or born. If the disability is one which a doctor negligently failed to detect in utero the child's claim is in essence that it was deprived of the opportunity of being aborted – the assumption being that if the mother had been properly advised she would have had an abortion. To date English law has not allowed these claims as the only English authority directly on this point, namely McKay v. Essex AHA [1982] makes very clear. McKay concerned a child, Mary, born partly blind and deaf in 1975 as a result of her mother catching German measles early in her pregnancy. Suspecting she might have been infected she consulted her doctor and blood samples were taken. Unfortunately these were not correctly analysed and Mrs McKay was told that neither she nor her baby had been infected with rubella. As a result she continued with her pregnancy. Mary claimed that her disabilities were caused by the defendant's negligence in allowing her to be born. In other words she would have been aborted had her mother been properly tested and informed. The Court of Appeal interpreted this as a 'wrongful life' action and rejected it. Furthermore, although Mary's action was brought under the common law (she was born before the Congenital Disabilities (Civil Liability) Act 1976 was passed) the court stated no wrongful life action could be taken under the Act either. Put simply all such claims were precluded, both at common law and by the 1976 Act. While the court's interpretation of the 1976 Act was controversial and also questionable – the relevant sections of the Act are in fact ambiguous and the intention may never have been to exclude them – until McKay is overruled it remains the only precedent.

Several public policy reasons are typically given to explain the Court's approach. First, to recognize a wrongful life action would, in effect, impose on doctors a duty to abort. Secondly, such a legal duty would compromise the value of human life by implicitly suggesting that a disabled child has a right to be born 'whole' or not at all. Thirdly, it would be impossible to assess the amount of damages because this would inevitably involve comparing the value of a life with disabilities with non-existence. These reasons are, however, not compelling especially as such claims have been recognized in the United States. The last one, in particular, is difficult to sustain in that other heads of damage such as 'loss of expectation of life' are equally difficult to assess and yet are still awarded. Moreover a wrongful-life action does not impose a duty on doctors to abort but instead requires them simply to tell the mother of her baby's condition. The choice of whether or not to have an abortion is then hers.

Case study 7.6
Nigel is born with Downs Syndrome which he alleges was due to negligence in prenatal testing. Can he sue for his disabilities?

No. Nigel's claim in essence a wrongful-life claim. In other words but for the negligent prenatal testing he would not have been born, i.e. had his mother been properly tested and advised he would have been aborted.

Case study 7.7
Lennie has syphilis. He is strongly advised to tell his wife given the potential harmful effects of the disease on any child they may conceive. Lennie ignores this advice and infects his wife. Their daughter, Glenda, develops severe disabilities several weeks after birth . Can she sue Lennie?

Glenda's claim is most probably a wrongful life action in which case it will fail. In other words knowing of the risk to her health Lennie nevertheless failed to take precautions. As a consequence Glenda was born with disabilities. His negligence was thus in failing to prevent her from being born. On the other hand it is at least arguable that Glenda could sue her father under the Congenital Disabilities (Civil Liability) Act 1976 in that he clearly breached the duty of care he owed to Glenda's mother by not telling her of his infection. He therefore directly caused Glenda's disabilities.

'WRONGFUL BIRTH'

'Wrongful birth' is a claim that the defendant breached a legal duty owed to a parent to give information or to perform a medical procedure with due care, resulting in the birth of a child with disabilities. It arises out of exactly the same circumstances as a wrongful-life claim, notably negligent prenatal screening or counselling – for example, a couple may be wrongly advised that there is no risk, or only a very minimal one, of a genetic disorder being passed on. If, acting on that advice, they conceive a child with the disorder, they will almost certainly have a right to sue. 'Wrongful-birth' actions, although very rare, have been recognized in the English courts. Damages awarded are intended to cover pain and suffering and the additional costs of raising a disabled child over and above the cost of raising a healthy child. However, they will only succeed if the ordinary common law principles of breach of duty and causation are established. So, in a claim based on negligent genetic counselling a woman must prove that she would not have become pregnant if she had been properly advised. And if the negligence was a failure to detect foetal abnormalities, success will depend on proving first that an abortion was available (i.e. the Abortion Act 1967 applied) and secondly that she would have had one.

'WRONGFUL CONCEPTION'

These actions arise from negligent contraceptive advice or treatment – typically a failed sterilization or failed abortion as a result of which a woman remains or becomes pregnant. Despite policy objections to these kinds of claims – which imply that the birth of a healthy child, albeit a 'mistaken' one, is an injury – they have now been recognized in the English courts (see, for example, Thake v. Maurice [1986]). Damages awarded are intended to cover the cost of bringing up an unplanned child and the pain and distress of pregnancy.

FURTHER READING

Dickens, B. (1989) 'Wrongful birth and life, wrongful death before birth and wrongful law'. In S. McLean (ed.), *Legal Issues in Human Reproduction*, Gower, Aldershot.

Fortin, J. (1987) 'Is the wrongful life action really dead?'. *Journal of Social Welfare Law*, 306.

Law Commission of England and Wales (1974) *Report on Injuries to Unborn Children*, Law Com. no. 69, CMND. 5709.

Montgomery, J. (1994) 'The rights and interests of children and those with mental handicap'. In A. Clarke (ed.), *Genetic Counselling: Practice and Principles*, Routledge, London.

Pullen, I. (1990) 'Patients, families and genetic information'. In E. Sutherland and A. McCall Smith (eds) *Family Rights: Family Law and Medical Advance*, Edinburgh University Press, Edinburgh.

Whitfield, A. (1993) 'Common Law Duties to Unborn Children'. *1 Med. L Rev*, 28–52.

Research, organ and tissue transplantation

8

Few cases in recent years have provoked as much controversy as B v. Cambridge HA [1995]. It concerned an appeal by a 10-year-old girl suffering from leukaemia against the refusal by a health authority to fund further treatment (see Chapter 2 for full details of the case). Media and public interest was largely caused by the widespread belief that the main reason for denying B treatment was its cost, estimated to be £75 000. Not surprisingly, many thought limited resources and budgetary constraints were no justification for denying B what was undoubtedly her only chance of survival. There were, however, other health care issues raised by the case, albeit less topical ones, namely the legality of bone marrow transplants between sisters, the extent of parental authority to give consent on a child's behalf and when a child is old enough to make independent decisions. These kinds of questions are typically raised by bone marrow donation but apply equally to research involving children, likewise organ donation. Also relevant in this context is the legal regulation of embryo and foetal research.

RESEARCH

TYPES OF RESEARCH

While research on human subjects is now recognized as essential if advances in medical treatment are to continue, serious doubts are still raised about the legality of research on children, especially if it carries some risk of harm but is of no potential benefit to them. Other concerns focus on the extent to which the principles of consent (see Chapter 3) provide adequate safeguards particularly when children are too young to make their own decisions. The uncertain state of the law explains in part why it was only in the early 1980s that the complete embargo on non-therapeutic research was finally lifted. Research on children is, however, now generally accepted as an important means of promoting child health and well-being. But what is meant by the term 'research' and what activities does it include?

Many commentators, while acknowledging that there is a distinction between research and experimentation (sometimes also called unusual or more frequently innovative treatment or therapy), none the less often use the two words interchangeably. The generally accepted definition of research is that it involves a systematic course of scientific enquiry. Innovative treatment on the other hand is a much more speculative process despite frequently being an extension of usual treatment. Typically it is surgical in nature and involves a modification of an existing procedure in the expectation that it will work for an individual patient.

Research can be classified in several ways. One of the most common classifications is between **therapeutic** and **non-therapeutic** research. **Therapeutic** research (sometimes called clinical research) aims to benefit a particular group of patients by improving available treatment. It thus combines research with the care and treatment of patients. In contrast the principle aim of **non-therapeutic** research is to gain scientific knowledge. As such it is unlikely to confer any benefit on the research subjects who may well be healthy volunteers or existing patients. The distinction between therapeutic and non-therapeutic research is practically and legally important. First, it is adopted in all the guidelines and code of ethics covering research (see below). Secondly it is crucial in weighing the risks and benefits of a particular project. Thirdly, the nature of the research can determine the amount of information which has to be disclosed in order to ensure that consent is legally valid.

Another classification commonly made is between invasive or non-invasive research although sometimes the borderline between the two is blurred. **Invasive** research is essentially any activity which involves coming into contact with a child's body and can range from simple procedures such as measuring children or taking blood or urine samples to much more high-risk ones like biopsies or arterial punctures. **Non-invasive** research does not involve any contact with the subject's body and includes such activities as questioning and observing children, research into medical records and so on. Non-invasive research is far less legally problematic than invasive research, largely because it is only likely to carry minimal risk, if any.

NON-LEGAL REGULATION OF RESEARCH

Surprisingly perhaps except for embryo research there is no specific legislation on human research (unlike research on animals which was first regulated over one hundred years ago by the Cruelty to Animals Act 1876). In the absence of any special law the legal framework within which researchers must practise is therefore governed by the common law – mainly consent and negligence law and less frequently contract law. Exceptionally too the criminal law can be invoked in that the offences of battery and assault would be committed if a researcher used (or threatened to use) unlawful force. Failure to comply with the Medicines Act 1968 might also lead to criminal sanctions if those involved in clinical trials do not follow required procedures.

Before looking at how the common law regulates research a brief outline of non-legal (i.e. not directly enforceable by law) controls will be provided. This consists of the following.

GOVERNMENT CIRCULARS

Government guidelines on research were issued in 1991 by the Department of Health in the form of a NHS Management Executive letter and booklet (HSG(91)5). Essentially, as before the responsibility for regulating research was left to local research ethics committees (LREC). However, the new guidance was designed to improve the working practices and effectiveness of existing LRECs which were first established in 1967. The Booklet provides detailed guidance on (among other things) the establishment and function of LRECs, their adminis- trative framework, constitution and the ethical principles they should follow. Basically the task of LRECs is to consider research proposals and advise the relevant NHS body. They can also consider research proposals from the private sector. LRECs have proliferated in recent years but their effectiveness remains questionable. The most funda- mental problem being the absence of a clear and universally accepted definition of what constitutes an effective research committee. As such it is both difficult to ensure that research is ethical and what issues should be covered when projects are reviewed. Moreover the diversity and independence of LRECs means that generally they operate in isolation from each other with little or no coordination or formal central control mechanism. This means that it is almost impossible to make sure that minimum standards of practice are established and maintained.

ETHICAL CODES AND PROFESSIONAL GUIDELINES

The Nuremberg code is undoubtedly the most famous international code. It was published in 1949 as a direct response to the evidence which was given in the war-crimes trials a few years earlier that at least two hundred German doctors had performed criminal medical experiments which often resulted in death. The code lays down ten basic principles upon which research should be conducted. The code was later supple- mented by the Declaration of Helsinki. This was first drawn up in 1964 and was strongly influenced by the Thalidomide disaster which prompted worldwide demands for more effective regulation of the testing of new drugs. Since its publication in 1964 the Declaration has been revised several times, most recently in 1989. Although it is by no means comprehensive the Declaration is important since it forms the basis of the various national professional guidelines and thus underpins the conduct of all current research. Note too that the 'risk/benefit' test which is a fundamental consideration in all research involving human subjects derives from the Declaration.

Professional guidelines are also a fruitful source of guidance on research. These have been issued by e.g. the Royal College of Physicians and the Royal College of Nursing. In addition guidance relating specifically to research involving children has also been issued by the Medical Research Council (MRC) and the British Paediatric Association (BPA). Not surprisingly as far as children are concerned these are the most detailed and both stress how there is a strong case for research on children but that it is justifiable only if certain principles are observed. These are that:

- the relevant information cannot be gained by comparable research on adults;
- all proposals should be submitted to and approved by local LRECs;
- legally valid consent should be obtained from the appropriate person;
- while research which is not intended to benefit a child directly is not necessarily unethical or illegal it should pose no more than a negligible risk of harm;
- in the case of therapeutic research the benefits likely to accrue to a child should outweigh the possible risks of harm.

LEGAL REGULATION OF RESEARCH

In the absence of any specific legislation research on children is regulated mainly by the law of consent. The common law principles of consent were explained in Chapter 3 as were the consequences of acting without consent. In principal these apply equally in this context. Hence any research carried out on children without consent could result in criminal charges and a civil action for trespass. If consent is obtained but is flawed in some respect – the most likely contention being that it was based on insufficient information – then a negligence claim would be appropriate.

But should the principles governing consent to treatment be modified when they are applied to research? Many legal commentators contend that some of the criteria for valid consent, particularly those relating to disclosure of information, are unsatisfactory and provide inadequate legal safeguards. As a consequence they claim that the law should demand a higher standard of disclosure in a research context. While this 'informed consent' approach they advocate differs significantly from the 'professional' standard which governs consent to treatment (see Chapter 3), it is nevertheless one which almost without exception all the professional guidelines on research recommend. Arguably too a higher level of understanding and maturity than is normally required to satisfy the 'Gillick' test of competency is appropriate, especially if the research is non-therapeutic.

The rest of this section will therefore look at the principles of consent which are legally the most problematic in this context, namely the definition of competency and disclosure of information. In addition it will also cover voluntariness.

THERAPEUTIC RESEARCH

NATURE OF CONSENT

To be legally valid consent to therapeutic research must be freely given, i.e. obtained without coercion, undue pressure or influence. In practice, however, especially in neonatal research where procedures commonly need to be started very soon, sometimes hours or even minutes after birth when a mother may be in no fit state to take in let alone fully understand information she is being given, consent may be far from free. Similarly the voluntariness of consent may be questionable if parents of a very sick young child are asked to make a decision very quickly without sufficient support. As a result they may feel obliged to give consent, fearing that otherwise their child's care and treatment may suffer. Without time to reflect or an opportunity to discuss the research fully, consent is unlikely to be free. This is perhaps why the BPA guidelines deal with voluntariness in some detail and recommend:

- no financial inducements (other than expenses) should be offered;
- no pressure should be exerted;
- as much time as possible should be given (some days for a major study) to consider whether or not to participate;
- the project should be discussed with relatives, or primary health carers;
- children and their families should be told that they may refuse to take part, or may withdraw at any time (even if a consent form has already been signed);
- no reason need be given for withdrawing from the research;
- assurances should be given that the child's treatment will not be prejudiced by withdrawal from the research.

As regards disclosing information about the research project the combined effect of the various professional guidelines and DoH guidance appears to be that more information should be given than is currently required when consent is given for medical treatment. Most legal texts too assume that the courts would probably adopt an 'informed consent' standard based on what information a 'reasonable subject' would expect to be given – even though they have repeatedly rejected this higher standard in other contexts (see e.g. the discussion of the Sidaway case in Chapter 3). Indeed for the courts to do otherwise would mean ignoring all the current guidance available to researchers and thus what is considered 'accepted practice' in relation to research. Note too that the 'reasonable subject' standard is an objective one, i.e. based on what other reasonable subjects would expect.

But what does the 'informed consent' approach mean in practical terms? What information actually has to be disclosed, either to children themselves (if competent) or those acting on their behalf (if not) bearing in mind that the term 'disclosure' includes not just providing information voluntarily but also answering questions truthfully. It is widely accepted that information sheets (written in a style which is accessible) should be provided detailing the purpose of the research, the alternatives and the expected benefits to the subject and society. The fact that research is being combined with the subject's care and treatment should also be disclosed which means explaining the difference between therapy and research and the meaning of relevant research terms. In addition the BPA's guidelines recommend that 'the nature of each procedure, how often or for how long each may occur' should also be explained. And if the research is based on a randomized controlled trial (RCT) subjects should be informed of the random nature of the trial. As to the risks involved (both real and potential), not surprisingly information on these is crucial if the so-called 'risk/benefit' ratio is to be measured accurately. The BPA guidelines distinguish between minimal, low and high risk procedures and explain how potential harm is to be assessed. However in the absence of any other more specific guidance, arguably the law would expect disclosure of all risks which a 'reasonable' research subject would expect to be informed about. Beyond that subjects should be told of any other 'material' consequences of the research such as that they might have to stay in hospital for longer or return more frequently for check ups (as an in-patient or out-patient). Finally subjects should be told that they can withdraw from the research without suffering any adverse consequences.

As with consent to treatment the form of consent can be oral or written. LRECs normally recommend written consent forms especially if the research involves more than minimal risk.

Case study 8.1

Samantha is 16-years-old. Her baby, Rachel, is nearly ten weeks premature and has been delivered by Caesarian section. Samantha was just coming round from the general anaesthetic when she was told that Rachel was very tiny, weighing only 2 lbs. More seriously she was having breathing difficulties and so might suffer serious and irreversible brain damage. However this could probably be avoided if she was immediately given a drug which was currently being tested. The researcher then went to give details of the drug and the purpose of the research including information about its expected benefits, possible side effects and for how long Rachel would have to take the drug. Samantha was also told that she was under no obligation to agree to the research.

Samantha agrees to 'volunteer' Rachel for the research. Is her consent valid?

The main issues raised by this case study are, first, whether Samantha was given adequate information about the research, i.e. its aims, methods and risks. Secondly was her consent truly voluntary?

As to the disclosure on information while clearly no information sheet was provided this by itself does not render the research unlawful. However, even if adequate information was provided – which arguably it was – without time to take it in let alone discuss its implications it is doubtful whether Samantha understood what she was being told. Moreover, given that she had just had major surgery and an anaesthetic, she was almost certainly unlikely to be capable of making a decision. It could thus be argued that her consent was not genuinely 'free', particularly as she was given no time at all to reflect but was 'persuaded' to make up her mind very quickly.

WHO MAY CONSENT?

The answer to this question depends on how the concept of competence is defined in relation to research. The relevant tests for assessing children's legal capacity to make their own decisions about medical treatment were explained in Chapter 3. But do these apply equally to research? This is the issue which needs to be considered here bearing in mind that if children are competent then their consent to research must be sought and obtained. Similarly their refusal must normally be respected. If they are not competent then someone else must give consent on their behalf.

As before it is necessary to divide children into different age groups.

16–17 YEAR-OLDS

The starting point for assessing competence in this age group is s.8 of the Family Law Reform Act 1969 which provides that the consent of 16- and 17-year-olds is valid providing they are competent. In this context what this means is that they are able to understand the nature and purpose of the research, its benefits and short- and long-term risks (both real and potential). However, competence is a flexible concept with no rigid criteria. This means that if the research is complex or involves high-risk procedures with potentially serious side effects then a higher standard of comprehension will be required than if the research was relatively innocuous, for example collecting blood samples.

On the face of it s.8 seems to give competent 16- and 17-year-olds the legal authority to give independent consent to research. But this depends on the words in s.8, namely 'surgical, medical or dental treatment' being widely interpreted to include therapeutic research. However, many legal texts, likewise several (but not all) of the guidelines doubt that the words are capable of such a broad meaning. Instead they maintain that the legislation is limited to treatment only and does not cover research at all, even if it is therapeutic. To be on the safe side, therefore, it is recommended that legal authority for giving consent be found elsewhere, namely from the common law. In other words only if 16- and 17-year-olds pass the 'Gillick' test can they consent independently to research. That said, however, a relatively high standard of understanding and maturity would normally have to be reached unless the research posed only minimal risk. Whether or not a minor is competent to give consent in any particular case would, of course, ultimately turn on the facts of each case.

If a competent 16- or 17-year-old refuses to participate in research researchers would be ill advised to rely solely on parental consent but should respect the minor's refusal (or alternatively seek the court's approval).

Finally it should be noted that there may be some circumstances, for example, where there is doubt about a minor's competency, to get parallel consent from a parent (subject to the minor's prior permission for parents to be informed).

UNDER 16-YEAR-OLDS

Minors in this age group can agree to participate in research irrespective of their parents' wishes providing they are 'Gillick competent'. Again however, the more invasive the research and the more serious its potential harm the more difficult it will be to reach the required level of maturity and understanding. Moreover because the Gillick test is notoriously difficult to apply with any uniformity it is not surprising that most of the professional guidelines (likewise DoH guidance) recommend complementing the child's consent with that of his or her parents unless this is inappropriate – because the child is not living at home, for example.

As with competent 16- and 17-year-olds the refusal of 'Gillick competent' under-16-year-olds to participate in research should be respected. Faced with such a refusal researchers should therefore seek a court's approval rather than rely solely on parental consent.

UNDER-16-YEAR-OLDS – NOT 'GILLICK COMPETENT'

Consent to carry out research on any minor under 16 who is not 'Gillick competent' (likewise incompetent 16-and 17-year-olds) must be obtained from a proxy – usually a parent, anyone else with parental responsibility or a court. A proxy's power to consent (or refuse) on behalf of a child is fairly extensive but is not limitless in that consent can only be given for research that is in the child's best interests. Regrettably there is no authoritative guidance of what the concept of 'best interests' means in a research context. Nonetheless it is widely accepted that it includes any research in which the benefits outweigh the risks.

It is also worth noting here that although not legally required – because a proxy's consent is sufficient legal authority – the BPA guidelines (and slightly less emphatically those of the MRC) recommend that researchers should nevertheless obtain the child's assent or agreement. Assent means getting the child's permission to carry out the research. It does not have the legal force of consent and so can be obtained at a much younger age – but probably not before the child has reached the developmental age of seven. If it is refused, however, the research is still lawful providing it is in the child's best interests. Whether researchers would in practice ignore a child's views is, of course, another question.

Finally are there any circumstances when research can be carried out without any consent? Although such situations are unlikely to occur very often and the issue has not come before the English courts, it is arguable that subject to specific approval of a LREC it would be lawful – providing the research was expected to benefit the child and it could not be postponed until consent could be obtained, i.e. the situation was one of extreme urgency.

Case study 8.2

John is nearly 16 and suffers from leukaemia. He has been in and out of hospital for several years but recently has had a relapse and does not seem to be responding to treatment. His mother, Ann, is distraught and desperate for John to try out any new treatment however experimental. For the last two months she has been trying to raise money so that she can take John to Mexico to try a new very controversial therapy which she heard about on the news. John's father died just under a year ago.

John's consultant, Mary, wants to include him in a research project she is involved with which is testing the effect of a new drug. So when Ann comes in to see John she raises the issue with them. Mary goes into great detail about the nature of the research, its purpose and how she hopes it will benefit John. She also explains the relevant procedures, some of which may have to be given intravenously and possibly intrathetically. They may cause John pain and considerable discomfort but Mary only briefly describes these side effects and fails to explain other potentially more serious consequences. She then tells Mary and John that she will discuss the new treatment with them over the next few days. On leaving, Mary hands Ann a consent form telling her that a patient information sheet is available if she or John wants one.

Several days later Mary bumps into Ann and asks her if she and John have decided what to do. She also gives Ann further details about the other serious side effects, saying she had not mentioned them earlier as she did not want to worry John too much. Ann tells her that she will not tell John either nor will she mention the vomiting and nausea he is almost certainly likely to experience because otherwise she fears John would refuse to participate in the research.

That same day John appears more upset than usual. Irene, a nurse who has got to know John well, asks him what the matter is. After a long conversation it becomes clear that although he has signed the consent form (as Ann has also done) he is very reluctant to take part in the research, partly because he cannot bear the thought of more tests, more visits to the hospital and more pain but also because he feels that there is no point to any more treatment. John also explains to Irene that he feels obliged to try out the new therapy for fear of upsetting his mother.

Is John competent to give consent?
Is Ann's consent necessary?
Is John's consent voluntary?
Has all the relevant information been given?
What difference would it make if John was 17 or 12?

Providing John is considered 'Gillick competent' then his consent alone is sufficient for the research to proceed. None the less, given the risks associated with it and the serious invasive procedures it involves, John would have to reach a relatively high level of maturity and understanding. Note too that in assessing his competence the effect of pain, medication or other treatment would also have to be taken into account as would his understanding of his illness and its prognosis.

If John is 'Gillick competent' Ann's consent is not legally necessary even though some of the guidelines advise that parallel parental consent be obtained.

Arguably John's consent is not truly voluntary in that it appears from his conversation with Irene that he is consenting only to please his mother. There is a strong case for claiming that her determination and desperation to obtain treatment for John is a form of undue pressure or influence which has the effect of denying John the chance to make his own decisions. Irene should therefore discuss her concerns (in accordance with UKCC guidance, 'Exercising Accountability' with Mary or other appropriate person, thus giving John more time to make up his own mind. If he ultimately decides not to participate in the research then his refusal should be respected and researchers should seek legal guidance before relying on Ann's consent alone.

In failing to give John full details of the side effects of the research, namely the nausea, vomiting and other more serious potential consequences, John has almost not received enough information on which to make a decision even though he has been told, albeit orally, about the nature and purpose of the research. In other words he could claim that his consent is flawed in that it is based on insufficient information. The fact that Ann knows all the details of the side effects is legally irrelevant because it is John's consent not hers which is legally effective. In Mary's 'defence' however it could be argued that the information is available in that it is contained in the patient information sheet which she has told John about.

IF JOHN WAS 17

There would be no difference in law if John was 17 since given the uncertainty as to the relevance of s.8 of the Family Law Reform Act 1969 researchers would in practice probably rely on the Gillick test of competency. Furthermore if instead they did look to the statute it would make no difference – if John was 'Gillick competent' then he would also be competent under the 1969 Act.

IF JOHN WAS 12

In this case, given the complexity and invasive nature of the research it would be unlikely that he would be considered 'Gillick competent'. Consent for his participation would therefore have to be obtained from his mother, Ann. Providing the research is in John's best interests she can consent to it.

As regards the disclosure of information then irrespective of whether or not Ann has actually seen the patient information sheet she, as proxy, has been given full and frank information, albeit verbally, about all aspects of the research, namely, its nature, purpose, expected benefits and risks as well as the actual procedures which will be carried out. Good practice was certainly not followed though in that Mary should not have left obtaining the information sheet to Ann – she should either have given it to her herself or made sure that someone else did.

If John decided he did not want to participate in the research, i.e. he did not assent to it, then it would still be lawful providing it was in his best interests.

NON-THERAPEUTIC RESEARCH

NATURE OF CONSENT

Non-therapeutic research, i.e. research which is unlikely to confer any potential benefit on a child (or only a slight or very uncertain one), can cover a wide range of procedures, many of which are typically relatively harmless while others can be more invasive. Once regarded as unlawful, non-therapeutic research on children is now widely accepted as justifiable in certain circumstances, even though it still poses several legal problems. These are essentially to do with consent, in particular when minors acquire sufficient maturity and understanding to make their own decisions about research which is primarily intended to benefit others. And when it is lawful for a proxy to 'volunteer' an incompetent child for research which is unlikely to bestow any direct benefit and yet might carry some risk.

Before looking at these issues – for which children need to be divided into the usual age groups – it is useful to outline what the various guidelines have to say, since in the absence of any authoritative legal decision or legislation these again set the standard against which the legality of research is likely to be judged.

Without exception all the guidelines give qualified support (albeit some more explicitly than others) to non-therapeutic research on children providing certain conditions are met. These are:

• comparable research cannot be carried out on adults;
• LREC approval is obtained;

- the research subject is properly informed;
- the risk to the child must be no more than minimal;
- appropriate consent must be obtained.

The first two of the above conditions are self-explanatory but the others require further discussion. As regards how much information must be disclosed none of the guidelines distinguishes between therapeutic or non-therapeutic research. However, some legal texts contend that it is at least arguable that a higher legal standard of disclosure of information is required when the research is non-therapeutic, especially if the research subjects are healthy volunteers. In other words the standard would be a subjective one based on what the actual research subject would want to know (rather than the objective 'reasonable subject' which it was suggested above applies to therapeutic research).

The other concept which needs to be explained here is 'minimal risk' (sometimes also called 'negligible' risk). The Institute of Medical Ethics defines this as a risk of death lower than 1:1,000,000, a risk of major complications less than 1:100,000 and a risk of minor complications of less than 1:1,000. The BPA guidelines define the term by describing the procedures it would include in this category, notably, questioning, observing and measuring children as well as collecting urine samples (but not by aspiration) or using blood from a sample that has been taken as part of treatment. Finally the MRC guidelines imply that a risk is minimal if it is no greater than the risks that reasonable parents commonly expose their children to in everyday life. It also describes which procedures it would include which are broadly similar to those specified by the BPA.

WHO MAY CONSENT?

16–17-year-olds

The Family Law Reform Act 1969 does not apply to non-therapeutic research which means that capacity to consent is governed by the common law, i.e. the Gillick test. Competence therefore depends on a minor's understanding and maturity as well as the nature of the research. Arguably too given that the research is unlikely to benefit the minor the law would require an even higher degree of understanding and maturity than for therapeutic research.

Given the uncertain legal position some of the guidelines also recommend obtaining parallel parental consent.

Under-16-year-olds

Children in this age group must be 'Gillick competent' before they can independently consent. But as with 16- and 17-year-olds the law would require a relatively high standard of understanding and maturity. Again, the younger the child the more prudent it is to obtain parallel parental consent.

Under-16-year-olds – not 'Gillick competent'

It is this group of children who pose the greatest legal problems (likewise incompetent 16- and 17-year-olds). These are, first, who can lawfully consent to non-therapeutic research on their behalf? The answer is: any person with parental responsibility – usually a parent or a court. Nevertheless even though such children do not have legal capacity the guidelines recommend that their assent be obtained, assuming, that is, that it can be meaningfully given – i.e. not before the child has reached the developmental age of seven. The second related question which is more difficult to answer is: what can incompetent children be 'volunteered' for? In other words what legal limits are there to the kind of non-therapeutic research a proxy can consent to? One answer is to fall back on the familiar 'best interests' approach. However in this context such a criterion is unhelpful given that research which is not likely to directly benefit a child is almost certainly not in its best interests especially as it carries some risk, albeit a minimal one.

One way of solving this dilemma is to adopt a broader less restrictive interpretation of a proxy's duty, namely that consent can be given for any research which is not against the child's interests. This criterion, while being less protective of the child, also demands less of a proxy in that it lets them off the legal hook if their decision turns out not to be the best one. But in the absence of any precedent on the nature and scope of a proxy's duty in this context, it is not possible to say with any certainty whether a court would endorse this lower standard. None the less most legal texts as well as the BPA guidelines assume that it would even though the legal authority they rely on to support their view is doubtful since it is based on the approach taken by the House of Lords in S v. S [1970] – a case concerning the legality of taking blood to establish paternity.

EMBRYO RESEARCH

As was noted earlier embryo research is the one area of research which is regulated by statute, namely the Human Fertilisation and Embryology Act 1990. Embryo research and experimentation raises many of the same legal issues as abortion and much the same controversy. Briefly there are two 'extreme' positions. Those who totally oppose it claim that the embryo should be given the same legal protection (i.e. the same rights and interests) as other human beings – and certainly the right not to be destroyed just for research. In contrast proponents of unrestricted research argue that its potential benefits are so enormous that it would be contrary to the public interest to prohibit it. It an attempt to reconcile these two divergent positions the Act tries to steer a middle way – permitting research in principle but only within a strict licensing and regulatory framework. As such the Act is best described as a compromise measure albeit a fairly liberal one given that embryo research is still banned in many countries.

THE LEGAL FRAMEWORK

Several basic principles underpin the Act. These are, first, that all embryo research is unlawful (i.e. criminal) unless carried out under licence. Secondly, licences can only be granted for certain specified purposes. Thirdly, certain activities are prohibited altogether. Fourthly, embryos can either be surplus ones (i.e. produced during IVF or other infertility treatment) or created just for research purposes.

PROHIBITED ACTIVITIES

The most controversial prohibited activity is that embryos cannot be kept or used after the appearance of the 'primitive streak', that is not later than 14 days from after the gametes were mixed. It is controversial because opponents of research believe that human life begins at an earlier stage than this, i.e. from the moment of conception when the process of fertilization begins. Other prohibited research activities include placing human embryos in animals or implanting animal embryos (or gametes) in humans. Nucleus substitution (more commonly known as 'cloning') is also prohibited.

LICENSED ACTIVITIES

As with infertility treatment (see Chapter 6) regulation of embryo research is left to the Human Fertilisation and Embryology Authority (HFEA) through its extensive licensing and supervisory powers. Subject to obtaining the necessary consents as required by schedule 3 of the Act it can currently grant research licences – which can last for up to a maximum period of three years – for activities which it considers 'necessary or desirable' for the following five specified purposes, namely: promoting advances in infertility treatment; increasing knowledge about the causes of congenital disease; increasing knowledge about the causes of miscarriages; developing more effective contraceptive techniques; and finally developing methods for detecting the presence of gene or chromosome abnormalities in embryos before implantation. Other purposes can be added to this list but as yet have not been. Note too while licences can be granted for testing human sperm (the hamster test) anything formed as a result of such research must be destroyed not later than the two-cell stage.

FOETAL RESEARCH

Although recognized as essential especially for understanding the effects of drugs during pregnancy foetal research and experimentation can be legally problematic largely because of the concerns it raises about consent but also because as with most other areas of research it is not regulated by any specific legislation (nor is it governed by the 1990 Act).

The legality of such research is thus determined by the common law of consent and the recommendations of the Polkinghorne Committee which although not having any legal force are the only relevant professional guidelines. A distinction must, however, be drawn between research on living and dead foetuses.

THE LIVING FOETUS

The Polkinghorne Committee was set up mainly because of the concern over foetal brain implants. It recommended that research on the living foetus was justified providing, first, approval was obtained from the LREC, secondly, risk to the foetus was no more than minimal and thirdly, appropriate consent was obtained. These recommendations are essentially the same as those contained in the various professionals guidelines on non-therapeutic research on children. However other possible legal implications do arise, in particular if the foetus is harmed by the research and as a result the child is born with disabilities. If this happened what legal action can the child take? Currently no action for 'wrongful life' could succeed. Nor would any negligence claim be possible against the mother under the Congenital Disabilities (Civil Liability) Act 1976 as she is exempt from claims by her child except for claims arising out of her negligent driving. A claim against the researcher under the Act would also almost certainly fail since the child's rights are derivative and so depend on a breach of duty owed to a parent. If the mother consented to the research then assuming that her consent was valid, i.e. she was given adequate information and so forth it is difficult to see how such a breach could be proved. The child's only possible claim would, therefore, be against the mother in negligence at common law (see Chapter 2).

THE DEAD FOETUS

Research on a dead foetus raises different legal concerns, notably how the death of the foetus came about. In other words if it resulted from an abortion rather than a stillbirth (according to the Stillbirth Act 1992 a child is stillborn if it has issued from its mother after the 24th week of pregnancy and did not at any time after being expelled breathe or show any signs of life) then the requirements of the Abortion Act 1967 would have to be complied with. The Polkinghorne Committee also recommended that LREC approval be obtained, likewise the mother's consent. However, there is some doubt as to whether this latter requirement is a legal one since her consent is only necessary if she has proprietorial rights over her dead foetus – a point as yet undecided in law.

FOETAL MATERIALS

Ovarian tissue such as the placenta can also be used in research. For legal purposes the main concern is that of the mother's consent but as with dead foetuses it is unclear whether or not this is a legal requirement. Note too that following concern over the use of the gametes from dead foetuses the Human Fertilisation and Embryology Authority recommended in 1994 that ovarian tissue could be used in research (subject to obtaining the mother's consent) but eggs and ovarian tissue from cadavers and dead foetuses should only be used for research into genetic diseases.

ORGAN AND TISSUE DONATION AND TRANSPLANTATION

Transplantation is now an established part of medical practice with heart, liver and even lung transplants almost so commonplace that they attract little or no media attention – except perhaps when they involve experimental therapy such as occurred in the notorious 1984 American case known as 'Baby Fae' in which a baboon's heart was transplanted into a 14 day old neonate with congenital heart disease. She died 17 days later. Kidney transplants too are relatively routine as are bone-marrow transplants. Yet despite the increasing frequency of these procedures legal problems remain which although similar to those raised in non-therapeutic research on children are not identical. The major legal concerns are essentially related to consent, in particular whether minors can validly consent to procedures which are basically altruistic yet can have very serious consequences and expose them to significant risks. And if very young children are required as donors what limits does the law impose on those consenting to donation on their behalf? In other words is donation and transplantation ever in the donor child's best interests'? Does it have to be? If not, what other criterion applies?

While issues of consent pose the most difficult legal problems in this context, other aspects of transplantation are also potentially contentious, notably the commercialization of organ donation. The law's role in regulating and controlling 'organ trafficking' will therefore also be outlined in this chapter as will the legal regulation of cadaver donations.

THE LIVING DONOR

Live donor transplantations are governed both by legislation, namely the Human Organs Transplant Act 1989 which regulates commercial dealings and the common law which deals with consent. Both however distinguish between regenerative and non-regenerative parts of the body as follows:

- **Regenerative**: These consist of blood, bone marrow, skin, semen and hair. They are all naturally replaceable or repairable and do not cause permanent or serious loss. As such their donation may involve certain risks, for example bone marrow donation is a more painful process and riskier than giving blood, but is unlikely to cause any irrevocable loss or harm.
- **Non-regenerative**: The major transplant organ here is the kidney. Other regenerative organs such as a heart, liver and lungs cannot be donated by a living donor in normal circumstances.

CONSENT

16- and 17-year-olds

The Family Law Reform Act 1969 is unlikely to apply given that donations are almost certainly not considered 'surgical, medical or dental treatment' however broadly these terms are interpreted. Nor does s.21 of the Act which enables competent 16- and 17-year-olds to give consent to the taking of 'bodily samples' apply to blood donations. This is because the Act defines 'bodily samples' as a sample of bodily fluid or bodily tissue taken for the purpose of 'scientific tests', i.e. taken to ascertain their 'inheritable characteristics'.

In the absence of legislation arguably the 'Gillick' test would be applied to determine the competency of 16- and 17-year-olds. Capacity would thus depend on the minor's maturity and understanding which would almost always have to be relatively high given that donation only confers psychological and emotional benefits on the donor, i.e. the procedure is aimed solely at helping another person. None the less as in all other medical contexts Gillick competency is a flexible concept and capacity would turn on the facts of each particular case, in other words whether the minor fully understood the proposed procedure, its seriousness and risks (both short- and long-term). If the procedure is fairly minor involving regenerative parts of the body, e.g. a blood donation, the Gillick test would be relatively easy to satisfy. It would be harder, however, the more serious the proposed donation, e.g. bone marrow donation which is both riskier and more painful. As to kidney donation most legal commentators doubt whether the law would ever consider a minor capable of reaching the required standard of comprehension. Consequently consent for such donation would have to be obtained from parents, anyone else with parental responsibility or preferably a court.

Under 16-year-olds

As with competent 16- and 17-year-olds minors under 16 who are 'Gillick competent' can give valid consent for donations which carry only minimal risk, i.e. blood, skin and with less certainty bone-marrow donations. In all other cases consent should be obtained either from someone with parental responsibility or a court. Whether or not this would be forthcoming in the case of organ donation is, however, doubtful unless the child could be held to benefit – for example because the death of a sibling could thereby be avoided.

Under 16-year-olds – not 'Gillick competent'

Consent to donations for minors under 16 who are not 'Gillick competent' (likewise incompetent 16- and 17-year-olds) must be sought from a proxy – usually a parent (or anyone else with parental responsibility), or a court. The crucial question here is: what can a proxy consent to? With no English authority directly on this point it is not possible to state with certainty what limits the law would impose on a proxy's power. None the less it is widely assumed that a court would adopt the test which applies to non-therapeutic research on incompetent minors, namely that the procedure must 'not be against the child's interests'. As was noted earlier this is a less restrictive interpretation of a proxy's power than the 'best interests' approach. As such it allows the proxy to consent to a broader range of medical procedures.

Case study 8.3
Hannah is four-years-old and suffers from leukaemia. She urgently needs a bone-marrow transplant. Following tests her older sister

Erica, who is ten, is found to be the most compatible donor and has agreed to donate. Can Erica's parents consent on her behalf? What difference would it make if Erica was 17 but refuses to be a donor?

As Erica is too young to have the necessary capacity consent would have to be sought from elsewhere. Since her parents are willing to give consent in principle they could consent on her behalf assuming that is that the donation is not 'against Erica's interests'. Generally although bone-marrow donation is painful and carries some risks it can be said to confer psychological and emotional benefits on the donor. As such it is 'not against Erica's interests' and therefore lawful. But if Erica had been coerced by her parents and had agreed to donate her kidney for fear of upsetting them it is at least arguable that the donation is against her interests and therefore unlawful.

If Erica was 17 it is unlikely that any court would force her to be a donor, especially as Erica would have to spend a short spell in hospital – possibly up to two days – and would have to have a general anaesthetic. In addition the procedure is painful and at the very least will cause considerable discomfort. The only comparable case in which legal action was taken to compel bone-marrow donation is the American case of McFall v. Shrimp (1978). It concerned a 39-year-old man (McFall) suffering from aplastic anaemia. Without a bone-marrow transplant he would certainly die. The only compatible donor was his 43-year-old cousin who, despite agreeing to be tissue-typed, later refused either to have more tests or to donate any bone marrow. McFall sued him claiming that by 'permitting himself to be tissue-typed and be demonstrating a four-tissue match he had obligated himself to continue'. Not surprisingly the court refused to order the defendant to submit to the transplant even though it described his refusal as 'morally indefensible'.

Case study 8.4

Paul and Harold are identical 14-year-old twins. Paul has a serious kidney disease and their parents have agreed that one of Harold's kidneys can be donated – it is a perfect match. Harold supports his parents, having made it clear that he cannot imagine life without his twin brother and would go through anything to help him.

Who can consent to the donation? What difference would it make if the twins were nearly 18?

While it seems that with one exception no live minor donor has ever been accepted as a live donor in the United Kingdom should such a situation arise the court's prior approval would almost certainly have to be sought. Most legal texts assume the court's approval would not, however, be forthcoming despite several American cases in which the court has sanctioned kidney donations by minors. In the case of Hart v. Brown (1972), for example, the court decided that a transplant from one healthy 7-year-old twin to her sister was lawful. Factors influencing the court included strong medical testimony that the procedure was a 'perfect transplant but also very persuasive psychiatric evidence that the healthy twin identified very strongly with her sister and would unquestionably benefit from the expected successful outcome but would suffer greatly if the donee were to die from her illness'.

If the twins were 17 a court's prior approval would still arguably be required even if the donor was 'Gillick' competent – which is itself questionable given the seriousness of the procedure. Again it is widely assumed that no English court would approve the donation but with no authoritative English precedent it is not possible to say that this would inevitably be the outcome.

THE HUMAN ORGAN TRANSPLANT ACT 1989

This Act was passed soon after several British doctors were disciplined for their part in a scandal over the sale of kidneys by impoverished Turkish citizens to wealthy private patients. One of the donors alleged he had no idea that his kidney was to be removed while others, although aware of the nature of their operations, had little understanding of the long-term implications of kidney donation. Not surprisingly the Act's main purpose was to stop the trafficking in non-regenerative parts of the body.

The Act applies to 'organs' which cannot be replicated. As such it covers the heart, liver, kidneys, pancreas, lungs, but not bone-marrow, blood products, semen, skin, gametes or embryos. It prohibits all commercial dealings in organs (whether from living or dead donors) which are intended for transplantation as well as related activities such as advertising and brokering. In addition the Act also restricts donations between those who are not 'genetically related' (widely defined in the Act to include natural parents and children, brothers and sisters, nieces, nephews, aunts and uncles and cousins whether of whole or half blood). This means that transplants between close family members (i.e. genetically related ones) are lawful and unrestricted by the Act except in so far as they are subject to the prohibitions against commercial dealings. The restrictions on transplants between people who are not genetically related are onerous in that criminal offences are committed by those who carry them out unless permission has been obtained from the Unrelated Live Transplant Regulatory Authority (ULTRA). This independent authority can authorise any transplant not otherwise allowed by the Act, for example between spouses or between grand-parents and grandchildren, but only if several conditions are satisfied. These are spelt out in some detail in the Regulations. One is that no payment has been or is to be proposed. Others focus on ensuring that donors have genuinely consented, have not been coerced or exploited and fully understand the nature and risks of the procedure.

THE DEAD DONOR

The law gives people very limited rights to decide what should happen to their bodies after they die. The few 'rights' they do have, for example, to carry a donor card or donate their bodies to medical research in a will, are not legally enforceable although as we shall see their wishes may be respected in practice as a result of the Human Tissue Act 1961 which governs cadaver transplantations. That said the law is far from satisfactory and is widely criticized for its technical and practical failures. A more fundamental criticism, however, is that the Act creates an 'opting in' system rather than an 'opting out' one. This means that the donor (or relatives) have to opt to donate whereas under an opting-out system – which many claim is the only way the supply of organs will ever match demand – organs could be removed unless the deceased has previously expressed his or her objection to donation. A less radical reform known as the required request system would impose a legal duty on health professionals to ask relatives if the deceased's organs could be used for a transplant. While the relatives could still refuse such a request it is thought that such a reform would overcome the awkwardness some professionals feel when broaching the subject. But neither of these reforms are likely to be implemented in the near future and may in fact be unnecessary if the new computerized organ donor register works effectively. This new database which is held alongside the national database of patients waiting for an organ transplant enables potential donors in the United Kingdom to register their intentions in a variety of ways, for example, through driving licence application forms, and other reg-istration forms widely available at post offices and so on. The database does not affect the provisions of the Human Organ Transplant Act 1989, however, which prohibits all commercial dealings in human organs. Accordingly payments cannot be made for donations from dead donors.

Under the Human Tissue Act 1961 there are two ways in which individuals can donate their bodies (or parts thereof) 'for therapeutic purposes or for purposes of medical education or research'. One is with the donor's express consent. The second relies on the consent of relatives.

EXPRESS CONSENT OF DONOR

s.1(1) allows individuals, either in writing at any time or orally in the presence of two or more witnesses during their last illness, to express a request that their bodies (or any part) be used for such purposes. Once such a request is made the person 'lawfully in possession of the body' may authorize that the deceased wishes be carried out. Written requests are often made in a will. However, minors cannot make valid wills although they can carry donor cards. But irrespective of whether the request is made in a will or through a donor card the person in possession of the body is under no legal duty to carry out the donor's wishes.

CONSENT OF RELATIVES

In the vast majority of cases organs from minors become available because a relative – typically a parent – has consented. s.1 (2) allows a person 'lawfully in possession of the body' to agree to organs being removed if 'having made such reasonable enquiry as may be practicable' he or she has no reason to believe either (a) that the deceased had expressed an objection to organ removal or (b) that any surviving spouse or relative objects. Several aspects of this section can be problematic. One difficulty in the past was the meaning of 'in lawful possession'. While this is now widely accepted as referring to the health authority responsible for the hospital if a minor dies in hospital (or is brought into hospital dead) or a parent if a minor dies elsewhere, other technical problems remain, notably the meaning of 'reasonable enquiry'. The only authoritative guidance on this is that contained in a DHSS circular (HSC(IS)156) which states that in most instances it will be sufficient to discuss the matter with any relative who has been in close contact with the deceased, asking his or her own views and those of the deceased and so forth. Regrettably too the Act does not define the words 'relative' – an omission which the circular picks up by suggesting that in some circumstances it should be interpreted very widely, e.g. to include not just those who are 'distant' relatives but also anyone 'closely concerned with the deceased'. Note that the relative's consent need not be obtained in writing but in some cases it is recommended that a post-mortem declaration form be signed (see DHSS circular HC(77)28). In some cases a coroner's consent may also be required, notably when an inquest may have to be held because the minor died as a result of a 'violent or unnatural death', e.g. following a car accident.

Once the relevant consents have been obtained one other provision still has to be complied with before organs can be removed. According to s.1(4) nothing can be removed (except eyes or part of eyes) until a registered medical practitioner has been satisfied through personal examination of the body that 'life is extinct'. In the absence of any legal definition of death this provision used to be problematic in relation to patients on life-support machines but is less so now given the wide acceptance of 'brain stem death' (see Chapter 9). This diagnosis of death is enshrined both in the Code of Practice on the Removal of Cadaveric Organs for Transplantation (1983) and the DHSS circular HC(88)63 (which provides guidance on the setting up of local transplant procedures).

Notwithstanding these guidelines notice was given in late 1994 by the English Office of the National Health Service that the practice of ventilating patients for the sole purpose of retrieving organs for transplantation (known as 'elective ventilation') was unlawful. The practice, although not widespread, was seen as an effective way of increasing the supply of organs. It involved patients with only a short time left to live being moved to intensive units and ventilated before or just after spontaneous respiration failure so that their organs can be harvested.

Case study 8.5
Colleen is 15 and is dying. On several occasions in the past couple of weeks she has told Nigella, a nurse, that she wants to donate her kidneys. Nigella's sister died two years previously due to a shortage of kidneys but she insists that she never broached the subject with Colleen but simply responded to her questions. Colleen has also discussed kidney donation with a cousin, Hilary, with whom she has become very close recently. Hilary, who is ten years older than Colleen, has just returned from working abroad where she has been for the previous five years. Three days ago Colleen signed a donor card which she put in a drawer next to her bed. Both Nigella and Hilary know that it is there. Colleen's parents are not keen on organ donation. They have had to leave the country for a few days and cannot be contacted for at least 48 hours. Colleen died unexpectedly a few hours ago.

Can her kidneys be used for transplant purposes?

Assuming that Colleen's life is extinct as required by s.1(4) of the Human Tissue Act 1961 the issue here is whether Colleen's parents can veto her intentions as expressed in the donor card. s.1(1) of the Act refers to express consent which arguably includes a donor card – although there is no case confirming this. If Colleen was competent to make a valid request then her wishes should be respected. However this requires authorization of the 'person lawfully in possession of the body'. As was noted above, if a person dies in hospital this refers to the health authority at least until Colleen's executors or relatives ask for her body to be handed to them. Accordingly Colleen's kidneys could lawfully be removed for transplant. Whether the hospital authorities would in practice carry out the procedure in view of Colleen's parents' strong objections is, of course, another matter.

If there is any doubt as to Colleen's competency to make a written request – for example, because Nigella put pressure on her to sign the donor card – consent for removal of her kidneys would have to be sought from Colleen's relatives under s.1(2). This allows the person lawfully in possession of the body to authorize removal if having made such 'reasonable enquiries as are practicable' he has no reason to believe that a surviving relative objects. Note that specific consent is not necessary, merely a lack of objection. What this means in practice will depend on the facts of each case. Typically it will be enough to discuss the matter with any relative who has been in close contact. But does Hilary qualify as the appropriate relative given that Colleen's parents cannot be contacted and a decision must be made quickly? The word 'relative' is not defined in the Act but circular HSC(IS)156 makes it clear that it can be interpreted in the widest sense, e.g. to include anyone who, although only a distant relative, is nevertheless closely concerned with the deceased. Arguably then it would be lawful to remove Colleen's kidneys following discussions with Hilary.

If Hilary is not considered an appropriate relative or she too cannot be contacted it is unclear what enquiries would have to be made. The Act is very obscure on this as it fails to specify (a) what a 'reasonable enquiry' is and (b) whether the practicability of making such enquiries relates to the hospital's or the relative's interests. That said, it would certainly be necessary to look at Colleen's medical notes to check if any objections have been noted. Beyond this it would be advisable to follow hospital policy (if there is one).

Case study 8.6
Bianca is 17 and has just given birth to an anencephalic baby, Rory.

In other words Rory was born without all or most of its forebrain. Transplant surgeons are keen to use some of Rory's organs for transplant purposes. Bianca has given her consent but the transplant team are concerned about the legality of the procedure given the difficulty of diagnosing brain stem death in a baby whose forebrain is missing but who is nevertheless still breathing and has a heart beat.

What is the legal definition of death in such a case?

Recognizing that tests for brain stem death are inapplicable to anencephalics a Working Party of the Medical Royal Colleges on 'Organ Transplantation' concluded in 1988 that:

> organs could be removed from anencephalic babies when two doctors (who were not members of the transplant team) agree that spontaneous respiration had ceased.

What this means is that the absence of a forebrain together with apnonea is recognized as death. However, it has been suggested that applying this criterion of death inevitably involves a form of 'reanimation ventilation', the legality of which is uncertain.

Case study 8.7
Emma is 16 and has just had an abortion. Is it lawful to use brain cells from the foetus to treat Parkinson's disease or other diseases in the elderly?

Foetal organs and tissue can be used for transplant purposes provided the death of the foetus was lawful. Assuming therefore that Emma's abortion complied with the Abortion Act 1967, i.e. the foetus was not aborted solely to obtain foetal tissue, there is no legal prohibition against the proposed transplantation. In the absence of any specific legislation on the use of foetal materials for transplantation the recommendations of the Polkinghorne (likewise those of the British Medical Association) should be followed, in particular Emma's consent should be sought although as with use of foetal material for research it is unclear whether this is a legal requirement.

FURTHER READING

British Paediatric Association (1992) *Guidelines for the Ethical Conduct of Medical Research Involving Children.*

Mason, J.K. (1992) *Legal Aspects of Organ Transplantation in Doctors, Patients and the Law,* (ed. C. Dyer), Blackwell Scientific Publications, Oxford.

Medical Research Council (1992) *The Ethical Conduct of Research on Children*, The Council, London.

Meyers, D.W. (1990) *The Human Body and the Law*, Edinburgh University Press, Edinburgh.

Nicholson, R.H. (ed.) (1986) *Medical Research with Children: Ethics, Law and Practice*, Oxford University Press, Oxford.

Royal College of Physicians (1988) *Research on Healthy Volunteers*, The College, London.

Royal College of Physicians (1990) *Research Involving Patients*, The College, London.

Royal College of Physicians (1990) *Guidelines on the Practice of Ethics Committees in Medical Research Involving Human Subjects*, The College, London.

Death, dying and the incurably ill patient

9

Deciding how to treat a dying or incurably ill infant raises what are by now familiar issues in that they focus essentially on the law of consent, in particular the right that parents and others have to give (or withhold) consent on behalf of minors who lack legal capacity. Different but none the less consent-related questions are also raised when older children and adolescents are terminally or incurably ill. But irrespective of who is the decision-maker decisions in this context are almost always likely to be more difficult and more controversial than they once were for several reasons. First, advances in medicine enable some patients to live longer than they would have done in the past. However, prolonging life may not always be in their best interests. Is it, for example, unquestionably bene-ficial to extend the life of a profoundly handicapped child so that it becomes a 'passive prisoner of medical technology' with no hope of recovery or improvement? If not, to do so is at least arguably unlawful. Secondly, a steady trickle of much-publicized cases in the early 1990s such as the trial of Dr Cox for attempted murder and the case of Anthony Bland, the young man injured in the football stadium disaster, ensure that the debate about treatment and 'life and death' decisions remain a focus for public debate. Thirdly, changing medical relationships, in particular the assertion of patients rights and the expectation that patients and their families should be more involved in decision-making increase the opportunities for disputes to arise. If the law is invoked to resolve these and reach the courts – as in the case of B v. Cambridge HA [1995] (see Chapter 2) – it is not surprising that wide public debate is generated, especially when claims are made, albeit from anti-euthanasia organizations, that decisions about whom to treat (and what for) mask what is in practice 'medical cleansing' of long-stay wards.

This chapter will look at the following aspects of death and dying, notably how death is defined in law, neonaticide and the treatment of terminally and incurably ill minors. It will also outline the 1994 Select Committee's Report on Medical Ethics. Note too guidance on care of the dying child which is contained in the Charter for Children with Life-Threatening Conditions and their Families and the recommendations in a report prepared by a Working Party on the Care of Dying Children and their Families by the British Paediatric Association in 1988.

THE LEGAL DEFINITION OF DEATH

Like so many areas in medicine, technological advances in the last 30 years have made what was once a relatively straightforward state to identify and define increasingly complex. So in the past when a person's heart or breathing stopped the law accepted unequivocally that death had occurred and the person was dead. For most deaths this traditional definition of death remains adequate but it is not appropriate when intensive treatment has been used to maintain a patient's vital functions. It is not uncommon now, for example, for patients to be resuscitated after a cardiac arrest. Similarly ventilation can be maintained artificially long after a patient has stopped breathing. Artificial feeding techniques are also fairly common-place. As such intensive care techniques have become a well-established part of medical practice, a different definition of death had to be developed which could be applied to patients on life support machines.

In the absence of any statutory definition of death the concept of brain stem death, i.e. the irreversible loss of brain function, is now accepted as a legal definition of death even though no English court has expressly endorsed it. The concept was developed in the mid 1970s by the Royal Colleges, first as a diagnosis of death and subsequently as a definition thereof. However, the concept is not applicable to all children even if they are comatose, totally apnoeic, and being ventilated. According to the British Paediatric Association Report in 1991 the diagnosis can be applied to children older than two months but can only rarely be confidently applied to infants between 37 weeks' gestation to two months old. Under 37 weeks the concept is inappropriate.

TREATMENT OF THE NEWBORN

This section looks at the treatment of infants who are born with major abnormalities, typically of the central nervous system. Withdrawing or withholding treatment from such infants is known as neonaticide (the term 'neonate' refers to infants up to four weeks old) or more commonly as 'selective non-treatment'. While the legal issues it raises are essentially no different from those which apply to terminally or incurably ill children or adolescents, most legal texts treat the subject as a separate issue for several reasons. First, infants cannot speak for themselves and unlike older children have never had the opportunity to express their views or imply their preferences. In short their wishes cannot be established nor can they be consulted. Secondly, very sick infants know of no other existence. Consequently their expectations and experiences are almost certainly going to be different from (and not comparable to) those children who have been well but who are now dying or are seriously ill. Thirdly neonaticide and some aspects of abortion are closely linked in that it is at least arguable that the legal distinction between terminating a pregnancy on the grounds of substantial risk of serious handicap (which is lawful) and the deliberate killing of a seriously handicapped neonate (which is not) is inconsistent.

Advances in neonatal intensive care now increasingly enable very premature infants and those with severe disabilities to survive. Yet in some circumstances a decision to withdraw or withhold treatment still has to be made. But when was it lawful to do so? Surprisingly it is only in the last decade that the law in this area has been clarified as the result of several cases – which have become known as the 'quality of life' cases, i.e. Re B [1981], Re C [1989] and Re J [1990]. In the absence of any professional guidelines or code of practice these currently provide the only authoritative guidance on treatment of the newborn (and other incompetent minors who are terminally ill or severely disabled). Moreover they are likely to remain so for some time as legislation is unlikely in the near future.

Questions which are commonly asked in this context include the following. What legal duty is owed to infants born with severe disabilities? Is there an absolute obligation to prolong life? What rights do parents have? Can the courts order health professionals to provide treatment? Can a baby be deliberately killed?

But before addressing these questions, the case of R v. Arthur [1981] will be outlined since despite being of very limited value as a legal precedent it was the first case to focus on the treatment of the newborn and expose medical practice to the scrutiny of the courts. Dr Arthur was a highly respected consultant paediatrician charged with murder following the death of an infant in his care. The infant had Down's Syndrome but otherwise seemed healthy. He was rejected by his parents and after a meeting with them Dr Arthur put in his case notes, 'Parents do not wish baby to survive, nursing care only'. He also prescribed dihydrocodeine. The infant died three days later – according to the prosecution of drug poisoning and starvation. The murder charge was later reduced to attempted murder because evidence was produced at the trial that the baby had several abnormalities which could have led to his death from natural causes.

Dr Arthur was acquitted. In the circumstances his acquittal was not surprising since apart from the contradictory evidence about the cause of death (which probably confused the jury and certainly weakened the prosecution's case) there was ample evidence that the infant was by no means the first Down's Syndrome infant to be treated in the way prescribed by Dr Arthur. In other words Dr Arthur, like other eminent paediatricians of his time, had followed accepted practice. Moreover it also became clear that the infant had not starved to death as was first claimed since he had been fed fluids and did not lose weight during his short life.

Despite the wide public debate the Arthur case generated it did little to clarify the law; in particular it shed no light on the extent of the legal duty owed to infants born with severe disabilities which is perhaps the central question in this context.

WHAT DUTY IS OWED?

Infants lack the legal capacity to make their own decisions about treatment. Consent to treatment must therefore be obtained from a proxy. As was noted in Chapter 3, a proxy, who is usually a parent, must act in the minor's 'best interests'. Notwithstanding the uncertainty as to the precise meaning of this term there is no doubt that it covers treatment which is therapeutic, i.e. intended to benefit the minor. But what does this mean in respect of an infant (or any other incompetent minor) who is incurably or terminally ill? Or to put it another way, what treatment does the law require health professionals to provide in such circumstances? Just as in other areas of treatment they must act in accordance with a responsible and competent body of relevant professional opinion (i.e. reach the Bolam standard). In this context this essentially means determining the infant's 'quality of life' – a term which the courts have, probably deliberately, refused to define precisely – but which appears to involve assessing the medical benefits, risks and adverse effects of treatment as well as the infant's potential for intellectual and social functioning.

Once assessed various treatment (or non-treatment options) are possible. Thus if an infant is dying (as in Re C [1989]) treatment can be lawfully withheld or withdrawn. Note that there is no legal distinction between withholding or withdrawing treatment even though the 'infant' case law discussed in this chapter concerns the legality of withholding treatment rather than withdrawing it. In other cases even if an infant is not facing death the prognosis may be so poor and he or she may suffer such disabilities (as in Re J [1990]) that again it is lawful for treatment to be withheld as it also can be when an infant's life is going to be 'demonstrably so awful' – for example because of his or her constant pain and suffering.

IS THERE AN ABSOLUTE LEGAL OBLIGATION TO PROLONG LIFE?

The cases of Re C [1989] and Re J [1990] establish beyond doubt that the law does not require every patient to be resuscitated or put on a life support machine. Health professionals do not therefore have to preserve life at all costs as there is no absolute legal right to life. This means that in certain circumstances it is lawful to let a patient die as the following cases illustrate.

Re C [1989]

C was born about five weeks premature suffering from a very serious form of hydrocephalus. She was made a ward of court for reasons unconnected with her medical condition because the local authority believed that her parents would be unable to care for her. Two weeks after her birth the court's permission was sought and obtained for the insertion of a shunt to relieve pressure on her brain. C's health did not improve and when she was 16 weeks old the local authority again referred the case to court when it became clear that C was terminally ill and suffering from irreversible brain damage resulting in very severe physical and mental disabilities – she was blind, probably deaf and had cerebral palsy of all four limbs. Her prognosis was described as 'hopeless' – she would not get better and no medical or surgical treatment would alter that fact.

The central question before the court was whether life-sustaining treatment such as nasogastric feeding or antibiotics had to be given if, as was inevitable sooner or later, these would be required to keep C alive. It decided that the hospital authorities should 'treat the ward to die' and should administer such treatment as might 'relieve her pain, suffering and distress'. Accordingly it would not be necessary to prescribe antibiotics or set up artificial feeding regimes. Essentially therefore the court ruled that medical treatment could be withheld.

On appeal by the official solicitor acting on C's behalf the Court of Appeal confirmed the High Court's order. However following the outcry over the words 'treat to die' it substituted the following words: 'That the hospital be at liberty to treat the minor to allow her life to come to an end peacefully and with dignity.'

Re J [1990]

Infant J was born 13 weeks premature (weighing 1.1kg) but by the time the case came to court he was five months old. Described as suffering from almost every conceivable misfortune, he had very severe and permanent brain damage and had been ventilated twice for long periods. But he was neither dying nor near the point of death – his life expectancy had been reduced at most into his late teens although he was expected to die well before then. Nevertheless even though he was able to breathe independently (and so in some respects his condition had slightly improved) his long-term prognosis remained very poor. He suffered from epilepsy, was likely to develop serious spastic quadriplegia, would be blind and deaf, was unlikely ever to speak or develop even limited intellectual abilities but would feel the same pain as a normal infant.

The central issue before the court was: if J suffered a further collapse which could occur at any time but was not inevitable, did the law require him to be reventilated? It decided that the doctors' duty to act in J's best interests meant that there was no legal obligation to reventilate him nor subject him to all the associated processes of intensive care if he could not continue breathing unaided unless to do so seemed appropriate to those treating him. None the less if he developed a chest infection he should be treated with antibiotics and maintenance of hydration.

The official solicitor appealed contending that except in cases of terminal illness or where a minor's life would be intolerable a court would never be justified in approving the withholding of life-saving treatment.

The Court of Appeal confirmed the High Court's decision in that given the unfavourable prognosis (with or without treatment), the hazardous and invasive nature of reventilation, the risk of further deterioration if J was subjected to it, it was in his best interests that treatment be withheld.

In addition it provided general guidelines about the treatment of infants with severe disabilities. These are as follows:

• A court can never sanction positive steps to terminate life.
• In deciding whether to direct that treatment need not be given to prolong life, the court had to carry out a balancing exercise. This involved judging the quality of life the infant would experience and the pain and suffering if his life were prolonged and the pain and suffering involved in the proposed treatment.
• The infant's best interests had to be looked at from his point of view giving the fullest possible weight to his desire – an approach which recognizes that even people with very severe disabilities can find a quality of life rewarding which to the unhandicapped may seem 'manifestly intolerable'.
• There is strong presumption in favour of a course of action which will prolong life.

Before concluding this section it is also worth noting dicta from the case of Re B [1981] (see page 185) which are relevant in this context, notably that it is lawful to withhold or withdraw treatment which would enable a child to survive a life-threatening condition if it is certain that the quality of the child's subsequent life would be 'intolerable to the child', 'bound to be full of pain and suffering' and 'demonstrably so awful that in effect the child must be condemned to die'.

In summary the combined effect of Re B, Re C and Re J is that it is lawful to allow an infant to die (i.e. treatment can be withheld or withdrawn) if:

- he or she is dying or will die irrespective of any treatment; in other words treatment is futile and death inevitable,
- while not terminally ill or even near death the risks of treatment outweigh its benefits bearing in mind the prognosis, the nature and extent of his or her disabilities, pain and suffering and quality of life if treatment is initiated or continued. In such cases death can reasonably be seen as beneficial or at very least as an improvement for the patient.

Finally it is important to emphasize that although the above precedents were established in cases concerning infants, they apply equally to the treatment or non-treatment of all terminally or incurably ill incompetent minors.

WHAT RIGHTS DO PARENTS HAVE TO DETERMINE TREATMENT?

While parents (or others with parental responsibility) have a central role in decision-making their wishes are not conclusive and can be overridden. This means that they do not have the legal right to insist that treatment is withdrawn or withheld nor that treatment is initiated. Nevertheless as the infant's proxy their views are very important and thus a significant factor in determining his or her best interests. Moreover it is beyond question that even though their wishes may not prevail they must be given appropriate information, such as the treatment options and their likely outcomes, benefits and risks as well as the infant's prognosis (with and without treatment).

Disputes about treatment are rare but do occur. Very occasionally they reach the courts as in Re B [1981]. The case concerned a baby girl born with Down's Syndrome and an intestinal blockage which would be fatal within a few days unless urgent life-saving surgery was carried out. Although only a relatively minor procedure her parents refused consent, believing it was not in her interests to have the operation because she would be very severely handicapped if she survived. Faced with their refusal the local authority became involved. B was made a ward of court and initially the surgery was authorized. B was moved to another hospital but on learning of the parents' objection the surgeon declined to operate. The local authority therefore went back to court but this time the same judge revoked his initial order deciding that B's parents' wishes should be respected.

The local authority appealed and the Court of Appeal authorized surgery which it held was in B's best interests after the following test was applied, namely,

> whether B's life was demonstrably going to be so awful that in effect she must be condemned to die, or whether her life was so imponderable that it would be wrong for her to be so condemned.

Despite uncertainty as to B's prognosis which could not be reliably made until she was two-years-old, it was nevertheless accepted that she would be severely mentally and physically handicapped and would not have anything like a 'normal existence'. Her life expectancy was about 20–30 years.

While acknowledging that great weight should be given to parents' wishes the Court of Appeal none the less overrode them. It was not convinced that B's life was going to be an 'intolerable one' as after the operation she would have the normal lifespan of a Down's Syndrome child 'with the handicaps and defects and life' of such a child. Accordingly it was not prepared to say that a life of that description ought to be extinguished. In short B had to be given the chance to live.

The case of B concerned a newborn infant but the precedent it established as to the wishes of parents applies equally to older incompetent children. In other words parents' wishes only prevail if they are in the minor's best interests but not otherwise.

But what if there is disagreement about the benefits of treatment – which doctors want to withhold or withdraw but which parents wish to continue? If agreement cannot be reached the case is likely to come to court as it did in the case of Re J [1992].

CAN DOCTORS BE FORCED TO PROVIDE TREATMENT?

Re J [1992] (see Chapter 1 for full details of the case) provides clear authority that the courts will not compel health professionals or a health authority (or NHS Trust) to provide treatment which in the bona fide clinical judgement of those concerned is contraindicated as not being in the best interests of the patient.

J was a 16 month old infant with a short expectation of life who had profound physical and mental disabilities including severe cerebral palsy, epilepsy and cortical blindness. He was largely fed by a nasogastric tube and was not expected to develop beyond his present level of functioning. J's consultant therefore decided that intensive therapeutic measures such as artificial ventilation would not be appropriate should he suffer a life-threatening event since any such procedure would only artificially prolong his 'vegetative state'.

Before the case finally reached the Court of Appeal the High Court ordered the hospital authority to use intensive measures including artificial ventilation for as long as they could prolong J's life. While J's mother was happy with this order the health authority (among others) was not and appealed. In allowing the appeal the Court of Appeal made it clear that it could not conceive of any circumstances in which it would order practitioners to provide treatment which was contrary to their clinical judgement. As Lord Donaldson said:

> No one can dictate the treatment to be given to the child – neither court, parents nor doctors. There are checks and balances. The doctors can recommend treatment A in preference to treatment B. They can also refuse to adopt treatment C on the grounds that it is medically contraindicated or for some other reason is a treatment which they could not conscientiously administer. The court or parents for their part can refuse to consent to treatment A or B or both, but they cannot insist on treatment C. The inevitable and desirable result is that choice of treatment is in some measure a joint decision of the doctors and the court or parents.

IS IT LAWFUL NOT TO FEED AN INFANT?

Although there has been no case directly on this issue in the English courts other than R v. Arthur (which as was noted above is unhelpful as a legal precedent) many legal texts contend that it would be unlawful not to feed an infant (or any other incompetent minor) who is capable of taking food by mouth. Accordingly any health professional who withheld normal feeding from an infant able to accept it would be in the same legal position as a parent who refused to provide food and thus almost certainly likely to face serious criminal charges. Nevertheless there is a contrary view which is that in some circumstances a failure to feed an infant by mouth may be lawful, that is when it is in the best interests of the infant to be allowed to die. In the words of one commentator,

> Waking up a person on his death bed merely to give him a life prolonging drink of water seems pointless, even cruel.

But the legal picture is more complicated when the term 'feeding' is further analysed given that it can include not just breastfeeding, spoon and bottle feeding but also feeding through medical and surgical intervention. This then raises the question as to whether there is a legal distinction between 'normal' feeding by mouth and artificial feeding using nasogastric tubes, gastrostomies and intravenous infusions. In other words is there a point when 'feeding' becomes medical treatment?

This question was one of the central issues in Airedale NHS Trust v. Bland [1993]. The case concerned a 21-year-old man who had been crushed in the Hillsborough football stadium disaster in 1989. For over three years he had been in a persistent vegetative state (PVS) but his brain stem was still functioning. In law, therefore, Anthony Bland was alive. He was able to breathe and digest (but not swallow) food independently but could not see, communicate, hear, taste or smell. His bowels were evacuated by enema and his bladder was drained by a catheter. He was fed through a nasogastric tube and lay in bed with his eyes open and his limbs crooked and taut. He had repeated infections and had been treated with antibiotics and other drugs. He had also been operated on for various urino-genitary problems. With constant care he could be kept in his current state for years, perhaps even longer, but he would never regain consciousness. In the words of one expert witness, 'Anthony Bland presented the worst PVS case he had ever seen.'

The House of Lords held:

- that artificial feeding (in Anthony's case this meant nasogastric hydration and nutrition) was a form of medical treatment; legally it was therefore no different from other forms of life-sustaining treatment, such as a ventilator or kidney machine and so could be withdrawn if not in the patient's best interests;
- that the actual process of withdrawing artificial feeding was an 'omission' (rather than an act) and so was lawful – in legal terms this is an important distinction because traditionally only positive conduct in the form of acts normally gives rise to criminal liability.

CAN AN INFANT BE DELIBERATELY KILLED?

The number of prosecutions of doctors for offences in connection with euthanasia are rare – four or fewer in any one year. Nevertheless it is beyond question that it is unlawful to terminate life deliberately whether the patient is dying or not. Killing a patient is murder and any health professional who takes steps which are solely intended to accelerate death is likely to face criminal charges even though juries have, at least until recently, been very reluctant to convict doctors who carry out what they regard as 'mercy killings'. The recent case of R v. Cox [1992], however, may mark a change in their approach. Dr Cox was convicted of attempted murder after his elderly incurably ill patient – who was in acute pain and had repeatedly asked him to kill her – died within minutes of being injected with potassium chloride.

But the verdict in the case could have been very different; indeed Dr Cox would never have been charged had he used morphine or some other drug with pain-killing qualities because then his primary intention would have been to relieve pain. As such his actions would have been lawful even if his patient's life had been shortened by the effect of the drugs. This practice – usually known as the principle of 'double effect' – is so common that it is widely accepted as unexceptional. Nevertheless many increasingly think it to be discredited in that it relies on what is arguably a hypocritical distinction between what is intended and what is foreseen. That said the well-established legal distinction between killing (an unlawful commission) and letting die (a lawful omission) is likely to remain unchanged given the Select Committee of the House of Lords on Medical Ethics (see further below) recommendation that the law should not be changed to permit euthanasia. As a consequence the statement made by the Crown Prosecution Service in its evidence to the Committee sums up the current legal position, namely,

> that the administration of pain killing though life shortening drugs to terminally ill patients is rendered lawful if the doctor is acting in the best interests of the patient, despite the fact the patient will die as a consequence.

Case study 9.1

Stephen was born 22 weeks premature. Following a full clinical assessment the decision was made not to give him any neonatal intensive resuscitation. Stephen dies two hours after his birth. His parents claim that he should not have been allowed to die and that doctors breached the duty of care they owed Stephen in that no attempt was made to keep him alive.

Are doctors legally obliged to provide treatment or can they withhold it?

Health professionals are under a duty to act in Stephen's best interests. This requires them to assess his chances of survival, taking into account not just his gestation age but also his weight, size and general condition. Once these factors are considered it is then possible to decide whether to resuscitate him. However, bearing in mind that it is rare for infants born at 22 weeks to survive except with very severe handicaps accepted medical practice (i.e. the Bolam test) has almost certainly been followed in withholding life-sustaining treatment from Stephen.

Case study 9.2

Tina was born severely brain damaged and is now 20 months old. She is blind and deaf and has no control over her limbs and is subject to fits but is not unconscious and cries constantly. She is treated with sedatives and is fed artificially through a hole in her stomach. Medical opinion is unanimous that she is unlikely to improve. It is uncertain whether or not she is in constant pain.

Her parents contend that she should be allowed to die and that artificial feeding should be withdrawn. Would it be lawful to do so?

Tina is clearly too young to express her wishes. This means that decisions – which must be in her best interests – have to be made on her behalf. While her parents' wishes are persuasive they are not conclusive and can be overridden. As Tina is neither dying nor near the point of death (unlike Re C [1989]) nor permanently unconscious (as in the Bland case) the withdrawal of treatment cannot be justified on the basis that further treatment is futile because death is inevitable. The term 'futile' was defined by the House of Lords in the Bland case as that which 'confers no medical benefit' or 'has no therapeutic purpose of any kind'. The legality of withdrawing treatment would thus turn on whether further treatment was considered 'futile' and her quality of life (both before and after treatment). In other words is her life going to be 'demonstrably so awful', so full of pain and suffering that it is intolerable? (See Re B [1981].) If the answer is yes, then artificial feeding – which is a form of medical treatment – can be lawfully withdrawn as can other medical treatment except that which is necessary to make her comfortable, i.e. pain relief. Similarly artificial feeding could be withdrawn if taking into account Tina's disabilities, prognosis and quality of life continued treatment can do nothing to improve her underlying condition or is such that its burdens and risks outweigh its benefits (see e.g. Re J [1990]). In short Tina's death is preferable to life.

TERMINALLY AND INCURABLY ILL MINORS

The legal principles established in the 'infant' cases (likewise Airedale NHS Trust v. Bland) apply equally to all incompetent terminally and incurably ill minors. But what about those who are competent? Does the law allow them to make what can in practice be life or death decisions? As was noted in Chapter 3, most notably in Re W [1992], there are circumstances in which the courts are prepared to override the wishes of competent minors who refuse life-saving treatment. In several cases too the courts have also been willing to disregard parents' views. In the case of Re E [1993], for example, a 15-year-old Jehovah's Witness was dying of leukaemia. With conventional treatment (which included blood transfusions) there was an 80–90% chance of full remission. An alternative treatment gave only a 60% chance of remission. But E refused to receive any blood products and was supported by his parents who likewise refused to give consent. Initially he was therefore given the alternative treatment but within two weeks his condition had deteriorated to the extent that his life was threatened. Consequently the hospital sought and obtained the High Court's permission to treat E as they considered necessary, including the transfusion of blood.

In the subsequent case of Re S [1994] the High Court similarly overrode both a 15½-year-old's refusal (and that of her mother) to life-sustaining treatment in spite of evidence that she would refuse treatment as soon as she was 18 (as had the minor in Re E who, on reaching his majority, had declined further transfusions and died). But the court was not convinced by the argument that it was thus cruel to subject her to invasive treatments which, in a few years' time, she would almost certainly reject.

In both Re E and Re S the High Court refused to accept that the minors were competent, contending that they failed to understand fully the consequences of their refusal, in particular the process of dying and the pain and distress it would bring. Nevertheless, even if a minor was competent, the courts would almost certainly act paternistically and override his or her informed refusal if it believed that treatment was in the minor's best interests.

But if a competent minor was dying (and so treatment was futile) or incurably ill and had no chance of getting better, would the courts be quite so willing to override his or her rejection of further treatment? In some circumstances it may at least be arguable that such treatment would not be in the minor's best interests given the minor's disabilities, pain and suffering, chances of improvement, risks of treatment and so forth.

But before looking at case studies on this it is worth noting the provisions of the Suicide Act 1961 which may be relevant in this context. Although the Act decriminalized suicide and attempted suicide it remains a criminal offence to 'aid, abet, counsel or procure the suicide of another, or an attempt by another to commit suicide'. Does this mean that a health professional who placed fatal pills within reach of a patient would face criminal charges under the Act if the minor used them and died? The answer is uncertain – there is no case directly on this point and it is unclear what the prosecution would need to prove. Much would turn on the professional's 'intention', i.e. whether by providing the means for suicide he or she intended the patient to take them.

Case study 9.3
Mark has just turned 17. For the last five years he has been a quadriplegic as a result of a swimming accident. He has been looked after mainly by his mother but she is now dying and reluctantly agrees to support Mark's wishes that he be allowed to die. Imminent loss of his mother's care and support has left him without any hope for the future even though he can read, watch television and operate a computer orally. Although his condition is irreversible he is not terminally ill and can live for many years as long as artificial respiration is maintained.

Is a court likely to declare withdrawal of the life support lawful?

There is no English case directly on this point in relation to minors although in Airedale NHS Trust v. Bland [1993] it was made clear that the law recognizes that 'an adult who is conscious and of sound mind is completely at liberty to decline to undergo treatment, even if the result of his doing so will be that he will die'. Moreover the right to refuse life-sustaining treatment applies whether or not the patient is terminally ill. However the court have recognized two exceptions to this well-established rule, notably pregnant women (see Re S [1992] Chapter 3) and minors (see above).

As Mark is still a minor the court could override his wishes until he reaches 18. But it can only do so if continuing treatment, i.e. artificial respiration, is in his best interests. This then is the crucial question, the answer to which would turn on such factors as (among other things) the nature of his disabilities and whether his condition was irreversible or could improve, whether he was competent and able to understand the nature and consequence of his decision, what future care could be provided for him, and what pain and suffering and distress he would endure.

Case study 9.4

Alison, who is 'Gillick competent', is 15-years-old and refuses to undergo another liver transplant without which she will die. Her reasons for refusing further treatment are based mainly on the pain and suffering the transplant will cause but also her firm belief that she will die anyway. The prognosis is in fact poor but indeterminate. However, because Alison's parents are very keen to try anything which may save their daughter's life, doctors are prepared to give them the benefit of the doubt.

What factors would a court consider in resolving the dispute between Alison and her parents?

Because Alison is a minor, consent for surgery could be obtained from anyone with parental responsibility. Except in an emergency though, it would be wise to refer the case to court rather than rely solely on parental consent. The court's decision must be based on what it considers to be Alison's best interests. Relevant factors here would therefore include Alison's wishes and the benefits and risks of a treatment, e.g. the pain and distress she will suffer if she has another transplant and whether it is likely to be successful. While the views of Alison's parents are also significant they are not conclusive.

Case study 9.5

Last year Dorothy, who had just had her 15th birthday, took a drug overdose. When she was taken to hospital a suicide note was found in her pocket. As a result of the overdose she suffered irreversible brain damage diagnosed as PVS. There is no chance that Dorothy will ever recover and her quality of life is described as nil. She is being fed artificially by a gastrostomy tube which has become dislodged. If she is to survive it must be replaced urgently. Dorothy's mother, Celia thinks she should be allowed to die telling doctors that on several occasions she has discussed with her daughter what should happen if she ever became a 'cabbage' – her firm wish was that all life support should be switched off. Furthermore Celia thinks that the suicide note is very strong evidence that Dorothy should be allowed to die. But her father disagrees. He wants the gastrostomy tube replaced immediately – a view not supported by Dorothy's consultant as she thinks reinsertion (i.e. life-prolonging treatment) to be against her best interests because no benefit will be conferred on her. In other words the legal justification for withdrawing or withholding further treatment is that it is futile.

Is a court likely to authorize withholding further treatment?

It should be noted that in the Bland case the House of Lords decided that withdrawal of life-sustaining treatment is in legal terms the same as withholding fresh treatment. As such, switching off a ventilator or withdrawing a nasogastric or gastrostomy tube is an omission to continue treatment and therefore lawful. Classifying these 'actions' as omissions is legally very important because there is no criminal liability for omissions unless there is a duty to act. What duty is owed to Dorothy depends on what is in her best interests. Given her underlying condition and the fact that health professionals do not have an absolute duty to maintain life at all costs it is at least arguable that continuing treatment would be against her interests and therefore unlawful.

The facts of this case study are similar to those in Frenchay Healthcare NHS Trust v. S [1994] in which the court authorized withholding treatment from a 24-year-old PVS patient. But unlike the previous two case studies Dorothy's wishes are more difficult to ascertain given that the suicide note and Celia's account of her daughter's views are the only clue as to her wishes. But even supposing Dorothy's views could be ascertained as she is a minor her wishes can be overridden in any event – e.g. by her father (assuming he has parental responsibility) who is willing to consent to the tube being reinserted.

But Dorothy is a PVS patient. As a consequence Practice Note (1994 2 All ER, 413) should be complied with. This states (among other things), first, that termination of artificial feeding and hydration for PVS patients will in virtually all cases require the court's prior sanction. Interestingly however, in Frenchay Healthcare NHS Trust v. S (1994) the Court of Appeal seemed to suggest that it would almost certainly rubber stamp any decision to discontinue feeding or other life support treatment providing there was sufficient responsible medical opinion to support that course of action. Secondly, the diagnosis of PVS should comply with the 1992 guidelines issued by the Medical Ethics Committee of the BMA (adapted in 1966) which specify that such a diagnosis should not be confirmed until the patient has been insentient for at least 12 months. Thirdly, the views of the next of kin, which are 'very important' should be made known to the court. Fourthly, the patient's previously expressed views should be a 'very important component' in any decision made.

Applying the practice note to Dorothy the following points are important:

COURT APPLICATION

The practice note appears to apply to all patients in PVS irrespective of their age. Since Anthony Bland's death seven other applications to remove feeding tubes have been heard in the English courts including Re G [1994] in which the court said its role differed depending on whether the patient is an adult or a minor. In respect of minors the court decides what should happen and authorizes a particular course of action. But in relation to incompetent adults the court's role is to state what is (or is not) lawful. Nevertheless in both the substantive legal question is the same, i.e. what is the patient's best interests. Accordingly unless Dorothy's case is an emergency one the court's permission not to replace the gastrostomy tube should be sought.

ADVANCE DIRECTIVES

Dorothy's previously expressed views are unlikely to amount to an advance directive (or 'living will') even though they do give some indication of her wishes. An advance directive is a document made when a patient is competent which indicates his or her preferences about medical treatment in the event of becoming incompetent. Advance directives can take several different forms and can be very specific or general but typically state in what circumstances life-sustaining treatment should be withheld or withdrawn. However, even if Dorothy had made such a directive it could be overridden because she is a minor – assuming of course that to do so was in her best interests (see e.g. Re W [1992]). The legal status of advance directives has yet to be specifically tested in the English courts. Nevertheless in Re T [1992] (see Chapter 3) and Airedale NHS Trust v. Bland [1993] the courts made it clear that in relation to adults an anticipatory refusal of treatment contained in an advance directive is legally binding, providing it fulfilled certain conditions. These are, first, that the patient was competent at the time of refusal; secondly, that the refusal was applicable to the current circumstances, i.e. he or she had contemplated the situation which later arose; thirdly, the patient had not been unduly influenced by anyone and finally that he or she had been informed in broad terms of the nature and effect of the treatment which was being refused, i.e. the consequences of non-treatment.

Other points worth noting here on advance directives are that they cannot authorize an act of active euthanasia, i.e. that health professionals end the patient's life with a lethal injection. Nor, according to the most recent guidance from the British Medical Association, should health professionals be obliged to comply with any request made in the directive that basic care and maintenance of comfort be refused. 'Basic care', according to the BMA, should be defined very generally to include 'those procedures essential to keep an individual comfortable', such as pain and symptom relief. Note too that the Law Commission, which has proposed specific legislation to clarify the validity of advance directives, rejects advance refusals of basic care (defined as 'alleviation of pain, maintenance of cleanliness and provision of direct oral feeding').

SELECT COMMITTEE ON MEDICAL ETHICS

The final section of this chapter outlines some of the recommendations made by the Select Committee of the House of Lords On Medical Ethics in 1994. It was appointed to consider:

the ethical, legal and clinical implications of a person's right to withhold consent to life-prolonging treatment, and the position of persons who are no longer able to give or withhold consent and whether and in what circumstances actions that have as their intention or a likely consequence the shortening of another person's life must be justified on the grounds that they accord with that person's wishes or with that person's best interests; and in all the foregoing circumstances to pay regard to the likely effects of changes in law or medical practice on society as a whole.

Although not specifically raised by its terms of reference the Committee recognized that medical practice in respect of infants could not be excluded from consideration of decision-making about the withholding or withdrawing of treatment.

The Committee published its recommendations in 1994. Many are expected to be eventually enshrined in legislation. They included the following:

- no change in the law to permit euthanasia;
- strong endorsement of the right of competent patients to refuse consent to any medical treatment;
- double effect is not a reason for withholding treatment as long as doctors act in accordance with responsible medical practice with the objective of relieving pain and distress, and without the intention to kill;
- treatment-limiting decisions should be made jointly by all involved in the care of a patient;
- support for a new judicial forum with power to make decisions about medical treatment for incompetent patients;
- no creation of a new offence of 'mercy killing';
- mandatory life sentence for murder should be abolished;
- no change in the law on assisted suicide.

FURTHER READING

Brahams, D. (ed.) (1990) *Medicine and the Law*, Royal College of Physicians, London.

British Medical Association (1995) *Advance Statements about Medical Treatment*, BMA, London.

British Paediatric Association (1991) *Diagnosis of Brain Stem Death in Infants and Children*, BPA, London.

Grubb, A. (ed.) (1993) *Choices and Decisions in Health Care*.

House of Lords Select Committee on Medical Ethics (1994) Paper 21, Vol 1: Report VII.

Khuse, H. and Singer, P. (1985) *Should the Baby Live?* Oxford University Press, Oxford.

Law Commission Report 231 (1995) *Mental Incapacity*, HMSO, London.

Lee, R. and Morgan, D. (1994) *Death Rites: Law and Ethics at the End of Life*, Routledge, London.

McCall Smith, R.A. (1992) *Ending Life in Doctors, Patients and the Law* (ed. C. Dyer), Blackwell Scientific Publications, Oxford.

Meyers, D.W. (1990) *The Human Body and the Law*, Edinburgh University Press, Edinburgh.

Mental health

10

Many different terms are used to describe children whose behaviour is considered 'problematic', such as mentally ill or disordered, aggressive, maladjusted, emotionally disturbed or difficult and beyond control. More often than not the 'labels' have no legal significance, especially as they are commonly used interchangeably. But in some cases they are very important as they identify in which of the four different systems children with very similar behaviour patterns have been (or could be) placed.

Briefly the four systems are: first, the criminal (or youth) justice system. In England and Wales the age of criminal responsibility is 10 years (children under 10 cannot be prosecuted). Although 10 is low by Western standards it is even lower in Scotland where criminal responsibility begins at eight. If convicted 'young offenders' can be subjected to a wide range of sentences, some of which may be custodial. The second system is the child care system. Children in this system are 'looked after' by a local authority. They comprise two main groups, those accommodated by voluntary arrangement and those compulsorily in care as a result of a care order (see Chapter 11). The third system is the education one, under which children are assessed for special educational needs. Once identified as having a 'learning difficulty' special educational provision should be made available (see Chapter 12). The fourth system is the psychiatric system. A child entering this system is likely to be referred to as 'mentally ill'.

Each of the four systems has its own distinct philosophy, legal framework and terminology. This means that each is governed by different legislation and different legal principles. As a consequence the way children are treated can vary significantly as can their legal status. However, all four systems can lead to children being removed from home and two of them, namely the child care and psychiatric systems, can involve non-consensual medical and psychiatric examinations and treatment. Note too that some children, especially young offenders (responsibility for whom lies with the Home Office), are denied many of the legal rights and protections which children in the child care system (controlled by the Department of Health) enjoy. None the less in practice there is considerable overlap between the various systems as a high proportion of children typically move from one to another – one recent study showed how as many as 73% had contact with more than one agency. While this process, called 'system spillage', is often necessary given that many children will require the services of more than one agency, it is not uncommon for the agency currently caring for a child to be unaware of the interventions of other agencies. It is also not uncommon for provision to be determined by the availability of resources rather than a child's needs as cutbacks and budgetary considerations in the system most suited to the child might result in his or her admission to another one simply because it has more resources.

This chapter will focus on children in the fourth system whose care and treatment is governed largely by the Mental Health Act 1983. Note that the Mental Health (Patients in the Community) Act 1995 has introduced a new power of supervised aftercare but this is unlikely to be used very often, if at all, in respect of children. First, two cases will be outlined which highlight how the law can treat 'disturbed' children.

The first case is Re R [1991]. It concerned a young woman of 15½ who had a long history of family problems and a disturbed childhood. Eventually she was taken into care but her mental health deteriorated and she suffered visual and auditory hallucinations. She absconded from a children's home and was found by police on a bridge threatening suicide. After a particularly violent incident when she 'ran amok' at her home, seriously damaging the building and furniture, attacking her father and assaulting her mother she was thought ill enough to justify an application for compulsory admission to hospital under s.2 of the Mental Health Act 1983. Initially placed in a psychiatric ward she was soon transferred to an adolescent unit but her condition deteriorated and permission was sought from the local authority (who had parental responsibility under the care order) to give her anti-psychotic medication. R refused the medication and because of doubts as to her legal capacity court proceedings were taken to determine whether she could be forced to accept treatment – even though by then it was clear she was no longer 'sectionable' as her mental health had improved (although she still needed treatment). When R refused medication she was lucid and rational and thus had sufficient understanding to make her own decision. In other words she had 'clear intervals' when her mental illness was in recession during which she was arguably 'Gillick competent'. But this state was neither permanent nor long-term and without medication the prognosis was that she would return to her earlier 'florid psychotic state' which would justify sectioning her again under the Mental Health Act 1983.

In a controversial judgement – influenced most probably by the unit's refusal to keep R unless it was given authority to use appropriate medication to control her – the Court of Appeal decided that despite R's rational periods during which she was undoubtedly able to make her own medical decisions she was not 'Gillick competent'. This was because Gillick competency required full understanding on a lasting basis and so no child who was 'only capable on a good day' could pass the Gillick test. As a result R could be forced to take medication against her will since to do so was in her best interests.

The second case was R v Kirklees Metropolitan BC ex parte C [1993]. It concerned a 12-year-old girl who had been taken into care following several burglary offences. Placed in an assessment centre she became violent and disruptive and was later assessed as a suicide risk – on a number of occasions she had cut herself with bits of broken glass and had threatened to jump out of the window. As C's self-destructive behaviour deteriorated the local authority gave their consent for her to be assessed – for which she had to be admitted. C absconded and claimed that as she had not been compulsorily admitted under the Mental Health Act 1983 her informal admission by the local authority against her will was unlawful. But the Court of Appeal decided otherwise on the following grounds. First, she was not 'Gillick competent' (and even if she had been her refusal to be admitted could have been overridden by the local authority). Secondly, her admission to an open ward in the hospital as an informal patient for assessment with the consent of the local authority (who had parental responsibility), was lawful at common law because it was in her best interests. This was so even though the Mental Health Act 1983 did not apply.

The decision in Re C is perhaps unremarkable given that it is now well established that in the case of minors (whether competent or otherwise) treatment which is in their best interests can be authorized by a court or anyone with parental responsibility. However, in some respects the outcome is disturbing in that it was conceded early on in the proceedings that C was not suffering from a mental disorder and did not require treatment (unlike R). How was it then that without any formal legal proceedings C could be compulsorily deprived of her liberty and confined to a psychiatric hospital? While the legal justification for treating her without her consent lies in the concept of best interests, it is at least arguable that compulsory hospitalization, especially at so young an age – which could well result in the stigma of mental disorder – was almost certainly not. Note however that the case was decided before the Children Act 1989 came into force. Accordingly if a similar situation arose now a secure accommodation order would have to be made under that Act.

MENTAL HEALTH ACT 1983

The above two cases highlight how young people with behavioural problems – albeit not 'Gillick competent' – can be treated and admitted into hospital against their will. Approximately 7000 young people are admitted each year for mental health treatment and the latest figures reveal that an increasing number are under 10. About one in ten are compulsorily admitted while the rest are admitted on a voluntary basis. Before looking at the respective rights of compulsory and voluntary patients, however, various terms used in the Mental Health Act 1983 (the Act) need to be defined.

The Act covers the reception, care and treatment of the mentally disordered as well as the management of their property. It is based on several fundamental principles which aim overall to protect the welfare and rights of patients and to reduce the risks they pose to themselves and others. The Act also is designed to ensure that whenever possible admission to hospital should be on an informal basis. The central concept in the Act is 'mental disorder' which is defined as mental illness, arrested or incomplete development of mind, psychopathic disorder and any other disorder or disability of mind. Oddly perhaps the term 'mental illness' is not further defined despite being the most important category of mental disorder. This inevitably means that its diagnosis is left entirely to psychiatrists but once diagnosed mental illness is sufficient on its own to warrant detention under the Act (unlike other cases where evidence of other abnormal conduct must be present). The Act defines other terms as follows:

- **'severe mental impairment'** means a state of arrested or incomplete development of mind which includes severe impairment of intelligence and social functioning and is associated with abnormally aggressive or seriously irresponsible conduct;
- **'mental impairment'** means a state of arrested or incomplete development of mind (not amounting to severe mental impairment) which includes significant impairment of intelligence and social functioning and is associated with abnormally aggressive or seriously irresponsible conduct;
- **'psychopathic disorder'** means a persistent disorder or disability of mind (whether or not including significant impairment of intelligence) which results in abnormally aggressive or seriously irresponsible behaviour.

Although the Act does not define 'any other disorder or disability of mind' it makes it clear that the law does not regard someone as suffering from any form of mental disorder simply because of 'promiscuity or other immoral conduct, sexual deviancy or dependence on alcohol or drugs'. Nor is the term 'abnormally aggressive or seriously irresponsible behaviour' defined although some guidance on how this should be interpreted is given in the Code of Practice (Code) which states that behaviour is 'abnormally aggressive' when it is outside the usual range of aggressive behaviour and causes actual damage and/or real distress occurring recently or persistently or with excessive severity. Similarly conduct is irresponsible when it shows a disregard of the consequences of action taken and where the result causes actual damage or real distress, either recently or persistently or with excessive severity (para. 29.5).

The Code, which was revised in 1993, makes recommendations and sometimes stipulations for 'good practice'. It does not impose additional statutory duties nor is there any legal duty to comply with it. Nevertheless failure to do so 'could be referred to in evidence in legal proceedings' under the Act.

Another central concept is 'medical treatment' which 'includes nursing care habilitation and rehabilitation under medical supervision'. According to the Code this covers the broad range of activities aimed at alleviating or preventing a deterioration of the patient's mental disorder. It therefore includes physical treatment such as ECT, and the administration of drugs and psychotherapy.

APPLICATION TO CHILDREN AND YOUNG PEOPLE

There is no minimum age limit for admission to hospital under the Act. However, the Code includes a special section on children and young people (see para. 30) in which it gives guidance on several issues of particular importance to those under 18. It states that practice for this age group should be guided by a number of principles, namely:

- young people should be kept as fully informed as possible about their care and treatment; their views and wishes must always be taken into account;
- unless specifically overridden by statute those with 'sufficient understanding and intelligence' should generally be regarded as having the right to make their own decisions;
- any intervention in the life of a young person should be the least restrictive possible and result in the least possible segregation from family, friends, community and school;
- all those in hospital should receive appropriate education.

In addition the Code stipulates that the following questions be asked whenever the care and treatment of somebody under the age of 16 is being considered:

- which persons or bodies have parental responsibility for the child? It is essential that those responsible for the child or young person's care always request copies of any court orders for reference on the hospital ward in relation to examination, assessment or treatment;
- if the child is living with either of the parents who are separated, whether there is a residence order, and if so in whose favour;
- what is the capacity of the child to make his own decisions in terms of emotional maturity, intellectual capacity and psychological state?
- where a parent refuses consent to treatment, how sound are the reasons and on what grounds are they made?
- could the needs of the young person be met in a social services or educational placement?
- how viable would be treatment of any under-16-year-old living at home if there was no parental consent and no statutory orders?

Note finally how the Code also emphasizes how it is the responsibility of all professionals and the relevant health authorities and NHS Trusts to ensure that there is sufficient guidance available to those responsible for the care of children and young people.

INFORMAL ADMISSION

Admission on an informal basis accounts for the vast majority – over 90% – of children and young people admitted to hospital who require treatment for mental disorder. This so-called 'voluntary' admission is governed by s.131 of the Act which encourages admission without any legal formality, similar in other words to the way in which patients enter hospital for physical disorders.

Not surprisingly the legal status of informal patients is very different from those detained compulsorily. Overall they have greater legal rights to do as they please, which means that in principle they can:

- go (and come) as they please, i.e. leave when they want to; and
- reject (or consent to) any form of treatment (psychiatric or otherwise), providing they are competent.

Yet despite their voluntary status informal patients are accorded few of the legal safeguards given automatically to compulsory patients; in particular they have no access to the Mental Health Review Tribunal nor are they within the jurisdiction of the Mental Health Act Commission. They do, however, have unrestricted access to the courts. Their legal entitlement to information is also minimal. In some ways, therefore, voluntary patients are significantly worse off than compulsory patients; especially, as is frequently the case with children, admission is not their own independent decision but that of their parents or some other person with parental responsibility (or a court). In addition children, whether competent or otherwise, have no absolute right to refuse medical or psychiatric treatment. In other words their wishes can be overridden.

CHILDREN AND VOLUNTARY ADMISSION

16- and 17-year-olds

The Act states (s. 131(2)) that minors of 16 or over who are capable of expressing their own wishes can admit themselves to hospital. This statutory right means that 16- and 17-year-olds can make their own decisions about informal admission irrespective of their parents' wishes (or of anyone else with parental responsibility). But once in hospital what rights do they have to determine treatment? What happens, for example, if they refuse to take medication? It now appears (see Re W [1992] Chapter 3) that the wishes of competent 16- and 17-year-olds are not conclusive. As such their informed refusal arguably to admission and certainly to treatment can be overridden either by anyone with parental responsibility or a court. Likewise incompetent 16- and 17-year-olds can be admitted and treated on the basis of parental or court authority.

Children under 16

As s. 131(2) does not cover this age group admission is governed by the common law. This means that a court or anyone with parental responsibility, e.g. a parent or local authority if the child is subject to a care order, could admit a child under 16. If the child is 'Gillick competent', however, then his or her decision both as to admission and treatment should be respected even if those with parental responsibility object. Should this happen, however, the Code recommends (para. 30.5) that the parents' views should be accorded 'serious consideration and given due weight'. It should be remembered that recourse to law to stop such admission could be sought. Note too that case law (notably Re R [1991]) has now established that the rights of competent under-16-year-olds (likewise, of course, incompetent ones) to refuse admission and treatment can be overridden by those with parental responsibility or a court.

RIGHTS OF INFORMAL PATIENTS

TO LEAVE HOSPITAL

In principle informal patients can discharge themselves (even against medical advice) at any time just like any other hospital patients.

However, their freedom to leave is qualified by the so-called 'holding powers'. In addition minors can also be prevented from leaving by virtue of secure accommodation orders under the Children Act 1989 (see page 205).

Doctor's holding power

s. 5(2) allows a patient to be detained for up to 72 hours if the doctor in charge (or his or her nominated deputy) reports to the hospital managers that an application ought to be made for compulsory admission. The nature of this power and the procedures which should be followed are spelt out in the Act and Code but basically it gives time for the patient to be assessed so that a decision can be made about compulsory measures, e.g. under s.2 or 3. In other words it can be used to stop a patient leaving before compulsory detention can be initiated.

Nurse's holding power

Nurses qualified in mental disorder have similar, albeit shorter, holding powers of up to six hours (under s.5(4)) in respect of in-patients who are receiving treatment for a mental disorder and who (a) are suffering from mental disorder to such a degree that it is necessary for their health or safety or for the protection of others for them to be immediately restrained from leaving the hospital and (b) it is not practicable to get a doctor to make a s.5(2) order. Important aspects of the nurses' holding power are that it can only be exercised in relation to patients who are being treated for a mental disorder and only if the doctor in charge is not available. Other guidance is provided in the Code which among other things stresses the emergency nature of the power, what the nurse should be assessing and what procedures should be followed, i.e. written requirements which must be complied with. It also stresses how the decision to detain patients is a personal one based on the nurse's own professional judgement. Should it be necessary to extend detention this can be done once the patient's doctor arrives and submits a report under s.5(2).

Secure accommodation order

According to the Children Act 1989 'secure accommodation' is 'accommodation provided for the purpose of restricting liberty'. This is generally interpreted as any practice or measure which prevents a child from leaving a room or building of his or her own free will. The definition would therefore clearly include locked wards in a mental hospital or locking a child in a room or a behaviour modification unit in a hospital. Whether other practices, such as restricting a child's movements by creating a human barrier, would be included is uncertain.

The criteria for restricting liberty are contained in s.25 of the Children Act 1989 which now applies to children accommodated by health authorities (including National Health Service Trusts) private health facilities and local education authorities, residential care homes, nursing homes and mental nursing homes. The Act does not, however, apply to children detained under the Mental Health Act unless they are on trial leave nor those detained under s.53 of the Children and Young Person's Act 1963 (which deals with the punishment of certain grave crimes). Note too that children accommodated under the following provisions cannot have their liberty restricted in any circumstances, namely (a) if they are over 16 and accommodated under s. 20(5) of the Children Act 1989 or (b) if they are any age but in respect of whom a child assessment order (under s.43) has been made and who are kept away from home pursuant to that order.

Local authorities have a duty under the Children Act 1989 to take reasonable steps to avoid the need for children to be placed in secure accommodation. Furthermore the Act states that children must not be placed or kept in secure accommodation unless it appears: (a) that (i) they have a history of absconding and are likely to abscond from any other description of accommodation; and (ii) if they do abscond they are likely to suffer significant harm; or (b) that if they are kept in any other description of accommodation they are likely to injure themselves or other persons. Without a court order children cannot be kept in secure accommodation for longer than 72 hours in any 28-day period. Detention beyond that requires a court order.

Secure accommodation is expected to be used sparingly which is why DoH Guidance and Regulations (1991) issued under the Children Act states that

> restricting liberty is a serious step which must be taken only when there is no genuine alternative which would be appropriate. It must be a 'last resort' in the sense that all else must first have been comprehensively considered and rejected – never because no other placement was available at the relevant time, because of inadequacies of staffing, because the child is simply being a nuisance or runs away from his accommodation and is not likely to suffer significant harm in doing so and never as a form of punishment.

Finally it is worth noting that the advice given in the Code (para 18.27) as to the use of combination locks and double-handled doors in relation to informal patients is debatable in that if there is no legal justification for such action it arguably amounts to false imprisonment (unless the Provisions of the Children Act have been complied with).

Case study 10.1

Carolyn is 16-years-old and was admitted to an adolescent unit a week ago following several months of substance abuse and other self-destructive behaviour. Over the last few days she has become increasingly violent and aggressive and on several occasions has assaulted staff and other patients. Yesterday she threatened to use a knife and was only stopped by being physically restrained. She has also refused to take her medication without which she is soon likely to become psychotic. Carolyn claims that it is unlawful to use physical force to restrain her.

Is she right?

The management of violent and aggressive patients (both informal and detained) is a controversial one, not least because of the questionable legality of certain 'management' practices. Extensive guidance is given in the Code (para. 18) about how to control patients 'presenting particular management problems'. These include physical restraint, medication and seclusion. In Carolyn's case the Code's recommendations appear to have been complied with – assuming that physical force was used only as a last resort and in an emergency, i.e. when there is a 'real possibility that significant harm would otherwise occur'. Note also that other non-physical attempts should initially be made and only if these have failed should physical restraint be used. This must however be 'reasonable in the circumstances and should never include either tying or hooking a patient (whether by means of tape or by using a part of the patient's garments) to some part of a building or to its fixtures and fittings.

Legal authority for restraining patients from doing harm to themselves or others, whether or not they are detained under the Act, is derived from statute and common law although there is considerable overlap between the two. In relation to Carolyn, for example, such force as is reasonably necessary to prevent a crime could be used. Similarly it is lawful to use reasonable force in self-defence or to defend other persons or property. But where physical restraint is used it must not be excessive. In other words it must be the least necessary to deal with the problem. If physical restraint is inappropriate, seclusion and medication may be justified. The Code gives detailed guidance about seclusion (which is not mentioned in the Act). It defines the term as the 'supervised confinement of a patient in a room which may be locked for the protection of others from significant harm.' Secluded patients should, however, be continually checked, kept under observation and their seclusion reviewed every two hours. If seclusion is in a locked room the provisions of the Children Act 1989 will also have to be complied with if the locked room constitutes 'secure accommodation'.

As Carolyn is refusing medication, and given the likelihood of her becoming psychotic, it might be appropriate to consider using the Act's compulsory powers under which it would be possible to treat her without her consent. Alternatively her refusal could be overridden by anyone with parental responsibility or a court (as in Re R [1991]).

RIGHT TO INFORMATION

The Code (but not the Act) stipulates that informal patients should be given as much information as possible about their care and treatment. In particular it should be made clear that they are allowed to leave hospital at any time.

RIGHT TO BE VISITED

Local authorities have a legal duty to arrange visits for child patients who are the subject of care orders and do whatever else would be expected of their parents (s.116).

COMPULSORY ADMISSION

Children are rarely compulsorily detained because there are several alternative ways of ensuring that they receive care and treatment, irrespective of their (or their parents') opposition. For example, under the Children Act 1989 care or supervision orders can be obtained (see Chapter 11). In addition that Act can be used to resolve any dispute about a child's upbringing (medical or otherwise). Furthermore, as was noted in Chapter 3, those with parental responsibility (likewise the courts) have wide powers to make decisions about medical treatment on behalf of children even if they are competent and so can override their wishes whenever it is in their best interests to do so. Nevertheless in some cases compulsory detention – usually referred to as 'sectioning' – is necessary and possible under the following provisions, none of which require a court order:

ADMISSION FOR ASSESSMENT (s.2)

Grounds for admission are: (a) that the patient is suffering from a mental disorder of a nature or degree which warrants the detention of the patient in a hospital for assessment (or assessment followed by treatment) for at least a limited period; and (b) the patient ought to be so detained in the interests of his own health or safety or with a view to the protection of other persons. The application for admission must satisfy several requirements which include (among other things) two 'medical recommendations' – one of them from a doctor with 'special experience in the diagnosis or treatment of mental disorder' (i.e. a 'section 12 doctor'). If practicable too one of them must have previously known the patient. In addition the doctors must have personally examined the patient (either together or separately). If they did so separately then no more than five days must have elapsed between the two examinations.

Who can apply?

The applicant can be either the 'nearest relative' or more commonly an approved social worker (ASW). The nearest relative is very broadly defined (see s.26) but in relation to children it usually is a parent or a local authority (if the child is subject to a care order). The nearest relative can pass his or her powers on to another person and if no-one wants to act the court can appoint someone. The ASW is an appropriately quali-fied social worker. Detailed provisions and guidance about the functions and duties of applicants, written requirements and so forth are contained in both the Act (ss.11–13) and the Code (para 2).

How long can the assessment last?

Up to 28 days although the patient can be discharged before then. Once an application has been made the patient can be taken to hospital which the Code stipulates should be done 'in the most humane and least threatening way, i.e. preferably by ambulance'. Although an assessment order cannot be renewed the patient may remain in hospital after 28 days as an informal patient. Alternatively detention can continue if a s.3 order (see below) is made.

DETENTION FOR TREATMENT (s.3)

Grounds for admission for this relatively long-term order are: (a) that the patient is suffering from mental illness, severe mental impairment, psychopathic disorder or mental impairment and his mental disorder is of a nature or degree which makes it appropriate for him to receive medical treatment in a hospital; and (b) in the case of psychopathic disorder or mental impairment, such treatment is likely to alleviate or prevent a deterioration of his condition; and (c) it is necessary for the health or safety of the patient or for the protection of other persons that he should receive such treatment and it cannot be provided unless he is detained under this section.

Several points need emphasizing here. First, the legal criteria for admission under this section are more stringent than for admission for assessment, in particular mental disorder by itself is insufficient to warrant compulsion as it must also require treatment in hospital. This means that if it could be treated in the community detention is not justified. Secondly, if the disorder is a 'minor' one, such as mental impairment or psychopathic disorder, it must pass the 'treatability test'. In other words treatment must be likely to benefit the patient. The medical recommendations are very similar to those required for s.2 admission although there are additional requirements, in particular reasons must be given for the diagnosis (which the two doctors must agree on).

Who can apply?

Either the nearest relative or an ASW. The application procedures are again identical to s.2 admission for assessment except that the ASW must consult the nearest relative before making an application for admission (unless it is not practicable to do so or would involve unreasonable delay). Furthermore, the nearest relative can prevent the application proceeding if he or she objects. If that happens the ASW can apply to court to displace the nearest relative.

How long can detention last?

Admission for treatment is a long-term provision which can last up to six months although the patient can be discharged before then. If further detention is necessary the initial six-month period can be renewed once for a further six months, and, thereafter for any number of 12-month periods. In other words detention can in practice last indefinitely, although each time the detention period is extended the criteria – albeit slightly modified – which justified the original detention must continue to be met.

When should s.2 rather than s.3 be used?

Because sometimes it may be difficult to determine whether a s.2 or s.3 admission is the most appropriate the Code (para. 5) provides several 'pointers'. Those supporting a s.2 (and particularly relevant to young people) include cases where the diagnosis and prognosis are unclear; where an in-patient assessment is necessary so that a treatment plan can be made; where the patient has not previously been admitted to hospital either compulsorily or informally. It also stresses how the choice of section should not be influenced by wanting to avoid consulting the nearest relative, who in relation to child patients is usually a parent.

EMERGENCY ADMISSION (s.4)

Emergency admission is the most controversial 'section' because the medical recommendations are much less stringent. Basically it is a 'short-cut' variant of ordinary admission for assessment to which it can later be converted. Grounds for admission are that there is urgent necessity for the patient to be admitted and detained under s.2 but complying with that section would 'involve undesirable delay'. The legal criteria are therefore the same as in s.2 admission for assessment but with the added criterion of 'urgent necessity'. Because of the urgency of the application there only needs to be one supporting recommendation given (if practicable) by a doctor with previous knowledge of the patient. Secondly, the doctor need not be a specialist in mental illness.

Who can apply?

As with all other applications either the 'nearest relative' or an ASW.

How long can detention last?

Up to 72 hours but it is possible to convert the emergency admission into a 28-day ordinary admission for assessment under s.2 by forwarding a second medical recommendation to the hospital managers. If the patient still needs to be detained after that (i.e. after 28 days from when he or she was first admitted) then providing the criteria for long-term detention for treatment are met (under s.3) the patient can be detained indefinitely.

When should emergency admission be used?

Emergency admissions should only be used in genuine emergencies when as the Code says (para 6.3), 'those involved cannot cope with the mental state or behaviour of the patient'. Hence there should be evidence of: the existence of a significant risk of mental or physical harm to the patient or to others; and/or danger of serious harm to property; and/or the need for physical restraint of the patient.

RIGHTS OF DETAINED PATIENTS

These include the following:

TO LEAVE HOSPITAL

Detained patients have the right to leave hospital as soon as the detention period has expired – assuming of course that it has not been replaced or renewed. However, the courts have said that they can and should be discharged before then if they are no longer suffering from a mental disorder. Otherwise a patient (detained under s.2 or 3) can leave hospital following a successful discharge application which in the case of children will normally be made by a parent (among others). But no patient will be discharged if he or she is certified as being a danger to himself, herself or others. Another way of leaving hospital is to apply to a Mental Health Review Tribunal (see page 212) which has the power and in some cases the duty to order a discharge.

If patients leave hospital without permission (called absence without leave) they can, depending on how long they remain absent, be taken into custody and returned to the hospital. In some cases, though absence can be authorized – short trial periods back in the community might be necessary for example, before a patient is finally discharged. Patients out on leave can be recalled. Other aspects of leave are well covered in the Code (para, 20) and the Act (s.17) which among other things gives detailed guidance about when leave should be granted and revoked.

TO BE VISITED

Child patients who are the subject of care orders must have visits arranged for them by the local authority who must also 'take such other steps as would be expected of a parent' (s.116).

TO INFORMATION

The Act (s.132) imposes a clear legal duty on hospital managers to 'take such steps as are practicable' to ensure that detained patients understand their legal position. Statutory information which must be provided includes: under what provisions they are detained and the effect of them; what rights patients have to apply to a Mental Health Tribunal; the Act's discharge provisions and those about compulsory medical treatment; the effect of the Code of Practice; and the powers of the Mental Health Act Commission.

The above information must be given both orally and in writing as soon as practicable after the detention has begun – leaflets published by the Department of Health are now widely available. There is also a statutory duty to give a detained patient's nearest relative seven days' notice of his or her discharge unless the patient or the relative objects. Note too that the Code emphasizes how duties in relation to information apply with equal force to patients under 18 and that in particular assistance should be given to enable their legal representation at any Mental Health Review Tribunal (para 30.10).

ACCESS TO THE MENTAL HEALTH REVIEW TRIBUNAL

MHRTs are independent bodies whose basic function is to safeguard the rights of compulsorily detained patients and make sure that their detention is regularly reviewed. Normally discharge applications will be made by patients themselves but they can also be made by the nearest relative. However, some patients never apply to a tribunal, which is why there is also a system of automatic review designed to prevent patients getting lost in the system. Accordingly child patients who have not applied to a tribunal within the first six months of their detention must be automatically referred as must those under 16 who after that time have not had a tribunal hearing within the previous year. Basically the role of MHRTs is to decide whether a patient should continue to be detained. They have several powers and duties including directing that patients be discharged (either immediately or in the future date) and recommending that a patient be granted leave of absence or be transferred to another hospital or into guardianship.

ACCESS TO MENTAL HEALTH ACT COMMISSION

The MHAC has several protective and supervisory functions which include reviewing treatment (under ss. 57 and 58) appointing doctors and others to carry out certain procedures under the compulsory treatment provisions in Part IV of the Act and monitoring how the Act's powers and discharge duties are exercised. Important too – increasingly so given the rise in referrals – is its duty to investigate complaints by detained patients about e.g. something which occurred while they were detained.

TO SERVICES

Certain patients, most notably those detained for treatment or following criminal proceedings, have a legal right to 'after-care' when they leave hospital. The Act (s. 117) requires district health authorities and social services departments to provide after-care until they are satisfied that such services are no longer needed. In addition a child patient may qualify as a child in need under the Children Act 1989 and thus qualify for services under that Act (see Chapter 11).

TO CONSENT OR REJECT TREATMENT

Part IV of the Act contains several provisions which authorize compulsory medical treatment. They apply irrespective of the patient's age to most detained patients (i.e. those detained under s.2 and 3 (but not under emergency s.4 admission or the s.5 'holding powers'). Some of the provisions, notably s.57 also apply to informal patients. Part IV only covers medical treatment – defined in the Act as including 'nursing, care habilitation and rehabilitation under medical supervision' for the patients' mental disorder. This means that treatment for physical disorders is governed by the common law.

There are four categories of compulsory treatment, namely:

1. Psychosurgery, i.e. any surgery which destroys brain tissue or functioning; and surgical implants to reduce sex drive.

These treatments are the most drastic and intrusive and are governed by s.57 and apply to almost all detained patients as well as informal patients. They can only be carried out with the patient's consent which must be verified by three independent people.

2. Electroconvulsive therapy (ECT) and long-term drug treatment, i.e. lasting longer than three months.

ECT is a controversial treatment which has long been the subject of debate although it is rarely given to children – a report in 1994 revealed that it had been used on 60 child patients in the previous decade. Long-term medication which includes both major and minor tranquillizers and anti-depressants is much more commonly used and can be given to detained patients (as can ECT) only if the several conditions are complied with.

These are contained in s.58 but they only apply to drug treatments if they are administered after three months has elapsed since the medication was first administered. Any medication given before then (i.e. for an initial period of three months) can be given without consent under s.63, see below.

The conditions are:

(a) that the patient consents (his or her consent has to be verified in writing by the patient's doctor or a second-opinion doctor (SOAD)); or

(b) a SOAD certifies in writing that the treatment is necessary notwithstanding that the patient either lacks capacity or is unwilling to give consent.

Note that consent once given can be withdrawn at any time, in which case a fresh consent must be obtained. There is also detailed guidance in the Code about capacity (likewise procedures for reviewing consent). If consent is not forthcoming or the patient is incompetent the SOAD procedures will have to be invoked which involve consultation with two people who have been professionally involved with the patient – one of whom must be a nurse.

3. All other forms of medical treatment (including medication) for the patient's mental disorder are governed by s.63.

This section allows treatment (apart from that covered by sections 57 and 58) to be given without consent under the direction of the patient's responsible medical officer, i.e. the practitioner in charge of the patient's treatment. It covers a wide range of therapeutic activities including in particular psychological and social therapies. And even though consent is not a legal requirement the Code (para. 16.16) stipulates that it should be sought, especially as many treatments could not be effectively carried out without the patient's acceptance and co-operation.

4. Urgent treatment is governed by s.62.

In certain circumstances this section allows ECT and long-term drug treatment (likewise psychosurgery and hormone implantation) to be given without the need to comply with the legal safeguards of ss 57 and 58. Neither are likely to be used in respect of child patients except perhaps if they are catatonic and might otherwise die.

Case study 10.2

Moira is 17 and suffering from anorexia nervosa. She has been sectioned under s.2 of the Act. Recently her consultant, Ayeesha, has become very concerned about her weight loss which is so extreme as to be life-threatening. Moira has refused all food for a week. Ayeesha thinks that Moira is competent and so does under-stand the nature of the treatment, its principle benefits and risks and consequences. But her assessment of Moira's capacity is challenged by Catherine, a nurse who has been 'professionally concerned' with Moira since she was first detained. Catherine contends that it is at least arguable that Moira is incompetent given that she refuses to accept that she is losing weight or that her life is in danger.

Ayeesha wants to know (a) whether force-feeding constitutes medical treatment for the patient's mental disorder under the Act and so can be given without Moira's consent and (b) if it would be lawful either to spoon feed her under restraint or failing that to sedate her and use a nasogastric tube?

Both these issues were raised in Riverside Mental Health Trust v. Fox [1994] where the Court of Appeal decided: first, that mental disorder as defined in the Act was wide enough to include anorexia nervosa, especially as it is now widely recognized by the medical profession (and the Mental Health Act Commission) as a 'mental illness'. Secondly, s.63 allowed treatment to be given for the patient's mental disorder irrespective of the patient's consent. As such force feeding (whether by spoon or nasogastric tube) could be given to an anorexic patient (competent or otherwise) without consent, since it was treatment for the mental disorder (rather than simply a procedure designed to keep the patient alive so that treatment can be carried out – in which case it would not be treatment for the mental disorder). This interpretation of force-feeding as treatment for anorexia – which accepts that relieving symptoms is just as much part of treatment as relieving the underlying cause – is controversial yet is one which is supported both by the courts (see also South West Hertfordshire HA v. Brady (1994) and the Mental Health Act Commission). The latter has stated that 'treatment of anorexia nervosa necessary for the health and safety of the patient including involuntary feeding and maintenance of hydration is permissible in patients whose anorexia is causing serious harm'.

There is now, therefore, clear legal authority that anorexic patients (competent or otherwise) can be comprehensively treated under the Act.

Accordingly Moira can be force-fed under s.63.

As Moira is a minor, however, it would be possible under the common law to feed her, despite her refusal relying on either the consent of someone with parental responsibility or the court (as in Re W (1992) see Chapter 3). It would thus not be necessary to invoke the Mental Health Act 1983 at all as she could be treated against her will, providing of course treatment was in her best interests.

Case study 10.3
Barry is 17½ and suffers from a psychopathic disorder. Following a fatal car accident in which his parents and brother were killed he is also suffering from post-traumatic stress disorder. Recently he has become very depressed and has cut himself deliberately several times – on the last occasion he needed several stitches. He has now been compulsorily detained under s.3 of the Act and prevented from physically harming himself but has refused all food. His weight has dropped so much that his life expectancy is at most two months.

His consultant wants to know whether he can be force-fed by tube.

This case study is similar to the one above (even though it does not concern an anorexic patient) that is whether force-feeding treats just a symptom (i.e. starvation) of the underlying psychopathic disorder rather than the disorder itself. In other words it could be argued that treating starvation does not treat the patient's mental illness and so is not treatment for mental disorder under the Act. The courts have, however, as with anorexic patients, rejected this fine distinction between procedures aimed at treating the disorder itself and those designed to treat its symptoms. In short they have decided that a broad view should be taken so that treatment for mental disorder includes treatment for its consequences. What this means in practice is that some detained patients who have capacity to refuse feeding can nevertheless be treated against their will for extreme conditions (i.e. extreme weight loss) if the physical condition is a consequence of their mental disorder. As such, and following the decision by the Court of Appeal in B v. Croydon HA [1995], Barry could be force-fed without his consent under s.63 of the Act.

OTHER TREATMENT

If detained child patients require treatment for a physical disorder which is unrelated to their mental disorder, for example, an appendectomy, Part IV of the Mental Health Act does not appear to apply – although some commentators claim that s.62 could apply in such cases. In other words the term 'any treatment' in s.62 can cover not just treatment for a mental disorder but also treatment for physical disorders if the treatment is necessary to save life. But this interpretation of s.62 is controversial and by no means universally accepted. The usual assumption therefore is that the common law applies (or the Family Law Reform Act 1969 in respect of 16- and 17-year-olds). Accordingly minors who require treatment for physical disorders must give their consent (if competent). Otherwise consent must be given on their behalf except of course in emergencies when non-consensual treatment can be given (see Chapter 3). Note, however that even if competent a minor's refusal to be treated can be overridden (see e.g. Re W [1992] and Re R [1991]). Note too that patients admitted under the emergency section 4 procedure and under the s.5 'holding powers' are not covered by Part IV of the Act. As a consequence their treatment too is governed by the common law.

Finally it is worth noting that although the Law Commission has recently considered the position of mentally incapacitated adults its recommendations which if implemented, would significantly affect the rights of incompetent adult patients, do not apply to minors.

OTHER POWERS UNDER THE ACT

In this final section some of the other compulsory procedures which can be used in respect of children with mental health problems will be briefly outlined.

GUARDIANSHIP (s.7)

This little used procedure is available only for over 16-year-olds. It is appropriate where compulsory powers are necessary, albeit limited ones, in that it aims to ensure that patients can receive care in the community but nevertheless be subject to some control and supervision. Grounds for an order are (a) that the patient is suffering from mental disorder, and it is of a nature and degree which warrants reception into guardianship, and (b) it is necessary in the interests of the welfare of the patient or for the protection of others that she or he be so received. Guardianship can last initially for six months but is renewable. Guardianship patients have access to Mental Health Review Tribunals.

EMERGENCY POLICE POWERS (ss. 135 AND 136)

s.136 enables the police to remove to a place of safety – widely defined in the Act but in practice normally a hospital or mental nursing home – anyone they find in a public place who 'appears to be suffering from mental disorder and to be in immediate need of care and control'. The police can only act, however, if it is necessary 'in the interests of that person or for the protection of other persons'. Detention can last up to 72 hours.

s.135 allows the police to enter premises, by force if necessary, and take a person to a place of safety. It enables them to deal with a crisis involving a mentally disordered person to whom they cannot otherwise gain access. It could be useful, for example, where a minor is threatening suicide but will not let anyone in. Removal is by warrant which magistrates can only grant if there is reasonable cause to suspect that a person believed to be suffering from a mental disorder; (a) has been, or is being, ill-treated, neglected or kept otherwise than under proper control or (b) is living alone and unable to care for himself or herself. This section again only allows detention for up to 72 hours.

It is also worth noting here that under the Police and Criminal Evidence Act 1984 (s.17) the police have the power to enter premises without a warrant to recapture a person unlawfully at large (a term which would include an absconding compulsory patient), or to save life or limb or prevent serious damage to property.

CRIMINAL COURTS AND DETENTION UNDER PART 111

Under s.37 the criminal courts can impose a hospital order, which authorizes admission and detention in hospital. s.37 covers all criminal imprisonable offences other than murder and has a similar effect to s.3 (see above). s.41 allows restriction orders to be added to hospital orders on juvenile offenders aged 14 or over but these can only be imposed if they are 'necessary for the protection of the public'.

FURTHER READING

Ayotte, W. and Harbour, A. (1994) *Mental Health Handbook*, Children's Legal Centre, London.

Cavadino, M. (1989) *Mental Health Law in Context: Doctor's Orders?* Dartmouth, Aldershot.

Department of Health (1993) *Code of Practice: Mental Health Act 1983*, HMSO, London.

Gostin, L.O. (1986) *Mental Health Services: Law and Practice*, Shaw & Sons, London.

Hoggett, B.M. (1990) *Mental Health Law*, 3rd edn, Sweet & Maxwell, London.

Jones, R . (1994) *Mental Health Act Manual*, 4th edn, Sweet & Maxwell, London.

Law Commission, No 231 (1995) *Mentally Incapacity*, HMSO, London.

Malek Mhemooda (1993) *Passing the Buck*, The Children's Society, London.

Child protection 11

When the Children Act 1989 (the Act) came into force in 1991 it was described as 'the most comprehensive and far reaching reform in living memory which would bring about a new beginning to the philosophy and practices of the child care system'. Yet despite this description and the Act's claim to strike a 'new' balance between the role of the state, the rights of children and the responsibilities of parents almost the whole Act was built upon and reinforced principles established in earlier legislation, namely the Children Act 1948 and the Children and Young Person's Act 1963. That said, however, few areas of existing child care law remained untouched by the Act and 10 volumes of accompanying official guidance. For health professionals, however, the Act's main impact is in relation to child protection work. Nevertheless several of its fundamental principles extend its impact well beyond that. For example, enhancing children's legal status and the relevance of their wishes, most notably by endorsing the concept of 'Gillick competence', has influenced the law of consent and significantly increased children's input into health care decisions (see Chapter 3). Redefining parental power in terms of parental responsibility has also had an effect on medical decision-making – primarily by making it easier to acquire and share legal responsibility for children. Consequently people other than parents may have the right to give (or refuse) consent to treatment on behalf of incompetent children and in some circumstances to override the wishes of competent ones too.

Other areas of the Act which are most likely to involve health professionals are those concerning welfare services for children 'in need' and the so-called 'private law' orders which can be used to regulate health care. To begin with, however, the legislation's underlying principles need to be outlined as they represent the Act's philosophy and the practices it is intended to promote.

GENERAL PRINCIPLES

THE CHILD'S WELFARE IS PARAMOUNT

The welfare (or paramountcy) principle emphasizes how children come first and their welfare (commonly referred to as their 'best interests') must be the paramount consideration whenever a court makes a decision about their upbringing. Yet despite the welfare concept being a central feature of the Act there is no statutory definition of its scope or nature other than the so-called 'welfare checklist' which the Act introduces. This is a list of factors a court must consider in most contested proceedings brought under the Act. It is intended to provide greater clarity and consistency and a more systematic approach to decision-making even though the factors specified are not in fact new since (with one exception) they repeat concerns which were considered important prior to the Act.

The factors are:

- the ascertainable wishes and feelings of the child concerned (considered in the light of his age and understanding);
- his physical, emotional and educational needs;
- the likely effect of any change in his circumstances;
- his age, sex, background and any characteristics which the court think relevant;
- any harm the child has suffered or is at risk of suffering;
- how capable each of his parents (or any other person in relation to whom the court considers the question to be relevant) is of meeting his needs;
- the range of powers available to the court under the Act in the proceedings in question.

PREVENTION RATHER THAN INTERVENTION AND THE PRIMACY OF THE FAMILY

One of the Act's most pervasive themes is the belief that children are best cared for by their families. It is most forcibly expressed in the 'non-intervention' principle (s.1(5)) which effectively creates a presumption against court action unless it is absolutely necessary and will positively improve the child's welfare. Local authorities are thus expected to use their powers and duties to keep children at home so that even when children are at risk compulsory intervention and their removal from home can be avoided. Other ways of reinforcing and promoting the family's central role and protecting it from unwarranted state interference include the new concept of 'parental responsibility' which emphasises that the responsibility for children belongs to their parents not the state and those provisions which seek to ensure that when children are living away from home their links with their family are maintained. In addition the Act imposes more stringent requirements on local authorities in an attempt to make them more accountable for their actions and to monitor how decisions are made.

PARTNERSHIP AND CO-OPERATION

The word 'partnership' does not appear anywhere in the Act none the less the idea of partnership is given statutory force to the extent that children and families are given greater rights than in the past to be consulted, kept fully informed and to challenge decisions which affect them. The essential principles supporting partnership are spelt out in detail in the Department of Health guidance: *The Challenge of Partnership in Child Protection: Practice Guide.* For the first time, also, specific reference is made in the Act to the need to consider race, culture and language when making decisions about a child's care.

The partnership theme is also intended to apply to how local authority social services departments interact with other departments (e.g. housing and health), the voluntary and independent sector and other relevant agencies. Co-operation and collaboration between authorities and other bodies is again for the first time given statutory force (see in particular ss 27 and 47).

THE CHILD'S VOICE

Perhaps the most important principle of all in the context of both child health and child care law is the Act's new emphasis on the child's voice. There are several provisions which are arguably designed to improve their legal status, recognize their capacity for independent action and acknowledge them as people in their own right rather than 'objects of concern'. These include new and greater rights to instruct lawyers independently, have their views presented to court, initiate court proceedings, be consulted and control certain medical procedures. The extent to which many of these 'rights' have been upheld in practice is of course another matter. The right to refuse medical and psychiatric examinations and assessments, for example, has been overruled (see South Glamorgan CC v. W and B [1992] see page 230) and other rights, notably those which allow children to start proceedings and be present in court, have similarly failed to give many the degree of autonomy they expected.

CHILD PROTECTION

THE ORGANIZATIONAL FRAMEWORK

Although local authorities have the primary statutory responsibility for the investigation and prevention of child abuse and neglect it has long been recognized that protecting children depends on multi-disciplinary teamwork. Joint working arrangements and procedures were therefore developed to provide a framework for inter-agency co-operation. However, in practice, these were often inadequate and inappropriate – almost all the 18 reports into the deaths of children known to (and often in the care of) social services in the 1980s highlighted how the failure of professionals to work together had contributed to their deaths. Developing a more effective framework within which all the relevant agencies could carry out their responsibilities thus became a major priority, especially once the Cleveland controversy erupted in 1987 and again exposed the deficiencies of existing inter-agency mechanisms – this time over the diagnosis and management of sexual abuse. The Cleveland inquiry prompted the publication of new and revised guidance the most important of which was the Department of Health's 1988 document *Working Together under the Children Act: A Guide to Arrangements for Inter-agency Co-operation for the Protection of Children from Abuse*. Revised in 1991 when the Children Act 1989 was implemented this document contains detailed guidance on the role of the health services (Part 4). While not having the force of statute it is expected to be complied with unless exceptional circumstances justify otherwise.

The current framework consists of three principle structures: Area Child Protection Committees; Child Protection Registers and Child Protection Conferences.

AREA CHILD PROTECTION COMMITTEE

The ACPC which comprises senior representatives of all the key agencies has overall responsibility for co-ordinating current practice and developing, monitoring and reviewing child care policy within a particular area. It does not deal with individual cases except when reviewing cases involving a child's death (where abuse is the cause or is suspected). Specific tasks include establishing, maintaining and reviewing guidelines on how cases should be handled, monitoring the implementation of legal procedures, recommending improvements to current systems and procedures and scrutinizing existing inter-agency training.

CHILD PROTECTION REGISTER

The CPR is a central record of all children in the area who are considered to be at risk. The register has no legal force nor does entry on the register mean that a child has been abused. The main purpose of the register is to provide a reference point enabling speedy checks to be made about whether a child is the subject of a protection plan and is therefore already being monitored. There are four registration categories: neglect, physical injury, sexual and emotional abuse.

CHILD PROTECTION CONFERENCE

The CPC or case conference is not a court and does not have any legal powers but it is subject to the rules of natural justice. It provides the formal setting within which professionals can share and evaluate information and agree a particular course of action. As such it is likely to include community-based health services and, if relevant, hospital-based services. Official guidance also strongly recommends that children, their parents and other carers should be encouraged to attend when appropriate and in particular that parents should only exceptionally be excluded, i.e. when there is strong risk of violence towards the child or professionals. There are two types of CPCs – the initial one and the child protection review. The initial conference makes decisions about the level of risk, whether there is a need for registration and what plans should be made for the future. The review conference monitors progress – whether registration is still justified, for example.

THE INVESTIGATIVE PROCESS

Because there is no mandatory reporting law in the UK (unlike most states in the USA) neither local authorities nor anyone else are legally obliged to report suspected cases of abuse and neglect. Nevertheless s.47 of the Act imposes a statutory duty on local authorities to investigate a child's welfare in a number of circumstances. Health professionals are also required by the Act to help with these enquiries as s.47(9) imposes a qualified duty on health authorities to 'provide relevant information and advice' unless to do so 'would be unreasonable in all the circumstances of the case'.

Health professionals are likely to be involved in the following:

RECOGNITION AND REFERRAL

They may be the first to identify or suspect that a child is at risk – in one study, for example, it was found that health service personnel, in particular health visitors, were responsible for referring 53% of children under five to social services.

EXCHANGE INFORMATION

Effective child protection depends on sharing and exchanging information but inevitably this process raises concerns about confidentiality. Guidance on this is provided in 'Working Together' (paras 3.10–11) and several codes (see e.g. UKCC 1987 advisory paper on confidentiality). Further guidance is also provided in the document: *Child Protection: Medical Responsibilities* which is expected to be used in conjunction with 'Working Together'. Overall these all emphasize that children's welfare is paramount. Accordingly knowledge or belief of abuse or neglect is an exceptional circumstance which will usually justify disclosure, albeit in a controlled 'need-to-know' basis.

COURT ORDERS

Of all the reforms introduced by the Children Act those relating to child protection were by far the most radical. New orders were introduced and existing ones were substantially amended. However, the central concept, i.e. the one which was designed to strike the right balance between protecting families from unwarranted state interference and its duty to protect children at risk, is that of 'significant harm'. It applies to all compulsory powers under the Act both short and long-term.

HARM (s.31(9))

Harm means ill-treatment or the impairment of health and development:

- development means physical, intellectual, emotional, social or behavioural development;
- health means physical or mental health;
- ill-treatment includes sexual abuse and forms of ill-treatment which are not physical.

The definition of harm is clearly very wide and so can cover every conceivable type of harm. Furthermore only one type of harm needs to be established. Note too that ill-treatment is sufficient harm in itself whether or not it results in damage to the child's health or development.

SIGNIFICANT (s.31(10))

Where the question of whether harm suffered by a child is significant turns on the child's health or development, his or her health or development shall be compared with that which could reasonably be expected of a similar child.

This section provides the only statutory guidance on what 'significant' means. Basically the 'test' of significance involves comparing the child with a (hypothetical) similar child, i.e. with similar attributes. In other words one of the same sex, age and ethnic origin and any other special characteristics. However, such a comparison (which is only necessary in cases of impairment of health and development) can be problematic. This is because while a child with learning difficulties must clearly be compared with a child with similar learning difficulties and likewise a child who is premature or deaf should be compared with a similar deaf or premature child, it is both contentious and uncertain how far social, environmental and cultural factors should be considered when making comparisons. As to other guidance on the meaning of 'significant' case law has now confirmed that it must generally be given its dictionary definition, i.e. considerable, noteworthy or important. Accordingly it should exclude so-called minor shortcomings in health care or minor deficits in physical, psychological or social development unless cumulatively they are having, or are likely to have, serious or lasting effects upon the child. Ultimately, though, whether the harm is significant is a factual one for the court to decide.

ORDERS AVAILABLE

These can be divided into two main categories. Short-term orders which authorize the child's temporary removal from home and long-term orders which give the local authority much more control over a child"s life.

SHORT-TERM ORDERS

Child assessment order (s.43)

This order (CAO) provides an opportunity to assess a child whose health, development or treatment is causing real concern but who is not thought to be in any immediate danger. It is therefore not designed for emergencies but for dealing with the narrow issue of examination and assessment. As such it is ideal for resolving the classic but not uncommon dilemma faced when informal attempts to see or examine a child have repeatedly failed.

However, in practice, the order has not (as was predicted by many commentators) been popular, largely it seems because social workers are reluctant to use it for fear of making parents even more unco-operative. Before granting the order the court has to be satisfied that the child is at risk. To summarize the relevant provision this means that the applicant must have reasonable cause to suspect that the child is suffering, or is likely (see page 229 for what 'likely' means) to suffer, significant harm but this cannot be established without a court order. Other factors which also have to be considered include the non-intervention and the welfare principle.

The order can only last for seven days but does not have to start immediately. Notice must be given of the application and it can be challenged. Ideally it should not involve the child leaving home but this can be part of the order if necessary since some assessments might require an overnight stay in hospital. Furthermore because the order does not affect existing parental responsibility then (unless the court has given permission) the applicant, i.e. local authority or NSPCC cannot do anything without parental consent. This means that those examining or assessing the child must ensure that they comply with any court directions about the child's assessment – which given the order's short duration is unlikely to go beyond an initial medical and social work assessment.

Action following a CAO will clearly depend on what it reveals about the child's health and development. In some cases voluntary arrangements may be appropriate while in others compulsory measures such as an emergency protection order will be necessary.

Emergency Protection Order (s.44)

Designed for genuine emergencies where immediate short-term protection is necessary, the emergency protection order (EPO) is one of the Act's most draconian compulsory powers. Among other things it not only authorizes the child's removal from home (or prevents his or her removal from a 'safe' place, such as a hospital) for up to eight days but also gives the applicant limited parental responsibility – enough to make short-term decisions such as arranging where the child should live and giving consent to urgent medical examinations or treatment. It can be extended once only for seven days and can be granted without notice. The order can be challenged in certain circumstances after 72 hours. To ensure that it can be effectively enforced, extensive powers can also be included in the order, most notably rights to enter and search premises and to have police and medical assistance (i.e. that of a doctor, nurse or health visitor). Other provisions also typically included relate to what contact a child should be allowed with his or her family and what type of medical and psychiatric examinations and assessments should be carried out.

There are basically two types of situations where an emergency protection order is appropriate, both of which require the court to consider the welfare and non-intervention principles. The first allows any person (usually this will be a social worker but could be a health professional) to cope with an urgent crisis. The court will grant the order if it is satisfied that there is reasonable cause to believe that significant harm is likely if the child is not removed to, or kept in, a safe place. The second type of order can only be granted to social workers or the NSPCC (in the case of the NSPCC slightly different criteria apply) and allows them to continue their investigations when there are urgent concerns about a child to whom access is being 'unreasonably refused'. It can be granted on a lesser standard of proof than the first order – one based on 'suspicion' of significant harm rather than a belief that such harm is likely to occur. Commonly called the 'frustrated access' grounds the intention behind them is to avoid the tragic consequences of not having access to a child. It reflects the recommendations of several child abuse enquiries where the failure to see and examine children and thus detect injuries caused by neglect and ill-treatment led to their deaths.

An EPO will either be followed by further compulsory measures, such as an interim care or supervision order, or it may result in the child returning home (with or without the provision of voluntary services).

POLICE POWERS

Included in this section, despite not requiring a court's permission, are the powers the police have under s.46 to prevent children being removed from a safe place or to remove them to suitable accommodation if they have reasonable cause to believe that they would otherwise be likely to suffer significant harm. These protective powers only last 72 hours and do not involve any transfer of parental responsibility although they are long enough to allow other orders to be sought (such as an EPO). Alongside these powers are those under the Police and Criminal Evidence Act 1984 which authorize the police to enter and search premises without a warrant to 'save life and limb'.

LONG-TERM ORDERS – CARE AND SUPERVISION

Long-term orders, namely care and supervision orders, typically follow the above child protection measures. Though the effects of the two orders are very different, both are based on the same grounds and the same principles apply. The choice of order depends on the amount of intervention which is considered necessary. Care orders give local authorities parental responsibility which they share with those who already have it (usually the child's parents). It therefore gives them considerable control over children, the care of whom they effectively take over, possibly for good. They also normally involve children leaving home even though they often return home on a 'trial' basis before the care order ends. Final (or full) care orders can last until a child is 18 but they may be discharged before then.

Supervision orders are ideal for less serious cases where some – albeit much less – intervention is needed. Their impact is therefore far less drastic. Not only are they much shorter than care orders lasting initially for one year (although they can be extended up to a maximum of three years) but they do not affect parental responsibility nor involve the child's removal from home (except possibly for short periods of time). But they do give a local authority the right to supervise certain aspects of a child's upbringing and care. In addition the court has extensive powers to impose a wide range of health-related requirements authorizing psychiatric and medical examinations and in certain circumstances treatment too (see Schedule 3 paras 4 and 5).

Before a final care or supervision order is made it is not uncommon for interim orders to be granted – usually when the court does not have all the relevant information and so is not in a position to make a final decision. Interim orders can initially be made for eight weeks with extensions of generally up to four weeks.

The grounds for care and supervision orders (which cannot be made in respect of young people over 17 or 16 if married) – the so-called 'threshold criteria' – are contained in s.31. This states that the court can only make an order if it is satisfied (a) that the child concerned is suffering or is likely to suffer significant harm; and (b) that the harm or likelihood of harm is attributable to either (i) the care given (or likely to be given if an order were not made), not being what it would be reasonable to expect a parent to give; or (ii) the child being beyond reasonable control.

A two-stage process is therefore established – the first step requires proof of actual (or future) significant harm, and the second step involves linking it either to lack of reasonable parental care or the child being beyond parental control. Nevertheless even when the threshold criteria are met an order is not automatic as the court must also consider other factors such as the welfare and non-intervention principles.

Some particularly important aspects of the threshold criteria worth noting are as follows.

- The phrase 'likely to suffer' is intended to allow local authorities to take action before any harm has actually occurred. Proceedings based on this 'future' event will typically fall into three categories: first, the parent may be suffering from mental illness or substance abuse; secondly, the child is already accommodated but there is concern as to what would happen if the parent resumed care; thirdly, it is alleged a child (either the one in question or another child in the family) has suffered harm in the past and is likely to do so again. But what does the word 'likely' mean? According to the House of Lords in Re H (1995) it is used 'in the sense of a real possibility; that is a possibility that cannot sensibly be ignored having regard to the nature and gravity of the feared harm'. Furthermore the word 'likely' bears the same meaning elsewhere in the Act, namely ss 43 (CAO) 44 (EPO) 46 (removal by police).

- The time when the threshold criteria must be established is immediately before a local authority started proceedings, not the time of the final hearing. This means that, when several protective measures have been taken with the result that a child is being well cared for, a care order can still be made (even though the child is currently no longer at risk). Any other approach would make it very difficult, if not impossible, for a local authority to prove present harm (see Re M [1994]).
- The approach required for deciding what a reasonable parent would do (or would not do) is both objective because it looks at what a 'reasonable' parent would do and subjective because it considers any special characteristics or needs the child may have. In other words the child has to be looked at in his or her particular environment. So if he or she has complex needs a higher standard of care may be required than would normally be necessary. Note too that even though parents may be doing their best (and harm is unintentional) this of itself does not preclude action being taken if the care being provided falls below a reasonable standard. This means that a child can be taken into care if a parent's mental or physical disabilities expose the child to significant harm.
- When a child is addicted to drugs or is suffering from a medical condition such as anorexia nervosa it may also be possible to satisfy the threshold criteria on the basis that the child is 'beyond parental control'.

COURT DIRECTIONS

MEDICAL AND PSYCHIATRIC EXAMINATIONS AND ASSESSMENTS

The court has wide powers to give such directions (if any) as it considers appropriate about medical, psychiatric or other assessments. Directions can be included in interim care and supervision orders, child assessment orders, emergency protection orders and full supervision orders. Exceptionally too, but only in full supervision orders, directions can be given about medical and psychiatric treatment. Directions can be given either when an order is made or subsequently and they can be varied at any time. In some cases the court will prohibit examinations or assessments altogether. But more typically the court will give detailed directions specifying what the examination or assessment should cover, where and by whom it should be carried out, perhaps even naming the child's usual doctor or other practitioner known to the family.

Consent to carry out the procedures must be obtained from the child if he or she is 'Gillick competent', otherwise it must be sought from any person with parental responsibility. Some orders, notably emergency protection orders, involve a transfer, albeit fairly limited, of parental responsibility to the applicant (usually a local authority) which means it has legal authority to give consent on behalf of the child. However, the Act specifically states that court directions do not override the right of children under 16 (and competent 16- and 17-year-olds) to refuse to submit to them.

It was initially thought that mature minors therefore had an absolute and conclusive statutory right of informed refusal, especially since the Act only has a very limited remit (i.e. with the exception of full supervision orders the right to say no only applies to medical and psychiatric examinations and assessments). Nevertheless in the controversial case of South Glamorgan County Council v. W and B [1993], the High Court, using its inherent jurisdiction, overrode the informed refusal of a severely depressed 15-year-old who had barricaded herself in her father's front room for 11 months. She hardly had any contact with the outside world and her contact with her family was largely confined to abusing them and giving them orders which she insisted they obeyed (if they did not obey she threatened to harm herself or commit suicide). Not surprisingly perhaps she objected to a direction in an interim care order that she be removed from home so that she could be assessed in a psychiatric unit. The court held that notwithstanding that she was 'Gillick competent' it was in her best interests to override her refusal since otherwise there was little that anyone could do to help her.

MEDICAL ASSISTANCE

In some cases – notably when an emergency protection order is being exercised – it may be necessary to provide immediate medical aid. Accordingly an order can direct that a doctor, nurse or health visitor accompany social workers exercising any of their powers under the order. Similarly, the court may direct that a doctor, nurse or health visitor accompany the police officer who is executing a warrant to gain entry into premises or access to a child.

Case study 11.1
Tom is just over a year old. His mother, Julia, is 19 and has recently split up from Tom's father Pete. She is finding it difficult to cope on

her own as Tom is a sickly child. The health visitor Anna is concerned about Tom as the last time she saw him he had what looked like an old cigarette burn on his arm. When she asked Julia what had happened she said she thought he had caught his arm on the stove but was not sure. Anna is also worried about Tom's hearing and wants him to have a check-up. Julia does not think anything is wrong and has repeatedly refused to arrange an appointment.

When Anna tells the GP about her concerns she is told to keep a close eye on things but not to involve social services.

Is Anna under any legal obligation to report her suspicions?

Can she examine Tom without Julia's consent?

If she is denied access to Tom what action could she take?

Anna does not have to report her suspicions as there is no mandatory reporting law in the UK. Nor does she have to initiate investigations into Tom's well-being under s.47. That section, despite imposing a qualified duty on health authorities to co-operate with local authorities (among others), nevertheless leaves statutory responsibility for investigation to local authorities.

Anna cannot examine Tom without Julia's consent because as Tom is too young to give consent it has to be obtained from someone with parental responsibility. As Tom's mother Julia automatically has parental responsibility.

If access to Tom is not an emergency because there are no urgent fears for his safety but none the less attempts to arrange a voluntary assessment have failed, a child assessment order should be sought. However, Anna cannot apply for one herself as it can only be granted to a local authority or the NSPCC. When granting the order the court could include directions as to the nature, type and objective of any medical or other examination or assessment which must be complied with when the assessment is carried out.

Case study 11.2

James and Graham are three-year-old twins. Their mother Doris lives with her boyfriend Andrew. Last week Doris took Graham to the surgery as he had a large cut on his face which she said had been caused when he fell off a chair. While cleaning the wound the practice nurse Megan notices several other burns for which treatment had clearly not been sought. She is more concerned about his weight, however, since he is very much thinner than his twin brother James. He is also very withdrawn and has a bad limp. When asked about his condition Doris is very evasive but does admit that Andrew is always picking on Graham and several times when she has left him to look after her son she has come back to find him in tears and very distressed. Megan and one of the practice GPs think that Graham should go to hospital but Doris refuses, saying she is taking him home and there is nothing anybody can do to stop her.

Can Graham be examined or taken to hospital without his mother's consent? What action can be taken to prevent Doris taking Graham home (or to remove him once he goes back)?

Could Megan or the GP initiate proceedings?

Although James appears well at the moment could any action be taken to prevent him suffering harm in the future?

Without the consent of someone with parental responsibility (or a court order) Graham cannot be examined nor taken to hospital.

An emergency protection order could be sought to prevent Doris taking Graham home if the situation was considered an emergency as it also could if he needed to be removed once he was there. In addition the police could invoke s.46 and remove or keep Graham safe if they had 'reasonable cause to believe that he would otherwise be likely to suffer significant harm'.

Anyone (including Megan and the GP) can apply for an emergency protection order which the court can grant if it is satisfied that there is reasonable cause to believe that a child is likely to suffer significant harm. An order gives the applicant limited parental responsibility, i.e. that which is reasonably required to safeguard or promote the child's welfare. This would allow the application to give consent to medical examinations or other assessments (likewise any necessary emergency treatment) – subject to any directions which may have been included.

All the compulsory orders in the Act can be granted on the basis of future harm, i.e. the child is not currently suffering any actual significant harm but is likely to do so in the future. While such proceedings are likely to be used in cases where a child has suffered past harm which is likely to recur they can also be used to protect a child who has not yet been harmed but who is at risk because of, say, a violent family history. If it is thought that James is at risk – from Andrew, for example – an order based on future harm could be obtained.

Case study 11.3

Linda is 14-years-old and the subject of a full supervision order. The order contains detailed requirements, both about the medical examinations she should undergo and subsequent medical treatment. Linda, who is 'Gillick competent', objects very strongly and refuses to submit to them. Does she have a legal right to refuse?

Schedule 3 paras 4 and 5 of the Act appear to allow medical and psychiatric examinations and treatment requirements to be included in full supervision orders only if children with sufficient understanding to make an informed decision agree. But the case of South Glamorgan County Council v. W and B [1993] (see above) makes it clear that despite the wording in the Act the court still has the power (under its inherent jurisdiction) to override their refusal. In other words the provisions of the Act relating to informed consent can be bypassed. Linda could therefore be examined and treated against her will if to do so was in her best interests.

WELFARE SERVICES

Part III of the Act covers the responsibilities of local authorities towards children and their families. It gives them a wide range of duties and powers aimed at supporting the family and ensuring that children can be brought up at home. In so doing it builds upon many of the provisions in previous legislation which recognize the link between protecting children at risk and supporting families who cannot care for children without help. However in emphasizing the positive benefits of service provision the new framework is designed to make support services less stigmatizing and intrusive than in the past and thus more likely to be used. Many services, which are either 'preventive' (i.e. preventing neglect and abuse and reducing the need for admission to care) or 'supportive' (i.e. aimed at supporting children at home) can be given not just to children themselves but to their families as well.

Almost all the duties and powers in Part III are targeted on a special group of children who are considered to be especially vulnerable. Such children are called 'in need', a term which comprises three groups of children, namely those with disabilities, those unlikely to achieve or maintain a reasonable standard of health or development and those whose health or development is likely to be significantly impaired unless services are provided. The definition of 'in need' (in s. 17) was deliberately wide – the intention being 'to reinforce the emphasis on preventive support and services to families'. But notwithstanding this official guidance research into policy and practice since the Act's implementation has consistently shown how services have been concentrated on children who are considered at risk. In other words the emphasis has been on child protection rather than on preventive and support work.

Despite local authorities having direct statutory responsibility for providing and regulating welfare services, the Act requires other authorities, notably health, education and housing authorities to co-operate in the provision of services (see s.27). Those which are most likely to involve health professionals including the following.

IDENTIFICATION AND ASSESSMENT OF CHILDREN IN NEED

The identification of children as 'in need' has been described as the 'gateway' to service provision because the label entitles such children to a wide range of services – from cash to accommodation. Official guidance stresses that a child's needs include physical, emotional and educational needs according to his or her age, sex, race, religion, culture, language and the capacity of the current carer to meet those needs. Although there is no statutory obligation to assess children 'in need' the duty to identify them implicitly requires effective assessment procedures to be developed. Furthermore assessment is a key element in service provision not just in establishing the extent of a child's needs but in ensuring appropriate services are made available.

REGISTRATION AND SERVICES FOR CHILDREN WITH DISABILITIES

For the first time children with disabilities who in the past were dealt with mainly in health and welfare legislation are included in children's legislation. The Act has several specific provisions which are intended to encourage integration of service provision for all children and ensure that those with disabilities are treated as 'children first' with common needs for care, affection and a stimulating environment, and disabled second. These include the duty to set up and maintain a register of disabled children – operated in some cases by a health authority on behalf of the local authority. In addition local authorities must provide services for disabled children which 'minimize the effects of their disabilities and give them the opportunity to lead lives that are as normal as possible' (schedule 2, para 6). When providing accom- modation they must also ensure that 'it is not unsuitable for their particular needs'.

OTHER SERVICES

Other services which may require an input from health professionals include day care, accommodation, services aimed at children living with their families (such as advice, counselling and guidance), family centres (which are of three types, namely therapeutic, community and self-help) and services aimed at preventing abuse and neglect (see further Part III and Schedule 2). Note also s.85(1) of the Children Act 1989 which imposes notification duties on any health authority providing accommodation for a child for a consecutive period of at least three months.

Case study 11.4

Nicholas is nearly two-years-old and his sister Inge is four. They live with their mother Janet, but have had no contact with their father, Julian, since he left just over a year ago. Janet has tried to trace him but without success. Nicholas was a premature baby and now suffers from repeated chest infections. He is also failing to thrive. Janet does the best she can but, with very little income and no support from Julian (who pays no maintenance), she is finding it increasingly difficult to cope, especially as she lives in very cramped and damp accommodation. With winter only a few weeks away Janet is getting more and more depressed as she cannot afford to pay for heating and wonders how the children's health will be affected by the cold and the damp. Inge seems to be developing normally but as Janet has no money to spare she has few toys or books nor anything else to keep her occupied. She rarely plays with children of her own age as Janet has no friends, having only recently moved to the area.

Janet's next door neighbour, Gillian, has a daughter Pam, aged two who has Down's Syndrome and has recently been diagnosed as having hearing problems in both ears for which hearing aids have been prescribed. There is also some concern about her development which is below average. At first Gillian coped well but recently life has become very stressful. Her husband, Bruce, was made redundant and with little to do all day but stay at home he has begun drinking heavily.

Are Nicholas, Inge and Pam children 'in need'? If so which services could be provided and what would be the likely involvement of health professionals?

Local authorities owe a general duty to safeguard and promote the welfare of children 'in need' within their area. Nicholas is almost certainly such a child in that he is 'unlikely to achieve or maintain, or have the opportunity of achieving or maintaining, a reasonable standard of health or development without service provision'. Arguably too his 'health is likely to be significantly impaired (or further impaired) without such services'. Less certain is whether Inge can be classified as a child 'in need'. But even if she is not she could still benefit from those services which local authorities can (but do not have to) provide. Pam, on the other is undoubtedly a child 'in need' as she is 'disabled' which according to the Act means 'blind, deaf or dumb or suffers from mental disorder of any kind or is substantially and permanently handicapped by illness, injury or congenital deformity or such other disability as may be prescribed' (s.17(11)).

Nicholas might benefit from some form of day-care support – such as a place at nursery or child-minding or playgroup facilities. Other appropriate services could include advice and counselling. Temporary accommodation (or even rehousing) might also be useful if the family's housing problems are the main cause of his failure to thrive. Discretionary services for Inge could also include day-care provision and possibly access to a toy library. As a disabled child Pam could benefit from a wide range of services, some of which should be specifically designed to minimize the effects of her disability and enable her to live as normal a life as possible. For example befriending schemes or domiciliary services might be especially useful including Portage. Pam's name could also be entered on the register of children with disabilities. If Gillian refused, her daughter's entitlement to services would not be affected.

Health professionals are most likely to be involved in identifying and assessing children's health needs in particular by contributing to the multi-disciplinary practices which the Act encourages. It does this by stating that assessments under the Act can be carried out at the same time as other assessments, i.e. those under the Chronically Sick and Disabled Person's Act 1970 and other related legislation. They may also be involved in the planning process which follows assessment, i.e. advising how the child's health and overall development needs can best be met.

PRIVATE LAW ORDERS

The so-called private law orders which can be used to resolve health-related disputes are known as the 'section 8 orders'. There are four orders, all of which can be sought by a broad range of people, extending well beyond close family members such as parents and grandparents to other relatives. Children themselves can also apply for them as can local and health authorities. Some applicants have automatic rights to initiate proceedings while others, such as health authorities (among others), have to get the court's permission first.

The orders are as follows.

RESIDENCE ORDER

This order is used for settling the arrangements about the person(s) with whom a child is to live. Typically these orders are sought by parents (whether married or not) but they can be made in favour of other people, for example, grandparents or step-parents. Complex provisions regulate the relationship between parental responsibility and residence orders. Briefly these are that existing parental responsibility is unaffected by the making of a residence order – divorced parents thus retain it irrespective of where or with whom a child lives. Similarly an order will not affect an unmarried father's parental responsibility. However, to make sure that other people with residence orders have the legal authority to make decisions about a child's upbringing, the Act provides that while they are in force residence orders automatically confer parental responsibility. The effect of these provisions is therefore that in some cases parental responsibility can be shared by several people at the same time – any one of whom can give consent to medical treatment on behalf of a child (subject to any court order to the contrary).

Note that local authorities cannot apply for residence orders and it is only the s.8 order which can be made in respect of a child in care.

Case study 11.5

Following her parents' divorce, Carol, aged nine, is living with her grandmother Charlotte to whom a residence order has been granted. One night she is rushed to hospital with suspected appendicitis and immediate surgery is recommended.

Who can give consent on Carol's behalf?

If no-one is available to give consent could an appendectomy be carried out without consent?

Charlotte has parental responsibility for Carol as a result of the residence order and so can give consent. Carol's mother or father could also give consent as despite their divorce they retain parental responsibility. Note that consent need only be obtained from one person with parental responsibility as the Act does not require all those with parental responsibility to consult each other before exercising it. In short, each can act alone and independently.

If no-one with parental responsibility is available to give consent hospital staff could operate without obtaining consent providing emergency treatment was necessary to save Carol's life. Otherwise they should postpone treatment until consent can be obtained.

Case study 11.6

Charles, aged four, is playing in his child-minder's garden when he has a bad fall. The child-minder, Ruth, thinks he should be checked over in hospital because he becomes very lethargic and is sick several times. She tries to contact his mother Sian but without success. Ruth therefore takes Charles to hospital herself where the casualty officer recommends immediate treatment.

Can Ruth give consent?

S.3(5) of the Act gives temporary carers, such as teachers and child-minders, the 'right to do what is reasonable in all the circumstances of the case for the purpose of safeguarding or promoting a child's welfare'. This includes the right to consent to emergency medical treatment. So if Charles' life is in danger and treatment cannot be postponed until someone with parental responsibility can be contacted Ruth can give consent.

CONTACT ORDERS

This order regulates who a child can have contact with. Like residence orders contact orders are generally used when parents split up and a child spends much more time with one than the other. Grandparents are also common applicants. Contact orders are rarely denied to parents except when continued contact is considered harmful, for example in cases of child abuse. Local authorities cannot apply for contact orders and, if a child is in care, contact is regulated by a different provision, namely s.34.

SPECIFIC ISSUE ORDER

This order is used to resolve a dispute which has arisen about a particular aspect of a child's upbringing. In the medical context this usually means controversial medical treatment. Basically the order deprives someone with parental responsibility (normally parents) of the right to make a decision and empowers the court to make it instead. Local authorities can seek these orders as can health authorities.

Case study 11.7
Rosalind, a premature baby, has respiratory distress syndrome and needs a blood transfusion but her parents Rachel and Norman are Jehovah's Witnesses and refuse to give consent.

Can a local authority or health authority apply for a specific issue order to resolve the issue?

In certain circumstances local (likewise health) authorities can seek a specific issue order. This means that a court will then decide whether it is in Rosalind's best interests to have the treatment or not (see the case of Re O [1993] in which the court authorized treatment in similar circumstances). Note that a specific issue order cannot be made in relation to a child who is in care. This means that if Rosalind was the subject of a care order the court's inherent jurisdiction would have to be used to resolve the dispute.

PROHIBITED STEPS ORDER

This order can be used to prevent a step which someone with parental responsibility would normally be able to take. Essentially preventive it is likely to be sought when one parent objects to something the other is proposing to do. Like the specific issue order it can be sought by local and health authorities and can be particularly useful in preventing controversial medical treatment such as sterilization. A prohibited steps order cannot be made in relation to a child who is in care but the court's inherent jurisdiction could achieve the same result, i.e. prohibit proposed medical treatment. (See Re S (medical treatment [1993] on the use of prohibited steps order in a medical context).

FURTHER READING

Department of Health (1988) *Diagnosis of Child Sexual Abuse: Guidance for Doctors: Standing Medical Advisory Committee Report*, HMSO, London.

Department of Health (1989) *An Introduction to the Children Act*, HMSO, London.

Department of Health (1990) *An Introductory Guide to the Children Act for the NHS*, Health Publications Unit, Heywood, Lancashire.

Department of Health, Department of Education and Science and the Welsh Office (1991) *Working Together under the Children Act 1989: A Guide to the Arrangements for Inter-agency Co-operation for the Protection of Children from Abuse*, HMSO, London.

Department of Health (1991) *Guidance and Regulations* (9 vols), HMSO, London.

Department of Health (1991) *Protecting Children: A Guide to Social Workers Undertaking a Comprehensive Assessment*, HMSO, London.

Department of Health (1992) *Child Protection: Guidance for Senior Nurses, Health Visitors and Midwives*, HMSO, London.

Department of Health (1992) *The Children Act 1989: What Every Nurse, Health Visitor and Midwife Needs to Know*, HMSO, London.

Department of Health (1992) *The Children Act 1989: NHS Study and Training Pack*, HMSO, London.

Department of Health, British Medical Association and Conference of the Royal Colleges (1994) *Child Protection: Medical Responsibilities*, HMSO, London.

Department of Health (1995) *The Challenge of Partnership in Child Protection: Practice Guide*, HMSO, London.

Hendrick, J. (1993) *Child Care Law for Health Professionals*, Radcliffe Medical Press, Oxford.

Mitchell, B. and Prince, A. (1992) *The Children Act and Medical Practice*, Family Law/Jordan, Bristol.

Stainton Rogers, W. and Roche, J. (1994) *Children's Welfare and Children's Rights*, Hodder & Stoughton, London.

Hospital welfare, health promotion and special educational needs

12

HOSPITAL WELFARE

PRINCIPLES OF GOOD PRACTICE

Despite the absence of specific legislation on the welfare of children and young people in hospital, their care and treatment has been the subject of several influential reports, in particular, the Platt Report on the Welfare of Children in Hospital (1959) which first recognized the special needs of children and their families and the Court report (1976) which focused on the need for integration of children's health services. The fundamental principles set out in these reports (and the subsequent White Paper 'Working for Patients') are now incorporated in a single document, *The Welfare of Children and Young People in Hospital* (the guide). Like other guidance documents this is not a 'legal' document and so does not impose legal duties. None the less it represents what is considered 'good practice' on the care of children in hospital and is thus expected to be followed.

The 'cardinal principles' underpinning the guide are: children are admitted to hospital only if the care they require cannot be as well provided at home, in a day clinic or on a day basis in hospital; children requiring admission to hospital are provided with a high standard of medical, nursing and therapeutic care to facilitate a speedy recovery and minimize complications and mortality; families with children have easy access to hospital facilities for children without needing to travel significantly further than to other similar amenities; children are discharged from hospital as soon as socially and clinically appropriate and full support provided for subsequent home or day care; good child health care is shared with parents/carers and they are closely involved in the care of their children at all times unless, exceptionally, this is not in the best interests of the child; accommodation is provided for them to remain with their children overnight; accommodation, facilities and staffing are appropriate to the needs of children and adolescents and separate from those provided for adults; like all other patients, children have a right for their privacy to be respected and to be treated with tact and understanding. They have an equal right to information appropriate to their age, understanding and specific circumstances.

In addition to these basic principles the guide provides comprehensive guidance on hospital services for children and how their special needs can be met. The following are those which have important legal implications.

EDUCATION

The Education Act 1993 (and relevant regulations, notably the Education (Approval of Special School) Regulations 1994) imposes new duties on local education authorities (LEAs) to provide education otherwise than at school where this is necessary to meet a child's needs. In relation to children who are not at school because of injury or illness this may involve a variety of arrangements, depending on local circumstances and needs. In some cases provision will be made through home tuition but in respect of children in hospital, it is more likely to be made through a hospital school (or tuition service) or an integrated hospital/home education service. Whatever the arrangement and despite the statutory responsibility for hospital education resting with education authorities effective arrangements and implementation of the law requires close inter-agency collaboration and liaison especially between education and health services.

The new legislation is intended to fulfil two broad aims. First, to minimize as far as possible the interruption and disruption to a child's normal schooling by continuing education as normally as the child's illness or incapacity allows. Secondly, to ensure that sick children's personal happiness, life and career chances as adults are not irretrievably disadvantaged. In short the intention is that children in hospital should have the same rights to education suited to their age, ability, needs and health as other children, even though the National Curriculum is not mandatory in hospital schools.

The role of the health services is spelt out in some detail in circular DH LAC (94) 10 which emphasizes the need for 'working together' in a number of areas. In relation to admissions, for example, they are urged to give teachers advance warning of a child's admission and an indication of how long he or she is expected to stay in hospital. Co-operation between medical staff and teachers is also essential in respect of the effect of medication and pain and other medical procedures which can, unless carefully planned, interrupt teaching time. Other aspects include guidance on children in adult wards, recurrent admissions, psychiatric care and children suffering from brain injuries.

PROTECTION FROM ABUSE

As was shown in Chapter 11 health professionals are expected to contribute to the investigation and prevention of child abuse – a process which may well involve hospital staff in that abused children may attend hospital accident and emergency departments as a consequence of injuries inflicted upon them. Accordingly the guide recommends that staff working with children should be trained to recognize the symptoms of child abuse and be aware of how they can obtain specialist expert advice and support. In addition provision should be made in contracts for specialist medical nursing staff to participate in multi-agency forums for the prevention of abuse.

DISCIPLINE

Anyone with parental responsibility in respect of a child has the right to administer discipline. Discipline can include corporal punishment providing it is 'moderate' and 'reasonable', i.e. appropriate to the child's age, health, physique, understanding and strength. Normally a child's parents will exercise discipline but they can delegate this power (see s.2(9) Children Act 1989) to, for example, hospital staff. However the extent to which this would justify corporal punishment of a child patient is uncertain, especially as corporal punishment is now banned in most schools and residential child care establishments. Note too that if a child's parents have indicated that they do not wish their child to receive corporal punishment their wishes should be respected.

VISITORS

While the Guide recognizes that parents and members of a child's immediate family should be encouraged and assisted to be with their child at all times occasionally this is not in his or her best interests (see also Health Circular (76) 5 which requires DHAs to provide facilities for parental and other visiting). But notwithstanding the presumption that parental contact is beneficial the guide makes it clear that when necessary, such as on medical grounds, parents can be excluded. In some cases it may be necessary to obtain a court order under the Children Act 1989 to restrict access to a child. Lawful visitors are those whom the health professional in charge of the ward expressly or implicitly allows to enter the premises. He or she also has the right to exclude visitors – either by refusing them admission or asking them to leave. Subject to hospital policy the professional in charge can also decide how many visitors to admit and how long they can stay. A visitor who refuses to leave is a trespasser.

LEAVING HOSPITAL

Guidance on discharge from hospital is given in Health Circular HC (89) 5 which requires health authorities to ensure that wards and departments maintain up-to-date discharge procedures which all staff with relevant interests must be made aware of. In addition the circular emphasizes the need for planning discharges and specifies the features of 'good quality' procedures. Children who are 'Gillick competent' (likewise competent 16- and 17-year-olds) have the right to leave hospital when they wish unless their rights to refuse treatment have been overridden (either by a court or someone with parental responsibility).

The decision to leave hospital in respect of incompetent children rests with those who have parental responsibility. Nevertheless if a child's removal from hospital is not in his or her best interests orders under the Children Act 1989 could be sought, for example, an emergency protection order. Alternatively the police could invoke their powers to prevent a child's removal. Even without the authority of an order under the Children Act 1989, however, it is doubtful whether any court would support the right of a parent to remove a child if to do so would threaten his or her life or health. Similarly, despite parental objection, emergency treatment could be carried out if that was necessary to preserve life.

COMPREHENSIVE ASSESSMENTS

Statutory assessment procedures may be required for some children in hospital under the Education Acts 1981–93 (see page 245), the Children Act 1989 and the Chronically Sick and Disabled Persons Act 1970 and Disabled Person's Act 1986. If so, hospital staff may be required to contribute to the assessment process to ensure that children can be assessed 'in the round'. The Children Act 1989 in particular provides for the assessment of children under that Act to be carried out at the same time as assessments under other legislation.

HEALTH PROMOTION

Health promotion in relation to children and young people is a key activity and a major component of the White Paper, *The Health of the Nation* (1992) which set out the Government's strategy for improving the health of the population of England. It consists of district-wide programmes and activities involving many agencies and individuals. Nevertheless despite this commitment to health promotion there is little specific legislation other than that which is contained in the National Health Service Act 1977. This states that health authorities have a duty: (a) to provide facilities for the care of expectant and nursing mothers and young children; (b) to provide for the medical inspection and treatment of school children; and (c) to provide for the dental inspection, treatment and education in dental health of school children.

The term 'health promotion' is not legally defined yet there are several provisions, in particular those relating to child health surveillance (see below) which seek to promote children's health by preventing disease, promoting a healthy lifestyle and health protection. In addition the *Health of the Nation* (Hall, 1996) identifies several priority health-promoting 'targets' which apply specifically to children and young people and to which all agencies (i.e. health, education, social services) both statutory and non-statutory must contribute. These are expected to take place in a variety of settings, namely, hospitals, schools and especially primary care because it is usually children's (some of whom are 'well patients') first point of contact with health services and should also ensure access to a wide range of professionals across the spectrum of mental, physical and social health.

Child Health Surveillance (CHS) is a major component of health promotion. It has two broad aims. First, that all children should have the opportunity to realize their full potential in terms of good health, well-being and development and secondly that remedial disorders are identified and acted upon as early as possible. While these are expected to be achieved by several methods the role of GPs is vital and is one which is now recognized by their contracts of service. While CHS is not a service GPs must provide they are encouraged to do so for those under five on their list. Regulations specify what it must cover, in particular (a) monitoring the health, well-being and physical, mental and social development of the child while under five with a view to detecting deviations from normal development, and (b) examination of the child.

Other 'health promoting' services which must be provided by all GPs irrespective of whether they have decided to provide CHS include: (a) giving advice, where appropriate, to a patient in connection with the patient's general health, and in particular about the significance of diet, exercise, the use of tobacco, the consumption of alcohol and the misuse of drugs and solvents, and (b) offering to patients where appropriate, vaccination or immunization against measles, mumps, rubella, pertussis, poliomyelitis, diphtheria and tetanus.

Note too the important role played by other health professionals in health promotion, for example, midwives who are legally required to provide midwifery care to a mother and baby during the antenatal, intranatal and postnatal periods.

SPECIAL EDUCATIONAL NEEDS

It has been estimated that about 20% of children may have some form of learning difficulty. Before 1981 such children were categorized for educational purposes by a process which was both stigmatizing and discriminatory – due largely to their segregation in 'special schools'. In an attempt to reverse this process the Education Act 1981 sought to integrate them, wherever possible, into mainstream schooling. To achieve this it set up a statutory framework with legally defined procedures for the identification and assessment of special educational needs. Although the Act did succeed in significantly reducing the number of children being educated in special schools it was not long before the new framework was criticized, in particular for the delays involved in making assessments, restrictive rights of appeal and the way it marginalized parents.

The Education Act 1993 (the Act) which builds upon and virtually replaces the 1981 Act aimed to remedy these defects and strengthen its effectiveness. Its most important reforms include stronger duties to identify and provide for children with special educational needs, time limits to cut delays in statementing children, a Code of Practice giving practical guidance to all those likely to be involved in identifying and assessing children (including the health services) and extended rights of appeal for parents.

According to s.156 of the Act a child has special educational needs (SEN) if he or she has learning difficulties which needs special help. This help is known as special educational provision. 'Learning difficulty' is a very broad concept which includes children: (a) who have significantly greater difficulty in learning than most children of their age; (b) who have a disability which either prevents or hinders them from using educational facilities of a kind generally provided for children of their age in the area; and (c) under five who are, or would be, if special educational provision is not made, likely to fall within the definition of (a) or (b) above.

Special educational provision means educational provision additional to or otherwise different from, that provided generally for children of the child's age in state schools.

Basically a child has a learning difficulty if he or she finds it much harder to learn than most children of the same age, or if he or she has a disability which makes it difficult to use normal educational facilities. The difficulty may be caused by a physical disability, sensory impairment (both hearing and visual), speech and language problem, emotional and behavioural difficulty or medical condition (e.g. congenital heart disease, epilepsy, cystic fibrosis and so on).

The Act's overall strategy is to continue the approach taken in the 1981 Act, namely to integrate children with SEN within mainstream schooling whenever possible. However it also reinforces and tightens up existing duties to identify, assess and make provision for children with SEN. In the vast majority of cases it is expected that such needs will be met by mainstream schools themselves, adopting the staged approach recommended in the Code of Practice (the Code). The first three stages are school-based (although stage 3 is likely to involve specialist help or advice from outside the school). While the needs of most children with special educational needs should be met effectively under the three school-based stages in a small number of cases the LEA will have to consider making a statutory assessment (stage 4) which may or may not be followed by a 'statement' (stage 5).

The role of health professionals in the identification and assessment of children with SEN is spelt out in detail in the Code and co-operation and collaboration between professionals is given statutory force by s.166 of the Act which imposes a qualified duty on DHAs to comply with any request for help in connection with children with SENs.

Health professionals are most likely to be involved in identifying children with SEN, in particular the extent to which their medical condition, disability or developmental delay is affecting their learning abilities. In addition DHAs and NHS Trusts have a statutory duty (under s.176) to notify parents (and the appropriate LEA) of children under five whom they believe have SEN. They must also provide the parents of such children with information about any voluntary organization whose services, such as counselling, might be useful.

The assessment process is the other aspect most likely to involve health professionals. While the needs of most children with SEN are expected to be met under the three-staged school-based process, any of which (but particularly stage 3) might involve health professionals, in a small minority of cases affecting no more than 2% of children the statutory involvement of the local authority will be necessary and a statutory assessment may be made. A request for a statutory assessment may come from a parent, a professional involved with a child such as a doctor (or other health professional) or the school itself. A statutory assessment is a very detailed examination and is likely to be made when a child's needs are very complex or so severe that immediate referral is appropriate. Children under 5 who are not yet at school (and so will by-pass the school-based stages) may also be brought directly to the LEAs attention.

The criteria for deciding to make a statutory assessment are detailed in the Code and relevant Regulations but the critical question is whether there is convincing evidence that, despite any action the school could take and any specialist support, the child's learning difficulties remain or have not been remedied sufficiently. If the LEA decide that a statutory assessment should be made (if they refuse parents can appeal to a Special Educational Needs Tribunal), they must seek written medical and psychological advice which should normally be provided within six weeks. According to the Code, medical advice should cover all aspects of a child's health and development, in particular evidence on any medical condition, medical treatment, general health or developmental problems, mental health problems, shorter term but acute medical problems (such as childhood cancer). In addition the medical advice should state the likely consequences for the child's education (see further Code, para. 3, 106–12).

For children with complex needs or specific difficulties or medical conditions the Code states that the health services should:

- ensure that there are no additional difficulties or disabilities affecting the child, and monitor the child's general health and development;
- help parents and teachers to understand the child's disability or medical condition and provide counselling and support to parents and children if required;
- provide access to any specialist advice or services required; and
- advise on any other matters such as access, provision of equipment, and administration of medication.

As regards psychological advice this should cover any factors which could affect a child's functioning such as cognitive functioning, communication skills, perceptual skills, adaptive, personal and social skills and so forth (see further Code paras 3.113–15).

Following a statutory assessment (which is likely to be rare for children under two) the LEA may decide to make a statement of SEN. This is a document that sets out all a child's needs and all the special help he or she should have. The main reason for one is, according to the Code, 'that the LEA conclude that all the special educational provision necessary to meet the child's needs cannot reasonably be provided within the resources normally available in mainstream schools in the area'. Health professionals may be involved in the statementing process, in particular those aspects which cover the child's 'non-educational needs and provision' such as speech and language therapy (which may or may not be regarded as non-educational depending on the health or development history of the child).

FURTHER READING

Audit Commission (1993) *Children First: A Study of Hospital Services*, HMSO, London.

British Paediatric Association (1993) *The Care of the Critically Ill: Report of a Working Party on Paediatric Intensive Care*, Critical Care Publications, London.

Department of Education (1994) *Code of Practice on the Identification and Assessment of Special Educational Needs*, London.

Hall, M.B. (1989) *Health for All Children – A Programme for Child Health Surveillance*, Oxford Medical Publications, Oxford.

Harris, N. (1995) *Law and Education, Regulation, Consumerism and the Education System* (2nd edn), Sweet & Maxwell, London.

Department of Health (1991) *Welfare of Children in Hospital*, HMSO, London.

MacFarlane, A., Seft, S. and Mario, C. (1990) *Child Health: The Screening Tests*, Oxford University Press, Oxford.

Platt Committee (Report of) (1959) *The Welfare of Children in Hospitals*, HMSO, London.

Recommended further reading

Brazier, M. (1992) *Medicine, Patients and the Law*, 2nd edn, Penguin, London.

Dimond, B.C. (1993) *Patients' Rights, Responsibilities and the Nurse*, Central Health Studies, Quay Publishing, Lancaster.

Dimond, B.C. (1994) *Legal Aspects of Midwifery*, Books for Midwives Press, Cheshire.

Dimond, B.C. (1995) *Legal Aspects of Nursing*, 2nd edn, Prentice Hall, Hemel Hempstead.

Dimond, B.C. (1996) *The Legal Aspects of Child Health Care*, Mosby, 1996.

Dyer, C. (1992) *Doctors, Patients and the Law*, Blackwell Scientific Publications, Oxford.

Finch, John (ed.) (1994) *Spellers Law Relating to Hospitals*, 7th edn, Chapman & Hall, London.

Jenkins, R. (1995) *The Law and the Midwife*, Blackwell Science, Oxford.

Kennedy, I. and Grubb, A. (1994) *Medical Law: Text and Materials*, Butterworth, London.

Korgaonkar, G. and Tribe, D. (1995) *Law for Nurses*, Cavendish Publishing, London.

Mason, J.K. and McCall-Smith, A. (1994) *Law and Medical Ethics*, Butterworth, London, 4th edn.

Rae, M. (1986) *Children and the Law*, Longman, London.

Richardson, J. and Webber, I. (1995) *Ethical Issues in Child Health Care*, Mosby.

Tingle, J. and Cribb, A. (1995) *Nursing Law and Ethics*, Blackwell Science, Oxford.

Young, A.P. (1989) *Legal Problems in Nursing Practice*, 2nd edn, Chapman & Hall, London.

Young, A.P. (1991) *Law and Professional Conduct in Nursing*, Scutari Press, London.

Young, A.P. (1992) *Case Studies in Law and Nursing: A Course Book for Project 2000 Training*, Chapman & Hall, London.

Appendix A
Table of cases

Note: The following abbreviations are used

AC	Law Reports, Appeal Cases
All ER	All England Law Reports
BMLR	Butterworths Medico-legal Reports
FLR	Family Law Reports
Med LR	Medical Law Reports
Med L Rev	Medical Law Review
QB	Law Reports, Queen's Bench Division
WLR	Weekly Law Reports

Cassidy *v.* Ministry of Health [1951] 1 All ER 574 35, 60

Clark *v.* MacLennan [1983] 1 All ER 416 30

Crawford *v.* Board of Governors of Charing Cross Hospital (1953) *The Times* Dec 8. 33

D, Re (A minor) (sterilisation) [1976] 1 All ER 326 111, 112

D *v.* NSPCC [1978] AC 171 84

De Martell *v.* Merton & Sutton HA [1991] 2 Med LR 209 142

Defreitas *v.* O'Brien and Campbell-Connolly [1995] 6 Med LR 108 29

Donoghue *v.* Stevenson [1932] AC 562 22, 23

E, Re (A minor) (medical treatment) [1991] 2 FLR 585 114

E, Re (wardship) (medical treatment) [1993] 1 FLR 386 190, 191

Edler *v.* Greenwich and Deptford Hospital Management Committee (1953) *The Times*, March 7 37

Fairhurst *v.* St Helens & Knowsley HA [1994] 5 Med LR 422 37

Frenchay NHS Trust *v.* S [1994] 1 WLR 601, [1994] 2 All ER 403 193, 194

Re F (in utero) [1988] 2 ALL ER 193 141

F, Re (Mental patient; sterilisation) [1989] 2 WLR 1025, [1990] 2 AC1 60, 62

G *v.* North Tees HA [1989] FCR 53 36

Gillick *v.* West Norfolk and Wisbech AHA [1986], AC 112 [1985] 3 All ER 402 7, 55, 65, 69, 99

Gold *v.* Harringey HA [1987] 2 All ER 888 59

H, Re [1995] 1 FLR 643 229

Headford *v.* Bristol and District Health Authority [1995] 6 Med LR 1 42

Hinfey *v.* Salford HA [1993] 4 Med LR 143 142

Hotson *v.* East Berkshire AHA [1987] AC 750, [1987] 2 All ER 909 40

Hunter *v.* Mann (1974) QB 767 78

J, Re (A minor) (medical treatment) [1990] 3 All ER 930 74, 181,182, 183, 184

J, Re (A minor) (medical treatment) [1992] 4 All ER 614 11, 76, 186, 187

Kay *v.* Ayrshire and Arran Health Board [1987] 2 All ER 888 39

Krali *v.* McGrath (1986) 1 All ER 54 41

Loveday *v.* Renton and Another [1990] 1 Med LR 117 39, 44

M, Re (A minor (Care Order: Threshold Conditions) [1994] 3 All ER 298 229

Maynard *v.* West Midlands Regional Health Authority [1984] 1 WLR 634, [1985] 1 All ER 635 29

Mitchell *v.* Hounslow and Spelthorne HA (1984) *The Lancet* 579 37

McFall *v.* Shrimp [1978] 10 PaD & C 3d, 90 171

McKay *v.* Essex Area HA [1982] 2 WLR 890 149

O, Re (A minor) (medical treatment) [1993] 2 FLR 149 75

P, Re (A minor) [1982] 80 Local Government Reports 301 109

P, Re (minors) [1987] 2 FLR 421 132

Q, Re (Parental Order) [1996] 1 FLR 369 129

R *v.* Adomoko [1991] 2 Med LR 277, 2 All ER 80 51, 52

R *v.* Arthur [1981] 12 BLMR 1 181

R *v*. Central Birmingham HA, ex p Collier [1988] Lexis Jan 6 11, 25

R *v*. Central Birmingham HA, ex p Walker [1987] 3 BLMR 32 11, 25

R *v*. Cox [1992] 12 BLMR 38 188

R *v*. Ethical Committee of St Mary's Hospital (Manchester), ex p H or Harriot [1988] 1 FLR 512 124

R *v*. Kirklees Metropolitan BC, ex p C [1993] 2 FLR 187 199

R *v*. Prentice and Sulman [1993] 4 Med LR 304 51

R *v*. Mid Glamorgan Health Services Authority and South Glamorgan Health Authority, ex p Martin [1994] 5 Med LR 383 89

R *v*. Secretary of State for Social Services and others, ex p Hinks [1980] 1 BLMR 93 10, 25

R *v*. Smith [1974] 1 All ER 376 107

R, Re (A minor) (wardship; medical treatment) [1991] 4 All ER 177 70,71, 198, 203, 216

Riverside Mental Health Trust *v*. Fox [1994] 1 FLR 614 214

Roe *v*. Ministry of Health [1954] 2 QB 66 33

Rogers *v*. Whitaker [1993] 4 Med LR 79 60

S, Re (adult; refusal of medical treatment) [1992] 4 All ER 671 63, 144, 192

S, Re (A minor; medical treatment) [1993] 1 FLR 376 74, 259

S, Re, (A minor) (Consent to medical treatment) [1994] 2 FLR 1065 191

S *v*. Distillers Co [1970] 1 WLR 114 41

Sa'd v. Robinson [1989] 1 Med. LR 41 27

Salih v. Enfield HA [1991] 2 Med LR 235 137

Saunders *v*. Leeds Western Health Authority and another [1993] 4 Med LR 355 36

Selfe *v*. Ilford & District Management Committee [1970] 114 Solicitors' Journal 35

Sidaway *v*. Bethlem Royal Hospital Governors [1985] 1 AC 871, [1985] 1 All ER 643 58, 59

Smith *v*. Tunbridge Wells Health Authority [1995] 5 Med LR 334 59

South Glamorgan County Council *v*. W and B [1993] 1 FLR 574 76, 221, 230, 233

South West Hertfordshire HA *v*. Brady (1994) Med L Rev 208 215

T, Re (Refusal of treatment) [1992] 4 All ER 649 57, 63, 195

Tarasoff *v*. Regents of the University of California [1976] 551 P 2d 334 87

Thake *v*. Maurice [1986] 1 All ER 497 151

Tredget and Tredget *v*. Bexley Health Authority [1994] 5 Med LR 178 41

W, Re (A minor) (Medical treatment) [1992] 4 All ER 627 55, 67, 68, 72, 190, 194, 203, 215, 216

W *v*. Egdell [1990] 1 All ER 835 85, 86

Whitehouse *v*. Jordan [1981] 1 All ER 267 14, 38

Wilsher *v*. Essex Area health Authority [1986] 3 All ER 801, [1983] 3 All ER 871 30, 31, 39, 49

X *v*. Y [1988] 2 All ER 648 85, 88

Appendix B
Table of statutes

National Health Service Act 1977 10, 12, 111, 124, 243
National Health Service and Community Care Act 1990 12
Offences Against the Person Act 1861 64, 110, 130, 137
Police and Criminal Evidence Act 1984 87, 217, 227
Public Health (Control of Diseases) Act 1984 62
Sexual Offences Act 1956 101, 102
Suicide Act 1961 191
Surrogacy Arrangements Act 1985 121, 122, 123, 131
Vaccine Damage Payments Act 1979 44

Index